The Pursuit of Happiness

The Pursuit of Happiness

John P. Houston

University of California, Los Angeles

Scott, Foresman and Company   Glenview, Illinois

Dallas, Tex.   Oakland, N.J.   Palo Alto, Cal.
Tucker, Ga.   London, England

Acknowledgment

Pp. 30–38. Adapted from INVITATION TO PSYCHOLOGY by John P. Houston, Helen Bee, Elaine Hatfield, and David C. Rimm. Copyright © 1979, by Academic Press, Inc. Reprinted by permission.

Library of Congress Cataloging in Publication Data

Houston, John P.
  The pursuit of happiness.

  1. Social adjustment. 2. Happiness—Social aspects.
3. United States—Social conditions. 4. Motivation
(Psychology) I. Title.
HM251.H678   158'.1   80–26472
ISBN 0–673–15421–1

1 2 3 4 5 - MAL - 85 84 83 82 81 80

Preface

Through the years that I have taught experimental psychology courses, students have often asked, "What good are all these theories based on laboratory data? How can they help me?" These questions are fair but difficult to answer. It is not a simple matter to translate technical psychological theories into genuinely helpful suggestions that may be tested in everyday life. And yet that is just what the student wants, needs, and deserves . . . someone to "humanize" psychological theory and to point out the ways in which it may be useful in our lives.

My goal in writing this book has been to present some techniques and procedures, all based on long-standing psychological principles, that can be helpful in the pursuit of happiness. These techniques represent what I see as some of the ways that psychological theorizing, often confined to academic circles, can be useful in our lives when we are troubled and frustrated. Because many of these methods are suggestions, the reader should select and test those items which seem to make sense to her or him.

The central concern of this book is that many Americans are unhappy, disgruntled, and frustrated in spite of an unprecedented standard of living. Why are Americans unhappy and what can be done about it? In attempting to answer these questions, the first portion of the book deals with the idea that our capitalistic system, so successful in many ways, clashes with our inherited capacity to experience satisfaction through need or drive reduction. The nature of our culture and our economic system lead us to want what we cannot have and to not want what is overly abundant. The book offers a number of actions we can take to break out of this unpleasant bind.

In the latter portions of the book, the second major conception of motivation, that of incentive motivation, is outlined in comprehensible terms. Here again our capitalistic system leads us into trouble. Specifically, it takes us to the point where we are receiving too much of some kinds of change, novelty, and complexity and not enough of other forms of variety. Suggestions that can be helpful in avoiding these unfortunate, but common, circumstances are provided.

This book is suitable for a number of different audiences. It can be used as a supplement in adjustment courses where it will provide an original perspective and a rather unique way of looking at the problems of adjusting to the complexities of a high technology capitalistic society. It can also be used as a supplement in experimental courses, and introductory courses, where its function would be to provide some relief from the more rigorous laboratory and theoretical work by introducing the student to some aspects of applied psychology.

I have tried to write clearly and simply and have used examples that I hope are engaging and entertaining. I have also attempted to maintain a sense of humor while writing about fairly serious matters.

This book is not an ordinary one in that it does not follow a formula, covering certain standard topics, as do so many psychology texts. It provides unique ideas about how to ensure happiness while it also covers some well-known adjustment problems and techniques. Some of these techniques have been developed over the years by a large number of psychologists. Others are new and speculative. In either case, I think it would be wise to take them as suggestions rather than as hard-and-fast, proven methods. It is also important to realize that if problems become severe or extreme, then qualified professional help should be sought. Many readers will find in the suggested methods cause for argument; I hope others will find pleasure and assistance, too.

J.P.H.

Contents

Chapter 1   Drowning in a Sea of Plenty   1

Going Under   1

The Psychology of Human Satisfaction   3

Frustration   4
   The Lack of Wanting / The Lack of Getting

Chapter 2   Double Frustration   6

The Curse of Superabundance   6

The Genetic Trap   12

Gimme, Gimme, Gimme   13
   The Need for Material Objects / You Can't Win /
   The Need to Achieve / You Still Can't Win /
   More, More, More

Chapter 3   What Not to Do   23

I'll Rip Your Face Off: Direct Aggression   23

Kick That Dog: Indirect Aggression   24

Who Gives a Damn? Apathy   25

The Baby Talk Syndrome: Regression   26

Dream On: Fantasy   26

Gobble, Gobble: Gluttony   26

Economic Slavery: Overborrowing   27

One Toke Over the Line: Drug Abuse   28

I'll Drink to That: Alcohol Abuse 29

Defense Mechanisms 30
 Rationalization / Reaction Formation / Repression /
 Suppression / Projection / Identification

Chapter 4 Having Your Cake and Eating It Too 39

Enjoying People 40
 Getting the Best out of Friends / Making Them
 Want You / Loving Living Together

Giving Children Less 47

How Entertaining (Yawn) 48
 Television / Dinner and a Movie, Etc. /
 Buying Tickets / Books and Magazines

Eating and Drinking 54

Appliance-of-the-Month Club 56

Spending Money 60
 Rule #1: Attack Your Budget / Rule #2: Spend Big /
 Rule #3: Spend Impulsively / Rule #4: Buy
 Investments / Rule #5: Upgrade, Upgrade / Rule #6:
 Use Cash Not Cards / Rule #7: Don't Earn Too Much

**Deprive and Indulge: A General Concept
and Some Examples** 67
 Meditation: Getting Away from It All / Smoking /
 So It Was a Flop? / From Insomnia to Sweet Dreams

Chapter 5 Wanting Too Much 76

It's All a Matter of Expectations 77

Level of Aspiration 78

Expecting Too Much 79

Getting It Down 81
 Insight / Look Down, Not Up / Readjust Your Sights /
 Choosing Less / You Can't Lose / Death at Any Moment /
 Admit Your Limits / Accept Inconsistency and
 Procrastination / Success Versus Happiness / Finding
 Common Denominators / Being "At One" with It All /
 "Cosmic" Perspectives / Standing Still Isn't All Bad

Aversion Therapy 93
 Stop Thought / Aversive Thought Conditioning / Summary

Chapter 6 **Expecting Too Little** 100

    Low Levels of Aspiration 100

    Reversing Learned Helplessness 101

    Assertion Training 104
        When We Should Say No / When to Ask for Yourself /
        How to Be Assertive

    The Ideal Level of Aspiration 109

Chapter 7 **Pushed and Pulled** 111

    The Lure of the Environment 111

    Try As We May 114
        Boredom / Nothing Lasts Forever / Satiation

    Preferred Level Theory 116

    The Natural Selection of Curiosity 117

Chapter 8 **Homogeneity in a World of Chaos** 120

    Too Much and Too Little 120

    Homogenized Life 121
        "Adjective-Animal" Restaurants / Love Those Banks /
        Fast and Identical / Polyester as the Bane of Society /
        Culprit #1: The Profit Motive / The Illusion of Variety /
        Culprit #2: Follow the Leader / Culprit #3:
        The Need for Security /Culprit #4: Snobbery /
        Culprit #5: Sexism / Canned Towns

    Increasing Uncertainty 131

Chapter 9 **The Cult of Extremes** 134

    Seeking Radical Change 134
        Entertain Me Please! / Compulsive Gambling /
        The Workaholic / Fill 'er Up / "Kinky" Sex /
        The Money Game / Shop, Dress, and Paint /
        ESP and the Occult / Summary

    Reacting to Chaos 142
        The Hell with It All / True Believing

Chapter 10 Restoring Balance   145

Getting Back into Your Preferred Level   145

Escape from Security   145
Satiation: People, Events, Things / When You're Done,
You're Done / Step #1: Recognize and
Rate the Problem / Step #2: Act /
Step-by-Step / Take a Friend Along / Trial and Error /
Romantic Attachments / The Payoff

More Versus Better   151

Invent-a-Game   153

Be a Supersnob   154

Follow the Leader . . . Once   154

Be Not Misled by Tinsel   155

Reject Sexism   156

Making Up a Hierarchy   158

Chapter 11 Time for Professional Assistance?   161

You Can't Do It All   161

Neurotic Behavior: Close But Still on Our Own   161
Anxiety Neurosis / Phobic Neurosis /
Obsessive-Compulsive Neurosis / That's Not All

Psychoses: Losing Touch   165
Schizophrenia / Manic-depressive Reaction /
The Causes of Psychoses

Therapy: Paying for a Captive Audience   169
Psychoanalysis / Client-centered Therapy /
Behavior Modification / Drug Therapy / Summary

Chapter 12 Help Is on the Way   173

Up or Down?   173

It's All in Your Mind   173

For Example   174

A Pleasant Irony   174

1

Drowning in a Sea of Plenty

Going Under

A recent Gallup poll indicated that well over half of all Americans find it impossible to describe themselves as fully happy. In fact, more than 20 million Americans characterized themselves as plain old unhappy. One might think that in this rich, advanced nation, where technology has eliminated many of the problems still confronting developing nations, most everyone would be pretty pleased with themselves and their lives. But such is not the case. Americans are seeking mental health care in unprecedented numbers. Suicide among young people is on the increase. Child abuse is widespread. Many people describe themselves as depressed, bored, and living a life without meaning.

Why do we so often lack peace of mind and a sense of self-satisfaction? The aim of this book is to explore this question, to tease out the roots of much of our anxious displeasure with our lives, and to outline some simple methods of increasing our satisfaction.

Of course there are many forms of unhappiness, and this book does not, cannot, address them all. For example, unhappiness may be caused by powerful environmental forces that are simply beyond our control. There is no denying that a great deal of unhappiness is caused by such things as disease, death, separation, and loss of employment. If an individual discovers she has terminal cancer, her life is bound to be filled with fear, sadness, anxiety, and despair. If parents discover that their thirteen-year-old daughter is pregnant, they will naturally feel great concern. If a laborer loses his or her job through massive industrial layoffs, then unhappiness will result. These and similar sorts of problems touch many of our lives and must be dealt with in one way or another.

But there is another subtler, more insidious form of unhappiness that is the main concern of this book. In a sense, this form of dissatisfaction is the opposite of the variety described above where the source or cause of the unhappiness is obvious and easily identified. Specifically, this subtler variety of displeasure seems most likely to crop up when nothing really seems to be wrong in the individual's life. For example, Robert X earns $50,000 a year working for a midwestern advertising agency. He has a wife, two children, a $100,000 home in a reasonably fashionable area, a three-year-old Mercedes, and some money in the bank. He and his wife lead an active social life, have no medical problems, and are almost guaranteed a financially secure life. And yet Robert X is desperately unhappy. He is bored much of the time. He is depressed. He feels his life has no meaning. Many mornings he can barely drag himself out of bed. The knowledge that he knows exactly what will happen to him for the rest of his life makes him uneasy. He can see himself following the same path all the way to the grave. He has just turned forty-four and has recognized that he has already spent more time than he has left. But he fears that the few decades he has remaining will be spent in the same meaningless, mark-time fashion that characterized the preceding years. He lacks very little in a material sense. Clearly, millions of people around the world would give anything to be in his shoes. And yet he has begun to drink heavily and to argue with his wife over trivial matters. He is going under.

It is this form of unhappiness, in which the individual seems to have almost everything our culture says is desirable but still feels miserable, that is the central concern of this book. The example of Robert X is an extreme one, but many of us sense that, by providing us with all these material benefits, our society has created a new sense of loss, a hollowness, and a dulled life experience. We sometimes feel smothered, confused, and helpless. It is this lack of excitement, this absence of gratification, and this aura of dull, never ending routine in the face of an unparalleled standard of living that must be altered if we are to enjoy life fully.

So, if your problems stem from some easily identifiable source, such as disease, death, or the Internal Revenue Service, this book will not be addressing the solutions you might want to consider. If you have a $45,000 loan coming due tomorrow morning and you have only $17 plus small change, this book won't help. Trouble with the Mafia is beyond the scope of this tome. This book will not help you outrun hot lead. But if you suffer from the form of dissatisfaction where everything seems all right but, at the same time, doesn't, then read on. This kind of unhappiness can be beaten.

The Psychology of Human Satisfaction

In our search for increased self-satisfaction we must do two things. First, we must discover what it is that brings us satisfaction. What is it, after all, that makes humans happy and fulfilled? We must understand the basic, general principles that govern and control the human sense of satisfaction. Second, we must become aware of what it is, within ourselves or our environment, that is blocking or thwarting that sense of well-being that we all so desperately need. We must recognize what we have done wrong in the ordering of our lives before we can bring about beneficial change. In this section we introduce the first of those issues: what are the basics of human satisfaction? In the next section we will explore some of the ways that human gratification can be thwarted or frustrated.

The field of psychology has something useful to say about human satisfaction. If one reviews the major psychological theories of motivation, including those of Hull, Freud, and Maslow, one is struck by the uniformity with which *satisfaction refers to the experience that accompanies the reduction of desire.* A sense of satisfaction is at its peak during the reduction of a desire. Although we can feel satisfied after we have finished eating, or making love, or drinking, the most intense feelings of pleasure and gratification occur during the actual events associated with the reduction of the desire. Getting something we want or need is what satisfaction and pleasure are all about. As we shall see, a great deal of our unhappiness revolves around the fact that we are often blocked or prevented, in a number of subtle ways, from satisfying desires.

Now, given that pleasure or satisfaction may be defined as desire reduction, what else does psychology tell us about the basic principles of human satisfaction? *Desire increases as time of deprivation increases.* This is just a fancy way of saying the longer we go without something the more we want it. For example, look at some of the basic essentials of life: food, sleep, water, air, and a warm body will suffice as a preliminary list. The body requires these elements much as a machine needs fuel. Without them the animal will die. The longer the animal goes without these elements the greater the desire for them. And, as a corollary, the greater the desire the greater the satisfaction or pleasure associated with the gratification of that desire. For instance, the longer we go without food, the greater our pleasure when we do finally eat. The longer and harder the workday, the greater our pleasure when we finally collapse into bed.

In other words, psychological theory implies that *to experience pleasure and satisfaction we must experience at least a modicum of deprivation.* If we have everything all the time we won't be able to experience pleasure . . . because we won't be able to reduce a desire . . . because desire only builds up through a process of deprivation.

Don't assume that this applies only to basic drives or desires such as the needs for food and water. Other, more complicated human desires, such as the need to achieve, the need to affiliate, and the need for power also operate according to this deprivation-gratification cycle. As we shall see in the next chapter, many complex and varied human needs can be subsumed under this analysis.

Frustration

We are arguing that the human being has the capacity to experience satisfaction or pleasure through the fulfillment of desires—both basic physiological needs and more complex psychological needs. The building up, through deprivation, and the subsequent gratification of these desires appear to be the essence of pleasure. Deprivation is essential to satisfaction.

We are an animal that is geared to become hungry and then to satisfy that hunger. Pleasure, for us, comes with drinking after we have been without water. Making love may be most exquisite after a period without love.

We all have the physical and genetic makeup to experience pleasure through the easing of deprivation states. But many of us don't seem to be gaining as much pleasure as we would like. Why? What's wrong? On a logical level there are at least two ways that the deprivation-gratification cycle may be blocked.

The lack of wanting

First, satisfaction or pleasure may be thwarted if we are not sufficiently deprived to enjoy the easing of a state of desire. Ironically, we must experience a relatively unpleasant state of hunger before eating is truly enjoyable. Eating a banana cream pie after just having consumed a banana cream pie is not as satisfying as the first bite after weeks without a pie. Making love fifty-eight times in a row might be fun, but not as pleasant as it is after a period of deprivation. The best night's sleep is often enjoyed after a troubled, insomnia-filled night. A warm fire never feels better than after you have nearly frozen outside. Receiving a radio for Christmas is more satisfying if you have no radio than if you already have four of them. Too much of anything can become tedious. Without deprivation, or lack, many of the pleasures of life are hidden from us. The lean and hungry edge can be taken away from our lives leaving us bored, bloated, and uneasy.

Animal trainers have long known that the best way to raise a healthy, happy animal is to keep it slightly deprived, slim, and in a state of desire. There is actually some evidence available which suggests that rats that are occasionally starved will live longer than rats given constant access to food. We are not claiming that rats and humans are the same, but this sort of evidence, taken along with so many other indicators, suggests that health and satisfaction require deprivation.

The lack of getting

The second logical way that this deprivation-gratification cycle may be blocked occurs when the individual wants something she or he just cannot have. A person who wants a new car but can't afford even an older one will feel frustration and dissatisfaction. Someone who wants an education but can't finance it will feel frustrated. Cars, houses, boats, free time, travel, clothes, and so on, all represent factors that may be strongly desired but absolutely unattainable for a given individual. To the extent that these are wanted but cannot be had the person will feel unhappy and dissatisfied.

In other words, we see two ways that pleasure can be blocked; either we may not want what we can have (we are not deprived enough), or we may want things we can't have. Either way we lose, unless we become aware of the source of our frustration and remedy it.

In this brief chapter we have noted that many Americans feel a general, vague sense of uneasiness and dissatisfaction in spite of the fact that their material wealth and level of security is the envy of the world. In our attempt to analyze this problem we have outlined the fact that the human biological machine is designed to obtain satisfaction through the fulfillment or gratification of desires.

We then outlined two ways in which this capacity to obtain satisfaction can be thwarted. First, we may miss out on some satisfaction if we are not, at least occasionally, deprived. If we do not desire something, or need it, then the possession or attainment of that something is a hollow, empty experience. Second, we may suffer from frustration and a sense of dissatisfaction if we desire things that we simply cannot have.

The trick is to make yourself want things that you can afford and to then go ahead and indulge in those things, rather than want things you can't have or stuff yourself with things you can have but don't really want. In pursuing these issues Chapter 2 describes how our prevailing American culture sets us up for dissatisfaction by (1) overindulging us in things we can afford and (2) encouraging us to want things we can't afford. Then, in Chapter 3, we discuss some of our natural, but desperate and self-defeating, attempts to cope with these forms of culturally determined frustration and unhappiness.

2

Double Frustration

The Curse of Superabundance

The old cliché "Money doesn't mean everything" has some validity. In fact, members of rich and powerful societies may well run into considerable emotional trouble just because they are wealthy and advanced. Progress, technology, and material gain are supposed to yield an environment that is more and more satisfying. America, so goes the popular myth, is a better way of life or a better standard of living. In some ways, this is true. We in America are less susceptible to disease and disaster than the members of many "less advanced cultures." We have more security, more material wealth, and more leisure time than others around the globe. But progress has its price. The American environment is supposed to be satisfying, and it is in many ways, but it also produces stresses and strains that contribute to emotional difficulties. Let's examine some of these less-than-perfect by-products of our cultural movement.

At an early age F. Scott Fitzgerald, the famous American author, observed that it is the becoming and not the being that is most satisfying. There is considerable truth in this statement. There is nothing quite so exciting for a politician as a victorious election night. Following a victory at the polls many politicians suffer a letdown. The high-school football hero never feels quite so elated as during those few seconds when he races toward the goal line and stardom. The student's slow, sometimes agonizing, progress toward the successful completion of a set of degree requirements can be more satisfying than possessing the actual degree. *Becoming* a poet or a writer or an artist can be more satisfying than *being* one. In fact, Fitzgerald points out that, following his early, heady successes, writing became a more and more odious chore necessary for the maintenance of his standard of living. In other words, attaining or reaching some desired state often represents a pinnacle of excitement.

Behind this notion is the concept of the human as a vital, striving organism that is built to struggle and to attain fulfillment of hungers through that struggle. We are perhaps happiest when we are meeting obstacles, overcoming them, and gratifying ourselves following the tussle. We are not particularly happy if all our needs are automatically and continuously fulfilled. If everything comes to us without effort on our part, we never experience need, and we never enjoy the fulfillment of that need. If we are automatically and passively fed, watered, clothed, and sheltered, we become bored and restless.

When the fight is taken completely out of life, when we are consigned to a state of passive and perpetual satiation, with all our drives at zero, we run into emotional trouble. Remember, our genetic makeup is such that we are probably happiest when we experience deprivation-based need and are able to satisfy that need. But if we are never deprived, then we never experience need. And when we don't experience need, we can't enjoy the reduction of that need.

This sad state of affairs is just what the American culture establishes in many ways. By heaping upon us the basic commodities of life, our culture robs us of much of the pleasure that can be derived from those commodities if we are first deprived of them for some time. In short, *we don't experience enough need for the things we can have because our culture is too quick to supply them.* It is the curse of overabundance and the first of the ways that progress and technological advance rob us of satisfaction.

Take food, for example. Fortunately, hunger is a drive that is quickly reinstated following the act of eating. Within hours we are hungry again. But, at the same time, we don't enjoy food as much as we would if there weren't so much of it around, if we were a bit more deprived, and if we had to work a little harder to obtain it. But ours is the food-at-your-fingertips society. Food can be had anytime and anywhere. There is hardly a town left where twenty-four-hour food is not available. Relatively few are starving in our country or, for that matter, very hungry. After all, we all just ate a few hours ago, didn't we? From the richest to the poorest we all have food. If you can't earn food, it will be given to you. This free food may not be the best, and it may be presented to you under rather demeaning conditions, but food you will get.

Food and eating become boring because, for many of us, there is no real deprivation involved. With a good solid twelve hours of not eating behind you even dog food smells good. But we are overfed, overweight, jaded, sated, and mildly disgruntled about eating. Food waste in this country is enormous. We throw away vast quantities of food because no one is hungry enough to eat and enjoy it.

Our fifteen-cubic-foot freezers are full. Our nation's grain elevators are bursting. Our streets are lined with restaurants. Our bodies are loaded with fats and sugars. The lean and hungry look is often replaced by the pear shape.

The fast-food concept adds to the problem. Not only are these fast-food establishments everywhere you look, but they perpetuate a further indignity. They go so far as to rob us of what little pleasure can be gained from waiting a few minutes for our food. Slam, bang, here is your fast, cheap, plentiful food. Stuff it in there, gorge yourself. We even have dial-a-food. Chicken, ribs, and pizza are all brought right to your door.

During a recent period when refined sugar prices were going up because of bad weather in the producing areas, a woman was interviewed on television. With a stricken look she exclaimed that she just didn't know what she was going to do without her ready supply of cheap sugar. This substance could easily be removed from our diets completely, but we have become so spoiled, so fat, so satiated that the mere thought of having to reduce the use of one unhealthy food substance sends us into a panic.

In many cultures about the world a great deal of satisfaction, pleasure, and peace of mind are associated with the production and consumption of food. In primitive cultures the gathering, growing, and preparation of food provides a satisfying focal point for life. Food is not always easy to come by; storms, drought, and pests sometimes reduce the food supply; these conditions add to the satisfaction that can be obtained from the food that is available. In the United States, with its overabundance and lack of any form of deprivation, food and eating often produce grumbling, dissatisfaction, and disharmony. "This steak is tough." "The service here is terrible." "This hamburger is cold and tastes like cardboard." Contrast this lack of satisfaction with the mighty pleasure a starving individual would experience if given but a single bite of the lowliest American burger. Because we have too much we are dissatisfied with what would make much of the rest of the world ecstatic.

Food isn't the only area where our technology has led to dissatisfying superabundance. There are other areas where we never really feel deprived at all and thus fail to experience gratification. Take cleanliness, for example. The hot shower is a great invention, capable of producing enormous pleasure. But you have to need and want to take a shower before this pleasure can be maximized. The best shower experiences are those that follow long, hot, dirty, tiring periods in our lives. But how many of those do we experience? Not too many. Many Americans get up in the morning and take a shower without really knowing what is happening. They aren't even very dirty, just having slept between clean percale sheets (which is another story). The average shower may be pleasant and may serve as a slap in the face, or stimulant, but it certainly can't compare with the pleasure that spray can produce after two weeks without a shower. It's no wonder we are robbed of shower-taking pleasure. Americans are surrounded by showers. Our homes have two or three of them. Tubs, too. And whirlpool baths. A home with only one bathroom is looked down upon by the average home buyer. An Eskimo might talk about one single shower experience for the rest of her or his life, while the American is blasé about the whole issue and often puts showering in the category of "things-I-gotta-do." Hair washing is another case in point. Many Americans wash their hair, not so they can feel the wonderful relief associated with flushing out assorted nits, dirt, and dandruff, but because they are worried about their appearance. They wash the living bejesus out of their hair using all sorts of weird chemicals to create as unnatural a fluff as possible. And then they worry because their hair still doesn't look right. Where's the pleasure in all that? Don't take so many showers and you will enjoy them more. No one cares about your hair (they are too busy worrying about their own) so wash it less. Remember, it's the becoming not the being. It's getting clean after being dirty that is the most fun. Walking around completely clean at all times is pretty tedious. Enough of life is just maintenance without having to be spotless at all times. Leave that to the worrywarts. Stand out in your crowd. Be a little shabby once in a while.

Sex is another case in point where superabundance and lack of deprivation leads to dissatisfaction. For many people, getting enough sex is a problem. But for others, even though they may not be aware of it, the problem is just the opposite. Imagine a typical middle-class couple who have been married for more than fifteen years. They have made love hundreds and perhaps thousands of times. The opportunity to make love is always available to them, day after day, month after month. At the slightest twinge of desire they can make love and reduce that budding desire to zero before it really gets off the ground. The sexual urge is a drive similar to hunger and thirst in that it builds with time. If not allowed the time it needs to build, and if gratified repeatedly at a low level of desire, then the entire sexual experience can become flat and listless.

It's not surprising that many people attempt to rejuvenate their sexual life in many different ways. Some try to spice up the experience with a given partner by turning to artificial stimulants, by having sex in new and unusual situations, and by wracking their brains for ways to make the event new, unusual, and exciting. This pursuit of novelty is merely an exhausting stopgap measure, for it does not get at the root of the problem, which is a lack of deprivation-based desire. Many turn to other partners, running through countless numbers, in an attempt to avoid a sense of inadequacy. But we should remember that if desire is great enough the lace panties and under-the-table positions with a stranger become superfluous.

Many people base a portion of their self-image and their sense of adequacy upon the amount of sex they have. For them, it is not so much the quality of the experience as it is the number of times they make love. Portions of our culture imply that bliss is continuous sexual intercourse. Anything less than this ideal is threatening. One solution to flagging interest in a once-passionate, long-standing relationship is to cut back, perhaps temporarily, on the frequency of lovemaking calmly and without becoming panicky or insecure about it. In this manner, desire is allowed to build naturally without artificial aids and without straining the individual's capacity to invent novel circumstances endlessly. But, for many, cutting back, even temporarily, on the frequency of lovemaking is very threatening. They wonder if something is wrong with them. They wonder if their love is dying. None of these need be the case. After all, in what book is it written that the human must engage in reproductive activities once every twenty-four hours or that human is classified as a flop?

Human sexual preferences vary widely. The rate of intercourse varies enormously. All these variations are normal in that none of them represents failure, inadequacy, or any other negative quality. Enjoy as much and whatever kind of sex you prefer and don't listen to anyone who tells you you *must* engage in a certain amount to be normal.

Why do we possess this sense that sex is required, that we must perform frequently? Again the villain is our culture. The mass media, advertising, the entertainment world, and even many forms of literature are constantly bombarding us with the same message in different forms: lots of SEX makes successful people. Millions of dollars a year are spent on messages drumming into our heads the ways that we can make ourselves more attractive, more alluring, and thus more successful with the opposite sex. Even more millions are spent by the public each year on the products advertised as surefire ways to become more attractive. The message behind all this, which we can't help feeling, is that we are somehow inadequate or inferior if we can't measure up to the supersex image touted by the culture. Thus we overindulge in sex and, in the process, miss some of the excitement.

No part of our body is safe from the implication that it is somehow less than perfect and needs to be brought up to "normal" sexual standards. Our hair is the wrong color, dull, and stringy. Our eyes, eyelashes, and eyebrows need perking. Our noses need to be reshaped. Our teeth are yellow disasters. Our lips are pale, dry, and boring. Our skin is not satin smooth and lustrous. It could also use a little tan coloring. Little things dangling from our ears will help them be more attractive. Female breasts need all sorts of help, we are told. They should be pumped up, pushed out, and generally moved around. Many parts of our bodies don't smell good. We are told, if we are to be adequate, we must spray under our arms, in our mouths, and between our legs, as though man- and womankind did not get along in a very sensual manner for ages before any of these devices were invented. Just so we won't get suspicious we are told many of these changes will make us look more "natural." Puffed-up, sprayed, colored hair is supposed to be natural when, in reality, slightly oily, unsprayed hair is the natural condition. Various parts of our bodies must be painted, particularly our nails. Hair must be removed in all sorts of random areas. Finally, we must go to great effort and expense to clothe ourselves properly if we are to assume we are adequate, "with-it" people. And not only must we go to all this expense but we must keep changing as well. We must "keep up" with the trends in clothing lest we fall into the morass of cloddiness and become "out of it."

None of this has anything to do with true sexuality. Sex can be had without the latest industry-proposed gimmicks. They weren't needed thirty thousand years ago so why are they needed now? Basically, this effort to convince us that we are potential disasters in the field of sex is here because it makes money.

Unfortunately, even the strongest, most individualistic of us is warped by this massive assault on our sense of adequacy. We all listen and, in spite of our better judgment, believe a little of what we are told. Maybe we aren't attractive if we smell like sweat. Maybe these superficial qualities do make a difference in our sex life and thus in our basic sense of adequacy. Maybe people who make love more often are more adequate. These worries can push us into the pattern where we force our lovemaking, where we feel we must make love or something is wrong with us. As a result we don't allow our natural desire to build up; we cut our desire short.

What we need to remember is that if desire is great enough it doesn't make any difference how dirty people are. We also need to keep in mind that amount of sex should not be equated with adequacy. The economics of the situation are such that more money can be made if the public believes that frequent sex is incredibly important and that sexual adequacy can only be attained through the continued purchasing of a wide range of manufactured goods. Both of these are myths. Can two shabby people who have sex infrequently be happy? The answer is yes if they can avoid being duped by the prevailing, economically inspired claptrap. If you are worried about not making love frequently enough or with enough intensity, lay off for a while. Your own body with its slowly growing washes of desire may surprise you. Without some deprivation, under conditions of continuous gratification, the satisfaction associated with sex must be diluted.

In many segments of American culture continuous intercourse is equated with the highest degree of adequacy. But many cultures do not indulge in this sort of self-defeating mechanism. To the contrary, many societies limit contact between males and females. Sometimes the sexes live apart and engage in sexual activity during prescribed specific times. One can only imagine the heat of those encounters. In other cultures sexual activity is delayed until relatively late in life. Certainly there is no social stigma attached to the infrequent or delayed sexual activity in these cultures. And one would be hard pressed to argue that desire is not allowed to grow. Perhaps we don't want to go quite so far in our efforts to spice up our sexual experiences. But there is a lesson to be learned.

Too much food, too much cleanliness, too much required sex. What other forms of American overabundance lead to dissatisfaction and unhappiness? Perhaps every form of consumption in American life is subject to some degree of overabundance. When it comes to basic needs we are just not deprived very often. We have more food, water, sleep, warmth, shelter, time, travel, social contact, information, cigarettes, alcohol, drugs, sex, and so on, than might be ideal for an optimal sense of happiness. It is the curse of having arrived. We've got it all and are thus robbed of the satisfaction of getting. Many of us are bored, jaded, satiated, bloated, and listless. We need to be starved a little, but we just can't seem to deprive ourselves of anything. Instead we go on consuming without enjoying as much as we could.

The Genetic Trap

One might reasonably ask why, if all this unhappiness is caused by a lack of deprivation, we don't just deprive ourselves of a few things and regain lost satisfaction. After all, if food tastes bland when we aren't very hungry, wouldn't it be a simple matter to go without food for a while and, in the process, begin to enjoy food more? The answer is no. It isn't a simple matter. The problem is that, in trying to deprive ourselves, we may be fighting against a naturally selected tendency to try to keep all drives at zero. Although this form of argument is very controversial, a case can be made for the notion that we are fighting against the dictates of our genetic makeup.

Think back along the course of human development. Through the ages the individuals who were most likely to survive were those with strong appetites and strong urges to locate and secure the essentials of life. Because the essentials of life were not nearly as abundant as they are in America today (in fact, they were often downright scarce), the individuals who were the most highly motivated to satisfy their desires would be the ones who would exert the most effort to obtain needed substances and would be the ones most likely to live to reproduce. Humans evolved under conditions of adversity and scarcity. Natural selection dictated that the most driven individuals would survive. We are genetically arranged to *reduce* drives. It is against our naturally selected nature to attempt to *increase* drives. No wonder we have trouble denying ourselves anything. Through the course of human evolution mutations that led to a desire to increase hunger or other bodily needs would die out. Supplies were scarce enough without the individual wanting to be even more hungry.

So all of us alive today may possess a genetic heritage which dictates that we always try to reduce drives. This heritage was established under conditions in which supplies were difficult to obtain and the impulse to reduce drives paid off in a greater likelihood of survival and reproduction. In fact, in many portions of the globe today a strong desire to reduce the needs of the body is still an asset. But things have changed in America and other advanced societies. Suddenly, and we mean in the course of several hundred years out of countless generations, the basic essentials of life are no longer scarce. Almost overnight, in terms of the evolutionary time scale, we have been inundated with food, water, shelter, and so on. Our technologies have accelerated to the point where obtaining the essentials of life are no longer a problem. And yet our genetic makeup lags behind. Our brains are essentially identical to those of our hunting-gathering Stone Age ancestors. Because natural selection moves slowly and technology has accelerated rapidly there is a gap between what our genes dictate we will be and what would be the best organism in our advanced technological state. Specifically, there is a conflict between our naturally selected desire to obtain and consume the essentials of life and the overabundance of these essentials provided by our technology. We can't resist that cheeseburger because our genetic makeup says, "Get all you can. It may be a long time before you see another." Food should be scarce for the happy, efficient functioning of creatures such as ourselves. But it isn't scarce. And we have trouble making it scarce through self-deprivation because we are just not built that way. Perhaps, in ages to come, natural selection will dictate that those who can refrain from opportunistic consumption will be more likely to flourish. But natural selection takes time that we don't have. We have to try to obtain satisfaction here, today, in spite of the conflict between what we are genetically and what technology has done to our environment. As we continue our line of reasoning, the techniques for remedying this schism will become clear.

Gimme, Gimme, Gimme

If you will recall, there are at least two ways that technological advances have led to dissatisfaction rather than satisfaction. We have just seen how technology can lead to boredom and unhappiness by providing an overabundance of the essentials of life. We now turn to the second source of dissatisfaction which has to do with the way that our culture encourages us to want things we can't have.

To make this source of unhappiness clear we must make a distinction between what psychologists call *basic drives* and *acquired drives*. Basic drives are the drives or needs we are born with such as hunger, thirst, sexual passion, and so on. We don't acquire those drives. They are innate and inherited. It is these basic drives that we have been discussing in connection with overindulgence. Basic drives often bring us little pleasure because they are so often overindulged. But there are other drives, the acquired drives, that lead to dissatisfaction in quite a different manner. Acquired drives are encouraged and then frustrated by our culture. We are encouraged to want things we can't have (and don't even need).

What is an acquired drive? Quite simply, it is a *learned* drive, or a need for something that is not an innate, inherited need like hunger. For example, the need for fancy cars is an acquired need. If not trained and encouraged to need or want several tons of metal and plastic, human beings will not, on their own, want such things. The desires to be wealthy, to be successful, and to wear elaborate clothing may well be acquired. Individuals will experience hunger no matter where they live. But acquired tastes vary from culture to culture. For example, native Americans of the Northwest United States felt the need to give away a portion of their wealth in what was known as a potlatch. But this need is not felt by the rest of Americans. It was not acquired. To the contrary, the remainder of Americans often seem to feel the need to give away as little as possible. Thus, what kinds of needs or drives an individual experiences are affected not only by innate factors leading to what we have termed the basic needs but by the social and cultural milieu in which the individual is raised as well. Learned or acquired needs vary from culture to culture while basic needs do not.

Before turning to the types of acquired needs that are fostered by, and then frustrated by, our technological, materialistic culture, let's spend a moment considering how a need is acquired. Just what is the learning mechanism behind the acquisition of this wide array of acquired needs? Experimental psychologists are not positive about how drives are learned. But they do have some good ideas. Consider the need to affiliate or to be with other people. This is a need that has received considerable attention in psychological literature. Some influential psychologists feel that this need is at least partially innate, that we are born with the need to socialize and spend time with other people. But other psychologists argue that the need to affiliate is largely learned, or acquired. They feel the learning comes about in the following, simple manner. If good or positive things happen to a person while in the company of others, then that person will begin to associate other people with pleasant experiences. The individual will begin to want to be with other individuals because, in the past, such social contact has been pleasant and rewarding. But if predominantly negative or painful experiences occur when the individual is in the company of others, then that individual will grow up with a low need to affiliate. Since most of us received warmth, food, and comfort from our parents and others when we were very young, we have a fairly strong acquired need to be with others. But some people suffer abuse and neglect as children. Many of these individuals may grow up with a low need to affiliate. Because their past experiences with people have been so negative, they are hesitant to expose themselves to others as adults.

So the theory behind the acquisition of a drive is simple. If an element, such as other people, is always associated with positive experiences or rewards, then we will begin to value, pursue, and desire that element.

Given that we now know a little something about what psychologists mean by acquired drives and how they are learned we may ask the important question: what kinds of drives does our particular culture foster and then turn around and frustrate?

The need for material objects

There are at least two important acquired needs that give Americans considerable trouble. We shall deal with them in order, beginning with the need for material objects. America has often been called a nation of materialistic individuals. We are characterized as a people obsessed with possessions. We seem to want more, more, more. We believe that by owning things we can be happy. Other cultures and nations throughout the history of humankind have emphasized the importance of ownership, but perhaps never to the extent that a preoccupation with objects has gripped Americans. The American dream is filled with new cars, boats, houses, clothes, and appliances. The despair of the American is not owning anything. Happiness and satisfaction are equated with ownership. This belief is so ingrained in our way of thinking that we sometimes have trouble believing that it is, after all, just an acquired taste, and not some innate, universal urge. But a perusal of other human cultures quickly reveals that ownership of material goods is not universal and is actively avoided in some situations. A Zen Buddhist, for example, has little use for Buicks and seeks to escape from the cloying burden of material objects. One of the major sources of conflict between the native Americans and the European settlers was that the Indians believed the land belonged to all humans equally. Dividing the land up into little plots to be owned by particular individuals was an alien idea to them.

There are several identifiable forces that contribute to our need to possess objects. First, ours is a capitalistic system. Capitalism is nothing more than a system in which most of the means of production are privately owned and operated for *profit.* Basically, the motivating force behind our system of production is greed. If you can produce more and sell more then you gain. Our economic system, geared as it is toward the production and the distribution of goods, provides the background for our acquired need for objects. This is not true in all cultures. For example, some "primitive" cultures lack the concept of private gain and profit. They are based upon simple sharing values where the success of an individual is shared directly by all.

But merely possessing a capitalistic system does not guarantee the establishment of an acquired need for objects. That capitalistic society must be a successful one. It must be able to produce goods. This is where our enormous capacity to generate an endless stream of physical goods feeds into the equation. Producers in this nation come up with more objects for sale and more apparent variety among them than was even imaginable a short time ago. And because the system is capitalistic and supposedly based upon competition, the producers must continuously come up with more, better, and novel objects. Because our technology, or the application of basic scientific principles, has progressed so rapidly we are inundated in a flood of material goods, some of which are worthwhile and some of which merely prop up the endless need to produce new objects in order to generate profit.

But there is, after the acknowledgement of a capitalistic system that can produce, one more element that is necessary before that capitalistic system can be called fully operative. Quite simply, the goods that are produced must be *sold* before profit can be realized. It is at this end of the system, the marketing end, where we find many of the mechanisms that produce an acquired need to own objects. First, our enormously sophisticated systems of mass communication allow messages concerning available goods to reach the consumer repeatedly and quickly. Never has a people been so bombarded with messages encouraging it to buy, buy, buy. Television, newspapers, radio, magazines, and billboards bring unending information about the products of our capitalistic system. We know more about what is available faster than ever before. Several hundred years ago it might have taken weeks or months for one end of a country to know what had happened at the other. A battle could be over before you even knew a battle was being contemplated. Major social, political, and economic news moved very slowly, to say nothing of the snail's pace dissemination of information concerning a new toy developed somewhere in the land. But today we know immediately. We even know ahead of time. We are told to anticipate and hunger for items that are "coming soon." Being used to instant and complete information about almost every single thing, we find it hard to imagine what it must have been like when sailing ships with skimpy news from Europe took months to arrive.

Finally, the great villain in the development of our inordinate need for objects is the advertising business. Advertising is absolutely essential for the efficient functioning of our capitalistic society. Without advertising all our mass communication, our ability to produce mounds of material goods, and our greed-based system of production would be mired down. It is, finally, advertising that sells the goods that support the profit system. But even though advertising is essential for the functioning of the system it has some negative side effects for the individual, for you and me.

It is advertising which encourages the acquired need for objects. If you will recall, an acquired need for something is established when that something is consistently associated with pleasant, good, positive events. In our example of the need to affiliate, we want people because we associate them with positive experiences. In a very similar manner, advertising contributes to our need for material objects by consistently associating the ownership of objects with positive experiences. We are constantly bombarded by the idea that people who own things are happier than those who don't. Flip on the television and what do you see? People being happy when they obtain some object or service. On a logical level, if we see enough people being bubbly and happy as they obtain new objects, then we are naturally going to want new objects too. It wouldn't be so bad if we were only occasionally exposed to this "objects bring happiness" message. But there is hardly a day in the life of the average American when this same message, in many different forms, is not received. In advertisements happiness is depicted as being the result of owning cars, deodorants, washday soaps, furniture, houses, refrigerators, wines, shoes, TVs, stereos, antiques, wallets, hats, pets, pictures, books, tools, lamps, curtains, trees, tire gauges, T-shirts, hams, pants, wheelbarrows, bird feeders, jewelry, tennis rackets, watches, gold, coats, bikes, and you name it. And what's more if you *don't* have all these things you will be unhappy. Your wash will be yellow, your boyfriend will back away from you, and the neighbors will look down at you. The general message is that we need everything. If we have everything we will be happy. If we don't we can never expect total satisfaction. The message is that we should go out and buy happiness.

The idea that objects lead to and are associated with satisfaction is dunned into us at every turn. A casual glance through a national magazine revealed an ad for a car. The following words were used in the brief ad:

most beautiful	more (6 times)
newness	great experience
attractive	value
innovative	complete
bright future	room
comfortable	highly respected
huge.	

Nowhere in the ad were the following words:

expensive	silly
trouble	pretentious
danger	plastic
necessity	fragile
ugly	rust.

An advertisement for a rug in the same magazine included terms like:

masterpiece	subtle
floating	dream come true
flowers	genuine
beauty	fairy tale
magic	happy
incredible	happiness
delicate.	

Similarly a brief ad for a resort hotel used:

secluded	romance
very	tinkling piano
tropical	clinking glasses
beautiful	sizzling crepes
white beach	strumming guitars
call of a sandpiper	excited applause
ripple of laughter	warm feelings
serenity	delight
love	vacation.

It didn't mention:

heat	uncomfortable travel
sunburn	expense
insects	noisy plumbing
poor service	drunks.

No wonder Americans believe objects equate with happiness. We are constantly being told and shown that this is true. No one is advertising calmness and stillness, or an uncluttered life per se, because they are not manufacturing those items and do not need to sell them (unless they have some object-related angle on these things such as a $900,000 home that will provide tranquillity). It is objects that they need to move so they present them as the harbingers of happiness.

Once instilled and supported by continuous advertising, the belief in "happiness equals ownership" becomes a social value. That is, it is believed and accepted by people and passed on both consciously and unconsciously from generation to generation. Suppose a young child sees her parents express great joy and happiness when a new appliance arrives. This represents one instance of the inculcation of the ownership value, one instance where the child sees that objects bring happiness. Without being aware of it the parents are teaching the child to value objects. They are building in the youngster an artificial need for objects.

Materialistic snobbery appears to be a common outcome of this capitalism-based acquired need for objects. If ownership of objects brings happiness, it follows that if you own more objects than your neighbors then you must be happier. In fact, if you own more than they do, you must be better than they are because you are all after the same things and you have been more successful at it than they have. Owning objects becomes doubly desirable. Not only does ownership allow you to join the ranks of happy owners, but you can justifiably feel superior to those who own less than you do.

You can't win

Contained within the system that prompts and encourages Americans to want and need objects are the very seeds that grow into dissatisfaction and unhappiness. Very simply, no individual can have everything. There is, after all, a limit to how much one can acquire. Personal limitations (e.g., lack of ability) as well as circumstances beyond our control (e.g., lack of opportunity, luck) define just how much we can own. And yet the economic and social system says nothing about the fact that we should all anticipate and expect a limit. Advertising never ceases telling us we can be even happier if we own more. The resulting social belief is that any person can acquire anything if they try hard enough. Yet this is simply just not the case. Americans have an unrealistic idea of how much they should be able to own. They have been conditioned to believe that ownership brings happiness and they are constantly offered an enormous array of objects which they can purchase on "easy credit terms." "Just pick up your phone."

It is inevitable that we shall all meet our own limit. Frustration and dissatisfaction result because we have been conditioned to want more than we can have. The snobbery mechanism outlined above contributes to our dissatisfaction. True we can feel superior to those who have less. But what about those who have more? We feel inferior to them and resent their success. There is always someone with more, and because there is always someone with more, we are bound to suffer. We eat our hearts out for objects that others have.

Middle-class children are given too much too soon. Their acquisitions might better be spaced out a little more. By the time they are young adults and ready to go out on their own they have already received a good portion, free and unearned, of the objects they will be allotted by their ability and circumstances. Because they have experienced effortless acquisition they have come to expect this Disney-like parade of incoming goods to continue. But, for most, it does not. Children are brought too quickly to the limit they will experience. The flow of free objects dries up and dissatisfaction is compounded.

In summary, we previously argued that Americans suffer dissatisfaction because they have more than they want, an overabundance in fact, of certain basic essentials of life such as food and water. They are never deprived enough of these elements to enjoy them. In the immediately preceding section we have outlined how this dissatisfaction is increased by the fact that our culture encourages us to want, desire, and value material goods in spite of the inevitable limit on the amount of those goods we can possess. Frustration of the acquired need for objects is inevitable. Our basic drives are overindulged while our acquired drives are frustrated and denied. In the next section we turn to a consideration of another acquired drive that leads to a great deal of dissatisfaction in our society.

The need to achieve

Another of the things that we learn to pursue in this culture is success. We all, to one extent or another, want to achieve, to do well, and to succeed in some way. We want to be the best, or at least very good at, something. We want to do well in school, in our careers, and/or in our social lives.

To achieve is to meet or exceed some standard. Americans, generally high in the need to achieve, want to excel in some way and often force themselves to try to do better and better. The businessman tries to arrange more deals and to accumulate more money. The actor wants bigger and better roles. The student strives for better grades. Parents want their children to be "the best." The population in general yearns for fame and fortune.

This urge to do better and to exceed standards is not necessarily innate. Many psychologists believe it is a learned impulse. They have found that those of us with the greatest need to achieve have been treated differently, as children, than have people who are not highly motivated to achieve. Specifically, it appears that people high in the need to achieve have been rewarded for, and been expected to engage in, independent behavior at an early age. For instance, many children who eventually grow up to be highly achievement oriented are expected to put themselves to bed when they are very young, rather than being tucked in and helped each evening. They are expected to entertain themselves and are rewarded for doing so. For example, they may be required to spend hours alone while other, eventually less achievement-oriented, individuals will be helped and attended to to a greater degree.

High achievement individuals also appear to be those who have been rewarded for achievement behavior at an early age. For instance, they may be required to earn and manage their own money while still very young. They will be praised and encouraged in all their independent, achievement-oriented behaviors.

You still can't win

It is true that people with a high need to achieve work harder and do better, in school, for instance, than those with a lower need to achieve. But built into the situation are the seeds of eventual, inevitable defeat and frustration. Quite simply, no matter how hard we work and no matter how much we accomplish, there is always one more standard, or level of excellence, above our own. We can never get to the end of it all, if we are truly driven to achieve. The skilled and driven individual near "the top of the heap" can be just as frustrated as the person toward the bottom. The frustration a U.S. senator feels in not being able to make it into the White House can be just as painful as the nursery school teacher's frustration over not being able to earn much more than minimum wage. Rich, successful, famous people can be just as frustrated as poor, unsuccessful, unknown people.

It all has to do with the fact that each of us, sooner or later, runs out of luck and talent. But there is always one more level of achievement staring us in the face. Each of us can go just so far. But the ladder of success never ends. Each of us will eventually reach the limits of our resources. And, if we are driven by the never ending need to achieve, this can be frustrating regardless of how far we have come.

The unsuccessful person scoffs and says, "If I could achieve what she has I would be content." But success is relative; what seems like ultimate, final success to one person is just another step on the ladder upward to another. And the ladder of success or achievement is endless.

As a result, many people in this highly success-oriented culture will eventually feel frustrated. Some manage to avoid these feelings of bitterness, but many do not. The need to achieve is one more example of the way our culture leads us into situations where we want what we can't have. Just as we all want material objects and are eventually denied, so too do we want success, only to be denied any further achievements in the end. It's a "no-win" situation.

The problem is compounded by the fact that we all tend to compare ourselves with those rare individuals who are on the very top of the heap. We look at the president of General Motors and say, "What does he have that I don't?" We think about that one lucky individual who wins the sweepstakes. We read accounts of fabulous wealth and fame. In other words, we look at the very top of the pyramid of success, and we feel bad because we are not right up there. What we tend to forget is that for every one of those success stories there are literally millions of people whose accomplishments and successes are more modest. But we don't think about all of those people. Their stories are not pounded into our lives by the communications media. When was the last time you heard a TV report about an average person bringing home an average paycheck? We usually hear about the rare, spectacular success stories. As a result we tend to compare ourselves unfavorably with those lucky individuals, rather than with the enormous mass of average individuals.

More, more, more

Americans, by and large, are spoiled in that they have been taught to expect more and more for less and less work. Just going along from year to year with our same relatively high standard of living is not good enough for us. We want, demand, expect more and more each year. We become angry when we don't get more. Business people are depressed if their profits stay the same from year to year, even though those profits may be incredibly high. Inflation is fueled by this never ending demand for more. The environment and our natural resources suffer because we hate and fear a constant level of income. At the same time we aren't willing to work as hard as we used to. As a result, wealth is drained from the country, going into those areas of the world where people will still work for less. The outcome is that we do, in fact, experience less growth than we might.

We become grouchy, grumpy, and demanding. Factions of the population compete with one another for the dwindling wealth. They try to take it away from one another, bickering over who is and is not doing their share of the work. In other words, when we expect more and more out of life we are, once again, caught in a no-win situation because, inevitably, the goodies of life have a limit.

3

What Not To Do

In Chapter 2 we saw how many of us are left not wanting what we can have (because we are not deprived enough to want it) and wanting what we can't have (because our culture teaches us to want more and more). Both of these lead to frustration, bitterness, and anxiety. In this chapter we deal with some of our most common reactions to frustration. Most of these don't do much good and can be called maladaptive, or worthless. But it is good to become aware of some of these reactions to frustration. By realizing what we are doing and feeling we can perhaps alter our behavior such that our negative emotions will be minimized.

I'll Rip Your Face Off: Direct Aggression

The well-known "frustration-aggression" hypothesis points out that when we are frustrated we will often attack whatever it is we believe is frustrating us. If one child takes a toy away from another, then that second child may directly assault the culprit in an attempt to regain the toy. If we are trapped in traffic, late for an appointment, we will often scream and yell at the offending drivers. If our romantic partner is taken away from us, we may become assaultive toward the competition.

In extreme cases, assault, and even murder, can be the result of frustration. We occasionally hear of employees killing their employers over blocked ambitions. We learn of family members murdering one another because of intense frustrations. Neighbors occasionally attack one another over frustrating disputes involving such things as noise, parked cars, and property maintenance. In other words, although aggression is not always the reaction to frustration, it is one of our major responses to being blocked in our desires.

Aggression can occasionally help, but not that often. If a child is bullied by other children, a show of aggressive behavior may help the child "earn some respect." But, more often than not, it seems aggression doesn't help very much within our complex cultural setting. If our neighbor's stereo is played too loudly, we can shoot out his windows and thereby stop the noise temporarily. But, more than likely, such direct aggression will create more trouble for us than we really need. Assaulting one another may ease our anger momentarily, but it eventually leads to trouble.

Thus, in general, although it is fairly common, direct aggression does not appear to be an ideal way to respond to the common frustrations of life. In the next chapter we will outline some frustration-reducing techniques that are much more adaptive.

Kick That Dog: Indirect Aggression

A husband arrives home after two hours on the crowded freeway. His request for a raise has been turned down. A business deal fell through. To top it off, the neighbor has left trash cans on his lawn. At dinner, the man's young daughter does a very ordinary thing . . . she spills her milk. On a better day this event might have been routine. But on this frustrating day the husband instantly flares and gives the child a smack. His wife protests and he yells at her. Everyone finishes the meal in sour silence. After dinner, the wife bangs the pots and pans around in the kitchen. The child sneaks off and teases her kitten.

All three people have engaged in *indirect aggression* in their efforts to reduce their frustration. When we are frustrated by something which might be dangerous to attack we often pick some weaker, less dangerous object and vent our anger on it. The husband wouldn't dare attack his boss (although he would dearly like to throw him out the window) so he takes it out on his family. The mother doesn't want to worsen the situation so she slams dishes around rather than going after her husband. The child seeks out the weak, helpless kitten and gives it a rough time because she is afraid to aggress toward her enormous, stern father.

The only thing that indirect aggression does for us is temporarily relieve the pent-up feelings of frustration. It is a temporary solution at best. It does not address the *cause* of the problem. For instance, no matter how good it felt to hit his child, the husband will still have to go back to his office and face his "failures."

We all use direct and indirect aggression to one degree or another. When the situation is a mild one (such as being caught in traffic) venting our anger can be helpful in that it gets it out. Try screaming at the top of your lungs next time traffic frustrates you . . . with or without windows rolled up. You will probably feel better even if a little foolish. But when the frustration is of a major, long-standing sort, then aggression does not seem to be the best answer. If you are frustrated in your career, in your social life, or in your love life, then any sort of aggression may momentarily help you, but, in the long run, it will either do nothing at all or it will make things even worse.

Who Gives a Damn? Apathy

Many times, when we are frustrated because we don't want what we can have and/or can't have what we do want, we become listless, apathetic, bored, and depressed. If a working person is turned down repeatedly in her efforts to move upward, she may say, "The hell with trying. It won't do any good anyway." A defeatist attitude is adopted. Rather than becoming aggressive and assaultive, the individual adopts just the opposite tack. She becomes enervated, weak, helpless, and despondent. She quits trying because she knows, she is convinced, that trying won't do any good.

Psychologists call this sort of response to frustration *learned helplessness* because they feel the individual has learned, through repeated failure experiences, that there is no hope. If things haven't worked out in the past, why should they be any better in the future?

This response to repeated failures, with its associated depression, is particularly insidious because it feeds on itself. Each time the person says, "Why bother trying?" she is reducing her chances of overcoming whatever it is that is frustrating. The more despondent and inactive the person becomes the less likely she is to overcome the problem.

Psychologists have begun to outline some method they feel might help in breaking this learned helplessness cycle. For example, they feel that if the individual can be encouraged, actually goaded, into being more assertive and even aggressive, then the cycle may be broken. They also feel that if the subject can be led through a series of *minor* successes (let's not try to conquer the world in a single shot), then some confidence can be regained. For example, if an individual is so far down and so depressed that he can barely get out of bed, that he has let his appearance go, and that he has lost all contact with his friends, then the process of building confidence in little steps can be helpful. If the depressed individual can be encouraged to take a shower, get dressed, and call a friend, and praised for doing so, then some progress has been made. The individual will begin to feel that he is not a total washout and can do something, after all, that will make life better. Next the individual might be encouraged to get a newspaper just to look for a job. Actually going on an interview would not be expected at this stage. Just thinking about what kind of a job might be a small step that could be praised and encouraged. By taking things little by little, step by step, rather than all at once, the sufferers can slowly regain confidence by succeeding in these small efforts rather than be overwhelmed by asking too much of themselves all at once.

Of course, this process of reversing depression by guaranteeing small successes, rather than demanding large victories, treats a condition that already exists. It would be better if we had some simple techniques that would help us avoid ever getting into that sad state of affairs where we have lost our confidence and feel as though nothing we can do will help us. Chapter 4 contains some suggestions that can aid us in maintaining a reasonable level of confidence.

The Baby Talk Syndrome: Regression

Sometimes, when we don't seem able to overcome frustration, we resort to behaviors that worked for us at an earlier age. Thus, the teen-age girl, unable to convince her parents that she needs a new wardrobe, may resort to some form of baby talk that had been very successful when she was younger. Or an adult, if reasonable discussion fails to achieve his aims, may return to demanding, temper tantrum-type behavior that was effective at an earlier time. A wife, feeling that she is losing her husband's affection, may attempt to make him jealous and aroused in a way that worked during their courting period.

Regressing to earlier forms of successful behavior when current, mature methods of dealing with problems seem ineffectual is something we all probably do to one degree or another. Sometimes it can help us over the rough spots. But when it becomes a primary method of dealing with frustration it precludes growth and fixates us at less mature levels of adjustment.

Dream On: Fantasy

When frustrated we can, and often do, escape into fantasy. We daydream; we imagine sweet victories and even sweeter revenge. We torture our oppressors, we vindicate our honor, and we show them all. There is nothing wrong with fantasy as long as it does not dominate our lives and prevent us from dealing with reality. After all, no matter how many times you send your employer to hell, she or he will still be there come Monday morning.

Gobble, Gobble: Gluttony

As we have seen, overabundance can lead to a form of frustration. Because our culture provides us with so much food and drink, so many forms of relaxation and entertainment, and so many excesses in terms of the basic necessities of life, we are never without these essentials long enough to really want, desire, and crave them. We are frustrated because we are not given the opportunity to want something strongly and then to go ahead and have it.

One response to this form of frustration is particularly sad—that of gluttony, or overindulgence. We desperately cram in more of everything, hoping in vain to recapture the exquisite satisfaction that can only be ours if we are first deprived. Continuous, massive consumption is a futile effort to gain satisfaction, and yet we go about it almost compulsively. We over-eat, we overdrink, we oversmoke, we run frantically from one form of indulgence to another, never gaining the satisfaction we could have if, for a while, we could deprive ourselves.

This response to frustration only increases the problem. If deprivation is what is lacking then compulsive overindulgence clearly is not the solution.

Economic Slavery: Overborrowing

We have already noted that, in various and subtle ways, our capitalistic system encourages us to want material goods. We all have, to one degree or another, a learned need to want *things*. The possession of things has been equated with happiness and superiority. And yet we have also noted that, sooner or later, we will feel frustrated in our desire for things because there is always a limit to how much we can possess. We run out of luck, resources, and talent. Some of us manage to possess more than others . . . but the person who possesses more is no less frustrated than the one who possesses less. The person with a Ford looks with envy at his neighbor who owns an Oldsmobile. The Oldsmobile owner wishes she had a Cadillac. The Cadillac owner eats his heart out because he can't afford a Rolls Royce. The Rolls Royce owner can't stand it when she pulls up to a stoplight and there is another, newer Rolls Royce in the next lane. And so it goes. No matter how much we have we always want more. And there is always someone out there with more to goad our feelings of envy and jealously.

So what do we do if we want more but have spent all our money? We borrow. We can have what we want right now. Just sign on the dotted line and worry about paying later. Refrigerators, vacations, microwave ovens, stereos, cars, clothes are all ours for the asking . . . as long as we sign on that line.

Because Americans are so driven to own things they often fall into the trap of overborrowing. In a sense, they sell their souls to the loan company. Sometimes borrowing is a good idea. For instance, if the thing you are buying, such as a house, goes up in value as time passes then borrowing can be a useful lever. But when the goods, such as clothes, appliances, and the like, lose value over time, then heavy borrowing can lead to even greater frustration, because there is a limit to how much we can borrow.

Once that limit is reached we are stuck with what we have and stuck with the odious task of trying to pay off loans for goods that have already lost their value and their novelty.

When we overborrow so that we can have things we want right now, our lives become restricted. We become overburdened with loan payments. We lose our freedom to move, change, and vary our lives because those loan payments keep coming due.

The last few years have seen a sharp increase in the amount of American consumer borrowing. Nearly everyone is in debt. Some manageable debt is fine. But when the borrowing becomes excessive it robs us of our freedom, and we become even more frustrated. Easy credit, high interest rates, a fear of continued inflation, and an acquired need to possess more and more all lead to the situation where we feel boxed in and enslaved by our own greed.

The loan consolidation scheme is one of the more insidious forms of economic slavery. A borrower, behind on his loan payments, is encouraged to "consolidate" his loans and reduce his payments to a single lower payment. The catch is that, even though the single monthly payment may be lower than the total previous payments, this lower payment must be made for a much longer time. The upshot is that by "consolidating" the borrower loses even more money and is in debt for a longer time. Almost no one gives money away. Loan companies always take some of our money, no matter how attractive their schemes may appear.

Overborrowing, as a response to the frustration we feel when we can't have what we want, can only lead to a greater sense of frustration. Once we are locked into a heavy payment schedule we have given up what little choice we had to begin with. Once our splurge of overborrowing is over, we can't even buy the occasional treat we used to be able to afford. All we can do is work and pay, work and pay, as we watch our stereos break, our cars fall apart, our children lose interest in their fancy gifts, and our clothes go out of style. There must be a better way, yes?

One Toke Over the Line: Drug Abuse

For thousands of years people have been swallowing, sniffing, injecting, and smoking a wide array of chemical substances in their efforts to relax, reduce anxiety, reduce pain, stimulate insights, sleep, perk themselves up, and feel happier. Obviously, there must be many reasons why people turn to drugs. But one of the reasons probably has to do with the kind of despair, frustration, and depression we have been talking about. If an individual's life seems blocked, going nowhere, and filled with unfulfilled desires, drugs offer an alternative solution. They can create some of the feelings of well-being that seem to escape the person in everyday life. Drugs can make a dreary, hopeless life more fun, at least temporarily. Unfortunately, many of the drugs currently in vogue carry a high price tag. Many of them can create mental or physical damage.

This is not to say that all drugs are necessarily evil. After all, drugs are merely chemical substances and mashed potatoes are chemical substances, too. Everything we consume has a chemical nature. But the problem with many of the narcotics, hallucinogens, stimulants, and depressants is that we are not sure of their long- or short-term effects. We just don't know enough about them to conclude that they are as harmless as foodstuffs. So there is a danger involved in the use of drugs and, for that reason, a dependence on drugs to alleviate the frustrations of life would seem to be a less than ideal solution.

I'll Drink to That: Alcohol Abuse

The use of alcohol seems to be particularly troublesome. Of all the drugs, this one seems to be most widely used and most often abused. Through history alcohol has had a checkered career in terms of its social acceptability. At times it has been held in high esteem, while during other periods of history, it has been regarded as the devil's work. At the present time it is used by millions of people in the pursuit of relaxation and a sense of well-being.

The trouble with alcohol is threefold. First, used in excess, it is physically harmful. If you want to do in your body, one of the surest, most direct ways is to poison it with a lot of alcohol. Second, alcohol is addictive. Alcoholism, or a dependence upon alcohol, is a dangerous and destructive form of addiction. Third, alcohol can fool you. It tends to make you feel confident when, in fact, it is impairing both your sensory and your motor capacities. It is entirely possible to feel extremely confident, and then quite bewildered, as you miss the driveway by five feet and end up parking in the roses. Automobile drivers are very susceptible to this false sense of security and competence that alcohol provides. It's just when you are least able to drive that you feel most confident. We can laugh at these little misadventures, but it is this sense of overconfidence that results in intoxicated people speeding off the end of the pier into the bay. Enormous numbers of deaths and injuries are the direct results of drunken driving.

Small amounts of alcohol don't seem particularly dangerous, especially when the drinker stays out of the driver's seat. A drink or two can lead to a fine sense of well-being. In fact, there is some evidence which suggests that people who drink small amounts of alcohol may actually live longer than nondrinkers. However, three or four drinks can seriously impair our mental and physical functions. In addition, drinking can lead to aggressive and violent behavior. Caution is the keynote when it comes to alcohol. Using alcohol as your primary means of gaining a sense of well-being is dangerous.

Defense Mechanisms

So far in this chapter we have discussed a number of behaviors which might best be avoided in our efforts to reduce frustration and anxiety. These have included aggression, apathy, regression, fantasy, gluttony, overborrowing, and drug abuse. In this section we want to consider an additional class of behaviors which, while not entirely maladaptive, are less than ideal solutions to our problems. These behaviors, called *defense mechanisms,* are normal in that we all, sooner or later, use them. But, at the same time, they are not completely satisfactory because, as we shall see, they involve self-deception and distortion of reality. The following description of these defense mechanisms parallels that presented by Houston, Bee, Hatfield, and Rimm *(Invitation to Psychology. New York: Academic, 1979).*

Rationalization

Let's begin with an example. Suppose a young man gets all dolled up and goes to a party looking, as always, for that one perfect thunderbolt of love and passion. After so many halfhearted and disappointing relationships he doesn't have much hope . . . but he hasn't quite stopped looking.

On this occasion the dream comes true, or so it seems at first. Across the proverbial crowded room he spots a woman who so strongly attracts him that he is left breathless. Cautiously, but with iron intent, he makes his way toward her. Screwing up his courage and doing everything he can to appear attractive, he attempts to strike up a conversation with her. She receives him politely at first. But as their conversation continues, he suspects he is beginning to bore her. He redoubles his efforts, she begins to look over his shoulder. He tries to think of humorous things to say, she looks irritated. Finally, she is openly rude to him. But he can't seem to leave. His ego is being lacerated, he is feeling smaller, less attractive, and more worthless by the moment. Then a large, hairy male breaks into their conversation and takes the woman away, much to her obvious relief. Later, out of the corner of his eye, he sees the woman talking to her smirking friends, pointing at him, and laughing.

Now what does our poor friend do with all this? What can he do? He wanted something he couldn't have. He has been ridiculed, scorned, frustrated, and made to feel anxious about himself. Without being aware of it, he begins to protect himself. He begins to use one of the defense mechanisms. First, eyeing her from across the room, he suddenly notices that that her calves are very bulky. In fact, her ankles are big, too. Piano legs! Who needs that? Then he thinks that even if she didn't like him she could have been polite about it all. She is obviously a crass, crude clod who doesn't deserve someone as sensitive and civilized as he is. Just look at that baboon she ran off with. Then he thinks, "You know, I was lucky to find out how bad she was before things went any further. Good riddance!" Following this line of thought our friend is able to regain his sense of well-being. He has successfully used the defense mechanism known as *rationalization.*

When we rationalize we reduce frustration and anxiety by saying we have not really been frustrated, or we haven't acted wrongly or foolishly. Let's look at a couple of additional examples. Suppose a student cheats on an examination and then finds she feels bad about it. What can she do? She can, without really being aware of the fact that she is rationalizing, tell herself that cheating is justifiable because *everyone* does it. If she didn't cheat she would be unfairly penalized in her competition with the other students. Similarly, a business person may cheat on income taxes, explaining the illegal act by saying that you can't make a profit unless you do cheat. And, anyway, the government just gives the tax dollars to welfare chiselers.

If students fail an examination, they can say to themselves that the failure was really a blessing in disguise, because it helped them realize that they weren't really interested in that subject anyway. If a business fails, the owners can say it was due to market conditions, or they can say they learned a lot from the experience, or they can reduce their feelings of failure by blaming the failure on their partners. Joe couldn't keep the books straight, or Barbara paid too much money for raw materials. There are always ways we can rationalize our own failures and reduce our anxieties.

Defense mechanisms are neither all good nor all bad. On the positive side, they *help us over the rough spots in our lives.* For example, if you fail to get a job you really wanted you can feel pretty miserable for quite a while. Some moderate rationalizing in this situation can be helpful. By rationalizing (e.g., I didn't really want that job anyway) you can give yourself time to get over the disappointment. You can gain time to find fulfillment and satisfaction in other ways. Rationalizing will give you some relief when your discomfort is most acute. Later you may even be able to look back on the situation and realize that you really did fail without feeling anxious. After all, we all fail sooner or later, don't we? No one is perfect.

Defense mechanisms are *unconscious* efforts to reduce anxiety and frustration in the sense that we are not aware that we are using them. We do these things, such as rationalize, without knowing we are doing them. If fact, if we *try* to use the defense mechanisms, if we attempt to use them consciously, they won't work. They just have to happen it they are to be effective.

For example, if a tennis player loses an important match and then says, "I will now blame this failure on my equipment, the officials, and the condition of the court, thereby excusing myself from all blame and responsibility," the sense of failure will not go away. The individual really has to *believe* in their rationalization. If they know they are simply making excuses, they will still feel bad.

The use of defense mechanisms, in moderation, is not abnormal. We all use them frequently, without being aware of the fact that we are utilizing them. They can help us over difficult spots in our lives. So don't be alarmed if you find you have been using rationalization as well as the mechanisms described below. We all do so. They are part of our everyday life.

But defense mechanisms are not all good. They do have some negative aspects. For example, they all involve *distortion of reality* and *self-deception.* When we rationalize we are actually kidding ourselves. We are denying or distorting reality because the truth is too painful. We can't accept our failures because they make us too anxious. We really did feel attracted to someone, or we did want a business deal to go through, but we pretend we didn't.

The lesson here is that, in *moderation,* defense mechanisms can be useful. But if things get out of hand, or if we start using defense mechanisms as our primary means of dealing with the environment, then one can begin to wonder at what point we are beginning to lose touch with reality. If an individual blames every failure on external causes, and never accepts any responsibility, then that person is overusing the mechanism of rationalization. Ultimately, such excessive use of rationalization will get a person in trouble in our culture. You just can't get away with it. People who rationalize too much will end up getting less out of life than they might otherwise. For instance, if a new employee in a department store *always* blames problems on customers, the other employees, the merchandise, the weather, and the general state of the world, that person may well end up looking for a new job.

Reaction formation

Our desires for things we can't have can lead to the use of other defense mechanisms. For example, suppose a young college student finally has his own apartment. His dreams of freedom, women, drugs, orgies all seem to be about to come true. But then he receives a phone call from an elderly aunt who, as it happens, took care of him when he was a youngster. She is now a widow without money. The young man immediately invites her to come and stay with him. But once she arrives things begin to go wrong. She disrupts his life, she nags him about his dirty socks, his dreams of sensual depravity begin to evaporate. And yet what can he say, for it is true that she gave up a good portion of her life for him? He begins to hate her. He has fantasies of throwing her and her little pile of belongings out on the sidewalk. He is horrified by these secret hostile thoughts. He feels guilty and anxious. What's wrong with him that he should want to hurt this unfortunate woman? But he does. He begins to wish she would have a heart attack and wonders what the probabilities of stroke are at her age. All of these thoughts seem sick, yet they won't stop.

This is where reaction formation, one of the defense mechanisms, may come to the rescue. In a reaction formation we act in a fashion that is just the opposite of what we are actually feeling. The young man may show his aunt great warmth and consideration, even though he really feels like screaming at her. He may become excessively polite and helpful even though his hidden desires are aggressive and hostile. In this manner, he acts as though there were nothing to be anxious about. He defends against his anxiety by acting in a manner that denies his feelings.

Repression

In repression we block out from our consciousness thoughts and feelings that make us anxious. For example, suppose, because our culture encourages it, a woman wants furs, jewels, status, power, cars, and all the other claptrap which a materialistic system values. But she is married to an unemployed envelope stuffer and has no skills of her own. What can she do? She can feel miserable by thinking constantly of all the things she wants but can't have, or she can repress these thoughts. Without being aware of it, she can refrain from thinking about these desired objects and events. In this manner she can at least partly reduce her yearning, her fear, and her sense of dissatisfaction.

Repression is a controversial defense mechanism because there is very little good hard experimental evidence for its existence. And yet it is a popular concept in many therapeutic and clinical settings. The argument is that each of us has buried within us repressed or unexpressed desires which, if we were to bring them into consciousness, would make us anxious. Many therapists believe these repressed desires cause trouble, even when they remain buried. They may still affect our behavior and our sense of well-being.

Dreams and repression. For example, many psychologists believe that repressed desires and frustrated drives show up in our dreams. The argument goes like this. We all have desires or impulses that are unacceptable to us because they make us feel guilty, anxious, or frustrated. So we repress them. That is, we just don't think about them, and we are not even aware that we have them. The classic impulses usually referred to in the analysis of dreaming are sexual and aggressive impulses. We are assumed to have strong, but unacceptable sexual and hostile impulses—you know, rape, murder, plunder. But to think about, or recognize, these nasty impulses makes us feel anxious as well as frustrated. So we hide them away. But the problem is that, even though they are repressed, we still have them. They don't go away. Dream theories often argue that these impulses are expressed in our dreams. As an example, let's say, we are frustrated because we were passed over for a promotion. Some punk kid got the job we felt we were entitled to. A classic case of what we have been talking about; we ran up against the limits of our ability. We wanted more than we could have. Our learned need to succeed led us to inevitable failure. The failure makes us angry. We want not only to personally destroy the people who gave "our" job to the younger person, but also to do away with that unsuspecting employee as well. We have murder in our hearts. But if we recognize and wallow in these hostile thoughts, on a conscious level, we feel guilty. It's not nice to want to murder people, so we have been taught by our culture. We will be made anxious if we think about these impulses consciously. So we repress them to avoid the anxiety they stimulate. But these little devils are still "inside" us somewhere. We still want to murder. So what can we do? If we can't think about murder consciously, but we still have the impulse, what can we do? We can satisfy our murderous impulse in a dream. We can get some relief from these aggressive impulses by attacking our persecutors in our dreams. We can fulfill our wishes in our dreams if we can't fulfill them by engaging in actual physical violence.

But wait a minute. That sounds all well and good but we still have a problem. Suppose we do murder our boss in our dreams. Suppose we do indulge our wildest desires. We create mayhem. Where does that leave us? When we wake up and remember the awful things we did in our dreams, we will *still* feel guilty. The moods and feelings experienced in dreams often carry over into our waking hours. If we have just brutally murdered our boss in our dreams, we are likely to feel a bit worried about the whole episode when we wake up.

So, according to dream theory, we *camouflage* our actions in our dreams. We hide our true intent, but still carry out the wish fulfillment. Then, when we wake up, we feel better because we have indulged our aggressive impulses, but we don't feel guilty because we don't recognize what we have really done. Our dreams often seem weird and incomprehensible. The argument is that this incomprehensibility is part of our protective apparatus. If we did understand our dreams we would be appalled.

To return to our example, we might, in our dreams, witness a murder committed by a stranger upon a stranger. Or we might dream of a huge wave sweeping over and destroying a city. Or we might dream of a judge dying from some horrible disease. Dream theory argues that each of these dreams expresses, in a hidden, disguised, camouflaged manner, our hostile impulses. *Symbols* are important aspects of this form of dream interpretation. A symbol is merely something which stands for, or refers to, something else. For example, the judge who dies from a disease is an authority figure who stands for, or represents, the employer we want to hurt. The disease represents, or stands for, the hostile acts we would like to engage in but can't. The disease does the job for us. In our dream, we kill off the boss (judge) through a hostile act (disease), but we don't feel guilty because we don't even recognize, consciously, what we have done.

Obviously, this form of dream interpretation is controversial. Many investigators object to this idea that dreams have hidden meanings, that they express repressed impulses, and that they use symbols to satisfy forbidden desires. On the other hand, many clinical psychologists believe hidden and repressed impulses can be expressed in our dreams.

The emphasis upon symbols is strong in this tradition. Much of the theorizing in this area has to do with sexual impulses, as well as with hostile urges. Thus it is not surprising to learn that such things as hoses, snakes, bullets, tree trunks, and elongated objects are interpreted as symbolic expressions of the male sex organ while ovens, closets, caves, hats, pockets, drawers, and the like are seen as expressions of the female organ. Riding horses, driving cars, climbing ladders, crossing bridges, and the like are seen as sexual intercourse.

The trouble with all of this dream interpretation, and the notion of repression in general, is that the facts have not been established conclusively. This is all pretty much guesswork, based upon clinical observation. No one has been able to prove, or to demonstrate experimentally, that anything is ever repressed or that repressed thoughts are expressed in dreams.

So if you try to understand yourself and improve your sense of well-being by analyzing your dreams and seeking your repressed impulses, you are delving into an area where speculation overshadows fact and where guesswork takes precedence over empirical knowledge. The position taken in this book is that there are better ways to pursue happiness. As we proceed through the following chapters we will discuss overt, concrete, *actions* which can be taken to increase our pleasure without having to refer to, or pursue, the illusive repressed desire.

Hypnosis and repression.   One of the areas of research that has been taken as providing evidence for repression is that of hypnosis. Many have claimed that repressed thoughts, normally unavailable to the individual, can be recovered under hypnosis.

Let's first consider a little background information. An individual must be willing to be hypnotized if it is to occur. In other words, you won't go into a trance unless you want to. In fact, what the hypnotist does is invite you to slip into or enter a hypnotic state. There are many ways to induce a trance, but in most of them the hypnotist, speaking in a soft, calm voice, invites the individual to relax, to become drowsy, and to become tranquil. The hypnotist suggests that the subject stop worrying. The subject is encouraged to relinquish control. People can be brought out of a trance at the snap of the hypnotist's fingers or upon the occurrence of some other agreed-upon signal.

Not all people will enter a trance. Many of us will be too busy watching, thinking, and analyzing to become hypnotized. Others will be too concerned about maintaining control to be receptive to the hypnotist's suggestions. Many different types of individuals can be hypnotized; there is no one specific personality type that is susceptible.

The trance itself is described as a state of calmness, detachment, and relaxation. People who are in a trance are not very active. They do not try to pay their bills or plan a vacation. They are passive and content to let the hypnotist do the planning. They are very receptive to the hypnotist's suggestions and will engage in all sorts of unusual behaviors when asked to do so, but they won't initiate very much activity on their own.

Depending upon the susceptibility of the subject and the depth of the trance, subjects can be encouraged to accept distortions in reality, such as "seeing" and petting a kitten that is not there, and to engage in unusual roles, such as "becoming" a police officer when asked to do so. Posthypnotic amnesia refers to the phenomenon in which a hypnotized individual is told they will remember nothing about the trance when they are brought out of it. If a subject is told, during the trance, that the number 3 will disappear from her mind, and she is then brought out of the trance, she will have difficulty counting correctly, saying, "1, 2, 4, 5," and, "20, 21, 22, 24, 25." Six fingers will be counted on one hand, "1, 2, 4, 5, 6."

Emotional behavior is very susceptible to hypnotic manipulation. People can be made to laugh or cry, to see something as funny or sad, when they are hypnotized. It is the ease with which emotions can be manipulated that makes hypnotism potentially dangerous. In the hands of an unskilled hypnotist, we can be made to experience quite unpleasant emotional states. Hence, as a word of caution, before you allow anyone to hypnotize you, be sure they know what they are doing.

Now, to return to our primary concern with repression. What evidence does hypnosis offer for the existence of repression? Well, there is a phenomenon called *hypnotic age regression* which many have claimed proves the existence of repression. In hypnotic age regression the hypnotist invites the subjects to "go back" in their life, in effect to become younger and younger. Often the hypnotized subjects seem to regress to their childhood. They begin to think and act like children. Many therapists feel that long-buried, or repressed, thoughts can be tapped into while the subjects are hypnotized. Old fears, conflicts, and desires, normally unavailable to the subject, are brought to the surface. Painful, disturbing, anxiety-producing thoughts and impulses are supposed to be released from the repressed state.

But there is considerable doubt about the validity of the age regression phenomenon. It does seem that some memories do appear under these conditions. But they don't appear to be any more accurate than memories produced under other conditions. They are just as inaccurate, just as full of gaps, and just as distorted as "normal" memory. In fact, the whole phenomenon of hypnosis is under attack. Some claim it is nothing more than an example of "role playing" wherein the subject wishes to please the hypnotist and so *acts* in accordance with the hypnotist's suggestions. Non-hypnotized subjects can, when willing, do everything that hypnotized subjects can do. In addition, it is impossible to tell the difference between a hypnotized subject and a nonhypnotized subject who is pretending to be hypnotized.

Still, age regression and repression are important concepts in many therapy situations. We will just have to wait for further research and study before we will be able to assess the true nature of regression.

Suppression

Sometimes, when we are irritated, frustrated, or made anxious by something we say, "I'm just not going to think about that!" If we wanted a color TV for Christmas, but someone was thoughtless enough not to give it to us, we can sometimes reduce our disappointment by saying, "I'm just going to think about other things!"

This technique, called suppression, is quite helpful in getting over some rough spots in life. But it is *not* a defense mechanism because it is used consciously. When we suppress unpleasant thoughts we do so of our own free will. We do it intentionally and, because it is not done unconsciously, it is not classified as a true defense mechanism.

Suppression can be a useful technique, especially when there is nothing we can do about the circumstances causing our discomfort. If we learn a close relative has terminal cancer, we might do well to at least occasionally avoid the inevitable feelings of fear and sorrow through suppression. But too much suppression can be dangerous also, especially when there *is* something we can do about our problems if we would only think about them. For example, suppose we have failed to receive a hoped-for promotion. We could bury our heads in the sand and avoid the whole unpleasant situation. But to do so might negate constructive steps that we could take if we faced our failure more directly. We might be better off thinking about why we failed and what should be done about it. Should we redouble our efforts to win the promotion in the future? Should we look elsewhere for satisfaction? These kinds of difficult but helpful questions won't even be asked if we suppress too much. In other words, if something can be done, suppression should be avoided.

Projection

Projection refers to the defense mechanism wherein we see in others our own unwanted attributes. A person who feels she is a failure may see the same quality in others. "Boy, what a loser he is!" A greedy person may see greed in others. "All he thinks about is money, money, money!" A dissatisfied individual may see dissatisfaction in all those around her.

Projection can help us feel less anxious about our own frustrations, failures, and shortcomings. For example, if we are anxious about failing, we can lessen that fear if we see the world as being full of failures. By comparison we do not appear to be so bad. If we are anxious about our own greediness, we can feel better if we conclude that everyone else is even greedier than we are.

Again, projection can help us feel less anxious. But, like all defense mechanisms, it involves distortion of reality and self-deception. Hence, there must be better ways to deal with our problems.

Identification

Small children can delude themselves into believing that they share the power of stronger children by walking, talking, and acting like the older children. In a like manner, adults can gain a sense of power, competence, and success by copying the behaviors of those they perceive as powerful and competent. We can identify with successful people and thereby gain a sense that we too are successful. If we drive the same kind of car, live in the same neighborhood, eat the same food, read the same books, and, in general, follow the lifestyle of successful people, then we too must be successful.

Again this defense mechanism involves self-deception. What we are doing is trying to gain a sense of worth by copying the superficial lifestyle of others.

These and other defense mechanisms are all well and good. But they do limit our possibilities for satisfaction because they involve distortion and denial in our efforts to cover up our anxieties. In general, it would be better if we could deal more directly with the causes of our anxieties rather than with their symptoms.

4

Having Your Cake and Eating It Too

Let's review what we have covered so far. First, we outlined how Americans often feel frustrated because 1) they don't want what they can have and 2) they desperately want what they can't have. Then, in the preceding chapter, we outlined some of the common and, for the most part, ineffective ways we often react to these feelings of dissatisfaction.

Because the "natural" reactions to frustration and dissatisfaction outlined in Chapter 3 are, at best, stopgap measures and, at the worst, downright self-defeating it behooves us to look for some new, alternative ways to deal with these problems. In this chapter we will begin to outline and describe some of our new procedures for gaining satisfaction. While these procedures are not guaranteed and are based on the opinions of the author, we hope you will find some of them to be helpful.

We have two problems to address or two forms of frustration to consider. The first, resulting from not wanting what we can have, will be addressed in this chapter. Basically, we will be suggesting that our desire for, and satisfaction with, many elements of modern life can be enhanced if we can manage to deprive ourselves of them for a while before we go ahead and indulge ourselves with them.

The second problem, having to do with feelings of frustration resulting from wanting what we can't have, will be addressed in the next chapter. For now, we want to concentrate upon the idea that we can increase our pleasure by waiting for that pleasure, or delaying it a bit longer than we are used to doing. If we can increase our drive, or our desire for it, then we will enjoy it more when we go ahead and indulge in it.

This chapter addresses a number of different areas of our lives where frustration due to overindulgence is common. We will consider relationships with other people, eating, work, entertainment, and so on. These topics are discussed in no special order. Some of them will be of more interest to you than others. But in each case the thrust of our argument will be the same: *by depriving ourselves rather than overindulging, we can enhance our eventual pleasure and generally feel better about the world.*

Enjoying People

Getting the best out of friends

People often say things like, "I'm bored with all my friends. I want to meet some new people," and, "If I hear about Nancy's problem with Bill one more time I think I'll scream." We often feel that our friends are driving us up the wall, are too demanding, are not entertaining, and are taking too much of our time. We begin to nod knowingly when we hear things like, "Friends . . . you can't live with them and you can't live without them." When we get to this point, when we begin to feel our friends are more trouble than they are worth, it is time to take stock.

One obvious solution to the problem is to stop being friends with your current acquaintances and to build a new set of relationships. Sometimes this solution is best, and sometimes it seems unavoidable. On the other hand, it is an extreme solution, isn't it? After all, you were drawn to these people for some reason in the first place. You do have things in common, and you have had affection for one another. To dump one batch of friends only to take on another group seems rather drastic. Basically, you will be doing little more than substituting one set of human problems and pleasures for another. There must be a better solution than this extreme form of housecleaning.

This is not to say that we shouldn't drop old friends and make new ones. As we grow, develop, and pursue our interests we are bound to change friends, at least some of them. On the other hand, there can be real value in trying to maintain and hold on to long-established relationships even though they occasionally seem boring and old hat. There are pleasures, joys, and ways of relating to one another that can only be reached after we have known one another for long periods of time. There is something valuable in living through a significant portion of life's stresses and strains with a given individual. Old friends can be the most comforting, the most helpful, the most intelligent, and the most entertaining just because they are old friends and have "been through it" with you. They know what you are talking about and why.

Still, we do sometimes become bored and restless in the presence of our oldest and dearest friends. When little of importance is occurring, old friends can become tedious. So what can we do, short of dropping the old friend completely? We can apply our simple notion that deprivation leads to increased desire. Quite simply, we must make an effort *not* to see our best friends when we run into the tedious phases of the relationship. It's like the old cliché, "Absence makes the heart grow fonder," with the added twist that we, ourselves, create the absence intentionally.

If we can stay away from our friends who have become boring for a while, we will find them much more entertaining when we do finally reunite with them. We can rekindle a sense of pleasure and interest in one another, without having to end the relationship permanently. We will really be ready to get right in there and talk about the nitty-gritty. Having been temporarily out of touch, we will have new experiences to relate to one another. We will have something new to talk about, rather than have to go over the same old thing one more time.

Many of us seem to establish this pattern without really thinking about it. We have old and close friends whom we do not see for long periods of time—weeks, months, even years. When we do get together it is stimulating and satisfying. On the other hand, we sometimes become wrapped into a pattern where we see too much of our close friends—and we chafe under the constant presence of one another. It is in these cases, where we are seeing too much of one another, that we need to take intentional steps to reduce the amount of contact with one another. We need to take *control*, intentionally, rather than just drift along.

How can we go about limiting contact without hurting our friends' feelings? It can be pretty tricky. (One can imagine a particularly sensitive friend asking, "Are you trying to avoid me?" and you answering lamely, "Yes, but only because I love you.")

Obviously, the most direct method would be making sure your friend knows what you are doing and why. But it takes a pretty strong person to be able to accept the statement that they are being avoided because being with them has become tedious. It's the old story, isn't it? Whenever a relationship is changed, the one who does the changing usually feels better than the one upon whom the change is imposed. "She left him" or "He left her" often makes all the difference in the world in how the involved parties feel about themselves. The one doing the changing usually feels more powerful, more in control, and happier. The one being subjected to change often feels threatened, weak, and worthless. "What's wrong with me? I'm not good enough."

So, to reduce the amount of time you spend with old friends in an effort to increase your satisfaction with the relationship is not always easy. A straightforward explanation of the situation can lead to bruised feelings and even the permanent end of the relationship. Perhaps it is better to use subtler methods. "Little white lies" can be helpful here. For example, unplugging the phone or taking it off the hook can be a surefire way of decreasing communication. If a friend has a habit of calling at a certain time, these techniques can help immensely. Some people even have the phone taken out of the home altogether in their efforts to reduce the overload and gain perspective on their lives and relationships. If you can't bring yourself to unplug your phone or take it off the hook, you might try the "handy excuse" method. When you find yourself in a vulnerable situation (e.g., near a phone or physically near your friend) have an excuse ready like, "Can't talk now. I've got an appointment with the IRS." Or, "I've got a meeting now." Or, "I'll catch you later; the kids are screaming for dinner." These are lies, of course, but they hurt no one and, in the long run, are designed to increase the satisfaction you obtain from the relationship. Honesty may not be the best policy in these sorts of situations.

White lies can be helpful in avoiding unwanted social engagements. For example, if you are at home in the evening, relishing your solitude, and a friend calls inviting you for dinner have an excuse ready. "We'll have to make it some other time. I've got to see my in-laws tonight." (In-laws, no matter how maligned they are, can be great excuses for all sorts of things.) The key here is to have your excuse ready *ahead* of time. Don't wait until the phone rings and the question is asked before you fumble around trying to think of something suave like, "A week from Saturday? Gee, sorry, I'm going to have the flu then."

Do your planning ahead of time. Be ready when the phone rings. If you are living with someone, get your signals straight. "If anyone calls, we are taking the dog to the vet." Excuses work better if they are preplanned because you can carry them off more convincingly.

Excuses are also better if they are specific. Saying something vague like, "Sorry, we're busy," makes the caller wonder if you are making an excuse. It's better to say, "Sorry, my sister is in town," or, "I wish I had known earlier. We've made plans to go to a cat show at the Forum."

But the real secret of excuse making lies in the ability to convince your caller that what you are going to be doing is a drag compared to what they want to do. "I wish we could, but I've got to take my car in for $300.00 worth of repairs." "I've been throwing up on the hour for the last eight hours." "You go ahead and have a great time. I've got to try to get the stains out of the carpet." "You remember my clown uncle from Des Moines? He's in town and wants to go to Disneyland."

Avoiding friends, to make them more valuable, without their knowing what you are doing, is the sort of maneuver that can be slightly exhilarating. Your intentions are of the best and yet you run the risk of hurting someone's feelings. So you have to be on your toes.

Making them want you

This business works both ways. Just as you will want them more if you don't see them quite so often, so too will they value you if they don't see you. By inventing excuses to avoid being with your friends, you build up their need to be with you as well as your need to be with them. Deprive them a little. Make them want you. Make them believe you are desirable and slightly difficult to get ahold of. The way to do it is to be elusive. Don't be available constantly.

There are certain cues that appear when you begin to be boring to your friends. Watch your conversations with them. If they begin to monopolize the time spent talking, you can begin to suspect that they find what you say to be less than scintillating. If, when you are talking, you have the uneasy feeling they are just waiting for you to stop talking so that they can start talking, it may be time to disappear for a while. In some sense, many of the best conversations are ones in which each party talks half the time and alternation between parties is fairly frequent. If your conversations begin to be one-sided with the other person doing most of the talking, it's probably because they find what they have to say more interesting than what you have to say. Sheer amount of time spent talking rather than listening can be a clue to how boring they find you.

There are other cues that indicate boredom. If they allow you to talk a fair amount of time but seem distracted, blank, or disinterested, you can bet they are just being polite. They may not look at you directly, they may turn slightly away from you, and when they do talk, they may not react to what you have been saying. They may start right off on their own concerns, unintentionally letting you know they find your words tedious.

So if you find your relations with your friends going flat, it's time to consider depriving yourself of them for a while—and depriving them of your own wonderful self, too. It's an easy thing to do. You just have to be aware of what is needed—time away from them. And you have to be willing to arrange your life and make the moves such that your contact with them is cut down. You have to be in control. The periods of being away from one another need not involve anger or bitterness. If you can convince them you are just in a busy period of life, they will feel comfortable.

These general guidelines hold true for all sorts of social contact. Many social groups "burn out," over a period of time, because they get together too often. Members often end up saying, "God, it's always the same old people saying the same old things." Circles of friends and acquaintances often stop getting together at all because they have been too persistent and too insistent upon gathering together too often. In the first deep blush of excitement groups will meet over and over again only to realize too soon that they are getting bored with one another. Over the long run an occasional party may be better than two parties a week without a break. The pleasure we gain from one another should be nibbled and conserved, not gobbled up too quickly.

Loving living together

People living together, as man and wife or otherwise, sometimes worry about what they are missing by being paired off in a relatively exclusive relationship. They see apparently gay and carefree singles moving from one relationship to another and wonder if they haven't boxed themselves in too tightly. What they tend to forget is that many of the singles often worry about what they are missing by not having a more permanent relationship. It's the old story—monogamous people are tempted by the dating game and singles are tempted by monogamy. Each, at times, wonders if the other method of relating to people might not be better.

In short, neither form of relating is perfect. Both involve good and bad points, and many people are unable to decide which method they prefer. Each can lead to pleasure and satisfaction. But there are times when the stresses and strains within each form of relating to others become particularly acute. For example, one common problem within a monogamous relationship is boredom with the other partner. It is when boredom and tedium creep into the relationship that a breakup can become likely. Staring face to face across the supper table with nothing to say, believing that exciting life is just minutes away, can be very depressing. Remembering the good times we used to have but can't seem to recapture can be depressing. Knowing that life is apt to go on in its present tedious unchanging way can be depressing. Knowing that there is a lot of unexplored world out there, but being unable to break loose and visit it, can be depressing.

Sometimes, although not always, this state of affairs can come about because two people have become too tightly bound together, too dependent upon one another, and too restricted in their lives. What starts out as an idyllic, charming little love nest can become a prison and a trap. In a sense, the deeper two people become involved with one another the greater the danger of their becoming a restrictive burden to each other. Because they are so in love with one another, they are likely to cut themselves off from the world and depend upon one another for stimulation and interest. That is all very well and good for a while—but it seldom can go on forever. Eventually the two will have heard all the jokes, learned all the moods, compared all the facts, shared all the interests, and explored all the intimacies that are available to them. It is at this point that boredom and dissatisfaction begin to creep in. It is at this point that the relationship is in jeopardy. It is at this point that something must be done.

The question is how to go about perking up a deep relationship that is going stale. How do we go about maintaining a relationship based upon deep regard, trust, caring, peace, and tranquillity? It's not easy, but there are some things that can be done. For example, one of the simplest techniques is to be sure you have enough time away from one another to build up an interest in one another. As someone once said, you probably need a good eight hours a day away from one another. This daily, persistent, and substantial separation does at least two things. First, it gives you something to talk about when you do reunite. Second, it allows you to build up a need for one another just as going without food builds up hunger. And just as food tastes better after a period without food, so too will you seem more delicious and exciting to one another after a period of deprivation. The optimal time interval varies with different people. Some should be away from one another more than others. A few hours apart may be enough to send one couple breathlessly into each other's arms while a few weeks, or even months, may be needed to heat up another couple's flagging interest in each other. In addition, the time interval may vary for a given couple. At any given point you may need more or less time away from one another.

Finally, one member of a couple may need more time alone than the other. Obviously, this can be a sore spot. Unless each member of the couple has a clear understanding of the other's needs, this differential need can be threatening. The one who needs to be alone may feel trapped. The one who needs to be together may feel deserted and threatened. It is a time when clear, honest communication is essential. The couple must discuss their feelings and, above all, *reassure* the other that what they want to do is in the best interests of the relationship. For example, if a woman feels she just has to be alone more, she should make sure her partner knows that she loves him and wants to stay with him. She must reassure him that she is not deserting him but that she merely needs "time out."

In summary, then, we believe the long-term health of a very close relationship can be aided if adequate time apart from one another is maintained. By being away from one another, by depriving each other of the wonderfulness of the other's company, a need for that company can be heightened and sustained.

There is another problem that develops in connection with the time-away-from-one-another solution and that has to do with what is *done* during the time the members of a couple are separated. If one member goes off and manages to have a wonderful, exciting, stimulating time, while the other sits at home waiting for time to pass, then the solution will probably not work. The one at home will feel bitter, inadequate, threatened, and unhappy. To avoid this sort of situation there has to be some careful and thorough negotiating. What must be arrived at are some *shared standards of behavior.* What this means is that the couple must agree upon what they will and will not do during their time apart from one another. The shared standards may vary widely from couple to couple. One pair may agree that they will pursue separate careers while they are apart and maintain strictly platonic relationships with members of the opposite sex. Another couple may feel comfortable with a situation where they both seek romantic involvements during the times they are apart. The shared standards can be as varied as are the personalities of the people involved. Clearly, what is best for one couple might be a disaster for another couple. But what is important in all cases is that both members communicate their needs to one another and that they both understand exactly what it is that they have agreed to.

Arriving at a position where degree of freedom is defined to the satisfaction of both parties can be painful and frightening. In fact, sometimes a clear and agreed upon course of action cannot be negotiated. In these cases the relationship either ends, or one or both members go on living in pain.

Reaching a definition of time-away behavior that is satisfactory to both parties often requires compromise. For example, suppose a man and woman have been living together for a number of years. They have been very happy, but now they are beginning to feel that they should spend some time away from one another. The man wants separate two-week vacations where each member is completely free to do as they wish. The woman finds this suggestion not only of little interest but threatening as well. Some compromise must be reached. The woman may have to agree to occasional separate vacations, or the man may have to agree to separate weekend vacations rather than two-week periods of being apart.

Occasionally members of a couple will have to "go to the wall" on a certain issue. That is, they will have to stand firm and say it's either going to be my way on this issue or not at all. This stance should not be adopted lightly or too often, as it can lead to the dissolution of the relationship, but there are times when it is essential.

Negotiating what will and will not be done during these periods when two people are apart should not be drawn out. The longer things "drag on," the more confusing and unpleasant they can become. In many cases there is no problem at all. Couple members instinctively and naturally choose activities that are acceptable to their partners. However, the decisions are often difficult, and indecisive, waffling behavior with unpleasant consequences can result.

The appropriate steps are simple. First, recognize that boredom and tedium are normal, acceptable consequences of spending too much time together. Second, increase the amount of time spent apart. Third, negotiate the nature of the activities to be engaged in during these times when you are apart.

In this manner you can have your cake and eat it too. You can enjoy a permanent relationship with all its goodies while, at the same time, you can maintain your sense of freedom, adventure, and independence. By spending time apart, you kill two birds with one stone. You build up your need for your partner, and you avoid being dependent upon them for stimulation.

Of course, there is another tack we can adopt in trying to cope with boredom within a relationship that does not emphasize doing things apart from one another. Quite to the contrary, we can fight off boredom by devising, inventing, and discovering new things to do together. The array of available hobbies, entertainments, and activities within our culture is almost limitless. Among these there is bound to be something new that you and your partner would enjoy together. The trick is getting up and doing something rather than sitting around feeling restless and irritable. Try something. If that doesn't work or isn't as interesting as it sounded, try something else.

Don't say, "Well, I'm not sure I will like that." Just pick something that seems it might have a chance of being satisfying to both of you and go ahead and do it. If there are five paths over a mountain and you don't know which is the correct one, it's better to pick one at random than to sit at the bottom of the mountain and worry about the situation.

Still, there are those times when new activities enjoyed together just don't seem to be the answer. There do seem to be times when we really have had enough of one another, and it is these times when being apart can sometimes bring us closer together. While being apart is not a scientifically proven method of helping a relationship, we believe it, like the other ideas discussed in this book, can be useful.

Giving Children Less

It is a common urge among parents to want to give everything to their children. We want our children to have everything we didn't have as children. We want them to have the best opportunities. This is all well and good in one sense. Specifically, the more stimulated our children are, the better they seem to develop. Understimulated and deprived children may fall behind, may be lacking in knowledge and techniques that are effective means of getting along in our world.

However, the situation can and does get out of hand. In our enthusiasm, concern, and anxiety many of us may give our children too much too soon. We shower them with so many of the goods and activities, at such an early age, that we are almost guaranteeing their eventual boredom and dissatisfaction. After all, as we have seen, the goodies of life are limited. Eventually we all meet our limit, as defined by chance and ability. And if a child has had almost everything by the time she is thirteen, then her limit will be met all the sooner. A child who is given clothes, money, toys, a pony, a TV, a stereo system, access to all sorts of entertainment, and freedom from work can be headed for trouble. This child just won't know what to make of the world when the hard reality of having to make a living looms on the horizon. She will already have experienced, free of charge, a good portion of the rewards that most of us work for. She will have "used up" much of the world at a young age. There just won't be that much left to attain. She may well become bitter, frustrated, and confused.

In our opinion, it might be better if we intentionally deprived our children a bit—actually held back some of the things we can afford to give them. We should dole out life's limited rewards in a careful manner. We don't want a spoiled, already jaded eleven-year-old. We need to deprive them, just as we deprive ourselves, so that when they do get something it will be appreciated. Many American children simply have too much.

They can't appreciate what they do have because they are given too much too fast. They are overloaded. A child living in an isolated rural area may experience exquisite pleasure upon being taken to a small, local carnival once a year—because the need is there. The same small carnival may be a total bore to the city child so used to major Disneyland-type attractions. A single toy may be loved and cared for by a poor child, while the child born into a richer family may have dozens of totally neglected toys tossed about her spacious room.

If we deprive our children, if we hold back on some of the rewards of life, we are doing our offspring a twofold favor. First, we are increasing their satisfaction when we do give them something because their desire will have been given time to build. Second, we are giving them a more realistic picture of the world. Presumably most of us won't be able to go on spoiling our children throughout their lives. Sooner or later they will have to make it on their own. The one who has had to wait, and sometimes work for, rewards will be less jolted by adult realities than the one who has always been given everything.

This tendency to want to shower our children with everything often leads us to give them things they are not yet ready for and cannot fully enjoy. For example, we give our children toys that are too old for them. We give them electric trains and bicycles and video equipment before they have reached a developmental stage where they can truly appreciate the gift. We often spoil things for them by giving things too early. We give them a toy that they are too young to enjoy. Then, when they have reached the proper developmental stage to truly enjoy the toy, they are no longer interested because they have already had it. It's old hat to them. They miss the intense pleasure they might have had if only we would have had the foresight to hold off on that particular toy until they were truly ready to enjoy it.

In summary, just as we can learn to deprive ourselves in order to increase our eventual satisfaction, so too can we restrain our understandable desire to give everything to our children. In the long run, they may be happier if they experience a buildup of desire before being satisfied.

How Entertaining (Yawn)

There are other areas of our lives where we don't seem to be getting as much satisfaction as we might reasonably expect. Often this is because we are getting too much of the things modern American life has to offer.

Bored? Nothing to do? Seen all the movies in town . . . or don't want to see them? Does the thought of going out to eat one more Friday evening make you want to scream? Does reading the latest magazines seem like a chore? Does the hassle of parking and shoving crowds make sporting events or cultural events seem more trouble than they are worth?

Do your tennis partners seem too predictable, and does your hang glider with all those struts and wires and that glaring sun set your teeth on edge? Are you tired of driving out of town (or into town)? Does the TV set make you think of your mother-in-law? When you pick up a best-seller, do you think about how much dough the author is making off you? Does the thought of throwing a party to dispel these feelings just make you more depressed?

Where's the excitement in life? What fun is all this "fun," if it isn't fun? What's wrong? What's wrong is that we've had too much of all these modern forms of entertainment. We're glutted with them. In spite of our constant crabbing about how much we have to work and how little free time we have, we really do have a lot of leisure time, and it often hangs heavy on our hands. So we fill the time with whatever is handy, and that happens to be the activities we've been talking about. We're overindulged in modern forms of entertainment. We never have a chance to miss them, because they are always too handy. Our interest never has time to build up, so our sense of satisfaction is limited.

It's time to take charge; to change your life around so you will get more satisfaction out of what you do. There are any number of simple things you can do to regain a sense of excitement.

Television

Television is a form of modern entertainment that can be subjected to our principle of deprive and then indulge. Often, without even thinking about it, we find ourselves, after a busy day, sitting like zombies watching situation comedies and soap commercials, without really experiencing much pleasure at all. Action on our part is necessary. TV is bad enough without drowning in it. We suggest two possible courses of action. If you feel your willpower is pretty good, just stick the TV in a closet. Leave it there for two weeks. Or, if you feel you might give in, remove your TV from the house. Leave it with friends or relatives. Make it, if not impossible to get back, then at least difficult and/or embarrassing.

Spend two weeks without TV. You'll find you won't miss it that much. Other interests will be rediscovered if you absolutely can't get your hands on a TV. You'll be forced to read or do puzzles or do *something* else besides fall asleep in front of the TV. Many of these interests will be things you used to do and enjoy but have stopped doing because it's "easier" to flip on the TV.

Reward yourself for abstaining from watching TV. Take yourself out to dinner and celebrate not having watched TV for a week. Brag about your efforts to your friends and family (it's better to brag to your mother than to your friends . . . she loves you even when you are obnoxious).

Then, after the designated time of deprivation has elapsed, go drag your TV back and flip it on. In our experience, we've found two common reactions to regaining access to TV. Some people love it, finding that it has regained some of its long-lost appeal. The jokes are funnier; the people more handsome, wittier, more insightful; the drama more powerful; the horses faster; and the commercials possessed of a certain beguiling charm. TV is interesting again. Of course, the effect doesn't last forever. Pretty soon, if you're not careful and start watching TV when you aren't particularly interested in it, you'll find it will go flat again. But if you're careful, making sure you feel a good strong interest before you turn it on, and if you avoid watching "because there is nothing better to do," then you can maximize your satisfaction with television.

The second common reaction to a long period without TV is the one where people find they like things better without TV. The alternative activities developed during the two-week period of abstention are more rewarding and more lasting in their value. For these people, returning to TV can be a depressing event, as though they are giving up their free will and becoming slaves again.

Advice for these individuals is simple. Put your TV out on the curb for the trash collector. Sell it. Give it away. It's clear you don't like it, don't appreciate it, and can get more out of life without it. Whatever you do, get rid of it. It's a seductive instrument and must be dealt with harshly. If you keep it around, you will probably start watching it again. Then you will experience a sense of disappointment in yourself, and you will feel flat, bored, and mildly grumpy as you switch from channel to channel looking for *something*. Television watching is seductive because it's so easy. It doesn't require any effort. But, at the same time, for these individuals, it is also much less satisfying than other activities which may require a little more personal effort.

Dinner and a movie, etc.

One of the standard forms of entertainment in America is to go out for dinner and then to a movie. Or to go out for dinner and then to a play. Or to go out for a few drinks and then go dancing. Or to go to a play and then out for dinner. Or to go to a concert and then out for a few drinks.

The combinations involved in these two-part evenings seem endless. But they aren't, and they can get pretty tedious. What often happens is that people fall into a pattern. *Every* Friday night Paul and Joan go dancing and then out for a late bite to eat. *Every* Saturday another couple goes out for activity X and then, inevitably, activity Y. It can get pretty boring, this double-segmented pattern.

It's like the woman who met the charming man who sent her one perfect rose every day. Every day. Day after day. Week after week. After a while she felt that if she had to see one more perfect rose she would lose control.

There are several things we can do to rekindle our flagging interest in the "evening out" concept. First, and most dramatically, we can just stop doing it for a while. Save money, stay at home, let "cabin fever" build up for a while. Then, when we do finally break out on the town, it will be with a refreshed and renewed sense of participation and enjoyment.

If you do select this method of rejuvenating your flagging interest in the evening out, reward yourself for staying home. Buy thirty dollars worth of steak and lobster and cook it at home, instead of paying for a cold fillet of sole and a condescending waiter. Spend the money somehow on something you really enjoy. You will probably feel smug and content and mildly relieved at not having to do the same old thing again. When you think about the money you have been spending on each of these evenings out and think about all the other delicious ways you could blow that money, you may end up permanently reducing the number of times you go out.

Here's another way to spice up the evening on the town. Instead of going out every week, or twice a week, or however often you do, go out one third as often. Save the money you would have spent on two successive evenings (put it in a jar so you can *see* it). Then take it, add the money for the third evening, and spend it all at once. Go to the places you don't usually go to because they are too expensive.

Mix it up. Save up sometimes. At other times go your usual route. You can also mix your activities. Many of us have the habit of falling into familiar patterns. We have our favorite restaurants and our favorite night spots. Sometimes favorite can become synonymous with "same old." When that happens it's time to shake things up. It's time to give the favorites a rest. Force yourself to go somewhere else or to do something different. Then, when you do return to your favorites, it will be with a sense of increased pleasure (and, sometimes, relief).

If you can't seem to get out of your favorite rut, involve other people in the decision. Invite friends over and allow them to influence the decision about what will be done.

Buying tickets

Don't ever buy season tickets to anything. If you do, individual performances or events can lose their special quality of excitement. You'll end up trying to give tickets away, feeling unsatisfied if they go to waste, but incapable of dragging yourself to the fortieth home game of the season. Buy tickets individually, picking your spots. It even helps to have to go to some trouble to obtain them. The event will mean a lot more to you if you do.

Rather than going to too many games or concerts and buying poor seats each time, do it this way. Pick the few events that appeal to you most. Then buy the best seats in the house. You will enjoy and remember the event. Again, save the money for the choice seats in a jar. Put the jar in a prominent, visible spot. Gloat over it as it fills up. Deprive and indulge, deprive and indulge.

Books and magazines

There is the story of the grade-school child who, after reading a book about penguins, wrote in her report, "This book tells me more about penguins than I really want to know." A book is only as good as your hunger for it. If you're not interested in a book, reading it can be an enormous chore. Many people say, "Oh, I should read more. What's wrong with me?" But maybe this isn't the best way to think about books.

Perhaps the way to think about books is to read only as many as you truly want to read. In fact, rather than listlessly picking up a book and plowing through a few pages in spite of your yawns each evening, you should simply put the book away until the thought of it becomes intriguing and exciting. You may end up cutting your reading in half, but who cares? You'll be enjoying what you do read much more. After all, why must we all be avid readers? Who says so? We should feel free to read as much or as little as we want to. Individuals differ enormously in the amount they read. Some have a need to read almost constantly while others hardly ever read. But to feel guilty about not reading is absolutely unnecessary.

If you can deprive yourself of books for a while they will regain some of their drawing power. We know of a young man, an avid reader, who did not read a book for six months because he was with an expedition. He reports that, upon returning, even the labels on cereal boxes took on new dimensions of pleasure and delight.

Books are wonderful because they allow you to experience so much of life without actually having to "be there." On the other hand, books only contain the words of people (or most of them do). So there is nothing magical about them. (This book, for example, is filled with suggestions and not absolute truths.) There is no need to feel that a person who does not read constantly is somehow inferior. God doesn't write books, only a certain species of symmetrical bipeds does. And who is to say they know so much more about life than you do? Read when you want to read. Allow your natural curiosity to be rekindled by consciously avoiding books for a while if they begin to bore you.

Consider, for a moment, all those magazines you subscribe to. How often do you read them? Certainly not all the time. When you come home and find three more magazines piled up against your door, you may have a sinking feeling. "Oh no, I'll never get through all of them." It's almost as if you're obligated to read the damn things. Not only are they not a source of pleasure, but they may actually take on the characteristics of a plague. You may feel guilty because you're not keeping up.

After all, don't all the advertisements point out that "thinking people," whoever they are, read such and such a magazine? Don't they try to point out to you that you are somehow inferior if you don't read their magazines? Well, forget all of that. Strike a blow for freedom. Throw off the shackles of unwanted and unnecessary printed material. Follow these five steps.

Step 1: Whatever you do, don't subscribe to any more magazines. Cultivate the art of slamming the door on those salespeople who are always insinuating that you are the only thing standing between them and higher education. Don't be drawn in by offers of free materials that will accompany your new order. You'll have to strain to choose from among the offered free materials . . . , and you'll probably never read them anyway.

Step 2: This is the critical step. *Cancel* all your existing subscriptions immediately. You'll get a lift out of this simple act. No one can do it but you. You will be taking charge of your own life. Do it with a mad gleam in your eye and the slightly demented cackle of a person driven close to distraction. Just think, once you cancel all those magazines you'll never be *behind* in your reading again.

Step 3: Go through your home like a whirlwind gathering up and burning all existing magazines, read or unread. Don't allow them to lie there gloating and accusing you. Toss them *all* out. Feel freed of a burden you never really wanted to take on in the first place.

Step 4: Now go without magazines as long as you can. The time will vary depending upon what kind of a person you are. Some will only last a few days. Others can go almost indefinitely. In any case, allow the need for a magazine to grow. Let it build up by itself. Allow your curiosity to be rekindled. After all, you are interested in the world around you, and you will eventually be interested in finding out what is going on . . . but only if you give your interest time to build. If piles of unmanageable information are crammed down your throat in the form of too many magazines delivered with too much regularity, you may gag. But if you cut them all off and deprive yourself of magazines for a while, you will find your interest will return. A new fresh curiosity will blossom. You will really want to read a magazine . . . any magazine if you hold off long enough.

Step 5: Now comes the final step. After a while the thought of a particular magazine seems especially intriguing to you. Go to your local newsstand and buy a *single* issue of the magazine. Take it home and spend three hours alone with it. Don't buy more than one magazine, and don't resubscribe to any of them. Always buy single issues, and only do it when you truly feel like reading *and* have the time.

Don't buy it if you're not interested. We often spot a magazine and buy it saying, "I'll probably want to read this later." Don't do it, because you may lose interest and then it, that single copy, will become a sore spot for you.

Don't buy unless you have the time to read immediately. If you buy one saying, "I'll probably have time tomorrow," chances are you won't have time, and the magazine may become one more tiny nag that you could live without. In summary, magazines are wonderful, but only if you need and want them.

Eating and Drinking

Eating and drinking are obvious areas where our principles of deprive and indulge can be helpful. If you are eating too much or drinking too much and suffering from a case of the blahs, it's time to take action. If you go to the market and suddenly realize, with a sinking sensation, that your choice of meat is limited, essentially, to the flesh of a handful of animals, then you are getting bored with food. If it seems as though all the supermarket has to offer are pieces of pigs, cows, and chickens, with an occasional sheep thrown in, it's time to do something. If you're tired of cooking or tired of having someone cook for you, if meals seems dreary, endless, and repetitive, if you find yourself eating just because it's dinner time, or because you haven't got anything else to do or because you're expected to eat, it's time to starve yourself a little. It's easily done and may help you lose some weight while food regains its appeal.

Start on a simple level. If you're accustomed to eating dinner at 6 P.M., delay the meal until 8 P.M. You'll find a couple of hours delay will whet your appetite. It's easy to wait if you use our technique of rewarding yourself for waiting. Choose some specialty that you like particularly but don't often have and eat all of it if you manage to wait the extra two hours. Prepare meals that *can't* be eaten early. Raw chicken just isn't very appetizing. So gauge your timing such that you put the chicken in when you're just beginning to get hungry. By the time it's done, you'll be famished.

If waiting around for food seems impossible, distract yourself with some rewarding activity. Go to a movie before, rather than after, dinner. If you do, you will avoid the theater crowds, get the early bird reduced ticket price, avoid all the inevitable trickles of sticky spilled Cokes around your feet, *and* be famished when you get home. Go after the baked chicken as if there were no tomorrow. Reward yourself for having waited. All it takes is a little planning and an awareness that we fall into eating habits which do not allow us to become hungry enough.

As a nation, we probably eat too much. We snack all day. We're told we shouldn't miss breakfast. We have bulging refrigerators. It's no wonder we're plump.

You should probably consult a medical doctor before you try skipping meals as a means of increasing your enjoyment and losing weight. But if your doctor agrees, this method can help. The thing to do is wait until you're face to face with a meal which just doesn't seem all that intriguing. It happens to all of us.

On some days we wake up and an egg and a piece of toast seem slightly repulsive. But we tend to eat anyway, remembering the old notion that breakfast is the most important meal. This may well represent food we neither want nor need. Skip the meal. Give the egg to the dog. You can always have a bite to eat when you get to work if you develop a headache. But in many cases you will find it will be lunchtime before you think of food. And when you do, it will be with greater relish than it would have been had you eaten that heavy little egg several hours earlier.

Or do it the other way around. Skip lunch. Eat a good breakfast and sail through until supper. You'll find *anything* sounds good by seven o'clock. Your companion, perhaps cooking away at home, will love you for it, wondering what happened to the picky eater.

Reward yourself for delaying or skipping meals. Use anything that will work. Some will want to reward themselves with extra special foods when they do eat. Others will want to reward themselves in other ways (e.g., going out, skipping an obligatory party, unplugging the phone and getting in bed at 7 P.M.).

Besides delaying meals and skipping meals (if your doctor agrees), there is a third method that can work. When you find yourself beginning to feel compulsive about food . . . "I gotta have just one slice of cheese," . . . go ahead and have one slice of cheese. But then stop yourself short with the following statement. "If I'm still hungry in a half an hour, I'll have some more." Wait, allowing the edge of your compulsive appetite to be blunted by the single piece of food. You may find, after the half hour has elapsed, that you can go for quite a while without eating anything more at all.

Delaying, skipping, and eating small amounts will only be possible if you plan and if you reward yourself for succeeding. In other words, you have to keep this problem of eating firmly in mind.

Each time you feel a hunger pang during the day and begin to move toward food, stop yourself by saying, "Now, I'll wait a little longer and then really enjoy it." Take pride in your efforts. Feel complacent and superior to all those clowns stuffing their faces. Feel like a fit, trim animal in control of her- or himself.

This section bears upon the whole issue of dieting. It seems there is really no substitute for eating less. I know, you can find diets of all sorts that promise easy outs. If you'll only eat x and y you'll lose weight. Stick to bacon and grapefruit, or grapefruit and chicken, or protein and certain pills, etc., etc. The promises are endless, but, in our opinion, what it all really comes down to is taking in less food. Although we could be wrong, it seems impossible to get around that fact.

The approach taken here is that you can reduce your food intake *if you make it worth the effort.* Delaying, skipping, and eating small amounts will naturally be rewarded by your increased hunger and the eventual satisfaction of that hunger. But, in addition, you must reward yourself in other ways. Buy yourself presents, go on vacations, do whatever you love to do if you succeed in eating less. Play a game with yourself; see how much control you can exert over yourself. Use high *quality* food as a reward for reducing *quantity.* For instance, eat roast goose, or filet mignon, or whatever it is that you adore, in small amounts, rather than stuffing in gallons of macaroni and cheese.

You can do it. Take charge. Start tonight. Delay your dinner for two hours and see how much you enjoy it!

Appliance-of-the-Month Club

There are other areas of modern life where a little deprivation, followed by gleeful indulgence, can lead to increased pleasure. Let's talk about modern conveniences; specifically the joys and wonders of modern appliances. The average American home is loaded with so-called timesaving appliances. Our bathrooms have electric shavers, hair dryers, electric toothbrushes, shaving cream dispensers, illuminated magnifying mirrors, heating pads, vibrators, curling irons, whirlpool baths, shower attachments, scales, deodorizers, and many other devices that you will be able to think of but we can't.

It's a wonder we can make our way through the tangle of wires, cords, tubes, motors, and plastic bodies. New, gimmicky appliances are being developed all the time, and we are told, by the advertising world, that we can't do without them.

Our kitchens probably have more modern conveniences per square foot than anywhere else on earth. Stoves, refrigerators, hot plates, electric fry pans, electric coffee pots, electric hamburger cookers, warming trays, electric can openers, electric knives, mixers, bottle openers, toasters, ice dispensers, dishwashers, freezers, garbage disposals, exhaust fans, telephones, soap dispensers, soda dispensers, electric popcorn makers, electric hot dog warmers, waffle irons, and blenders are but a few.

Our garages are filled with electric saws, power mowers, electric hedge clippers, edgers, drills, and assorted internal combustion engines. Our homes are filled with heaters, plumbing, pipes, faucets, sewers, TVs, radios, stereos, door bells, smoke alarms, outdoor lights, pool pumps, filters, air conditioners, fans, typewriters, and so on. The list is wonderful. Without knowing it, we have surrounded ourselves with dozens and dozens of appliances that hadn't even been imagined a hundred years ago. And yet, we can ask, are we really any happier now than people were before they had all these technological wonders crammed down their throats?

These appliances are touted as being time-savers. The idea is that you will be freed from the drudgery of life, you will be free to enjoy the higher things of life, if only you have a new vacuum cleaner. But these appliances are, at best, a mixed blessing.

Consider some facts. First, many of the so-called time-savers don't save time at all. Is it really any faster to open a can with an electric appliance than it is to open it by hand? Will you ever be able to write the great American novel during the time you save using an electric rather than an ordinary knife? How much more time does it consume to throw garbage away than to wait while your disposal grinds it up? Is a significant amount of time saved by the ice dispenser?

Admittedly, many of these appliances do save time. But many of them just represent expensive ways of doing things we could easily accomplish without them.

Appliances are also represented as making life easier. In many cases they do require us to exert less effort. But is exerting less effort always good? Probably not. It would probably be better for our physical condition if we used plain old nonpowered lawn mowers, if we sawed wood by hand, and if we cut food without the aid of electric knives.

So many of these appliances do not live up to their reputations. Many of them save us neither time nor energy, and many of them actually rob us of exercise.

But there are other problems with these technological wonders, too. For example, they are often more trouble than they are worth. They are designed to release us from some of the maintenance tasks which plague our lives. But once we own these appliances, we have to maintain them! We end up spending time and energy maintaining equipment which is supposed to free us from the boring maintenance jobs of life. It's the old "out of the frying pan and into the fire" story. There's no way we can get around it—life requires maintenance work. The question is whether we want to maintain machines which relieve us from ordinary maintenance work, or simply forget about a lot of these so-called time-savers and just do the job ourselves.

Think about your home for a moment. More than likely you will be able to think of at least two modern conveniences (perhaps better labeled modern inconveniences) which are presently broken. You've been thinking about them off and on, meaning to get around to them. But one probably needs a repair person, and all the wonderful lying and cheating that can involve, while the other requires that you buy an entire new unit, which is expensive. So they lie there broken and you carry around this nagging feeling.

Who needs that kind of aggravation? I mean, how important is a garbage disposal, after all? But wait, there is a solution. Join the appliance-of-the-month club. All you have to do to be a member in good standing is throw away an appliance when it breaks and not replace it. The next time your electric can opener gives out, toss it out the back door. Get yourself

one of those sturdy manual can openers and feel freed of one more technological pest. If your hair dryer breaks, dry your hair over a heater. Forget
about your broken electric toothbrush. As things break, often at the rate
of one a month (hence the name of the club), don't replace them. You'll
feel great. Reward yourself by blowing the money you would have needed
to repair or replace the unit. As you spend it think about the overcharging,
exaggerating repair person you won't ever have to talk to.

Begin slowly, eliminating the most obvious, outrageous wastes of your
time and money. These include the gimmicky sorts of things we have been
talking about such as electric pencil sharpeners. As you eliminate them
and begin to get into the spirit of the thing, you can begin to trash larger
and more expensive modern conveniences. The garbage disposal should,
without doubt, be completely eliminated from the American scene. It is
expensive and completely unnecessary. Just put your garbage in a plastic
bag and place the bag in the trash. Same amount of time and effort
involved. It eliminates those inevitable sessions with the broom handle
crammed into a jammed disposal, it eliminates clogged pipes, it eliminates
overloaded septic systems, and it eliminates repairs and replacement. Not
having a disposal can be a refreshing experience when it is your decision
about damn well not having one.

Automatic dishwashers can be eliminated once you have done in all
those nasty, irritating little appliances. The time spent rinsing dishes,
placing them in racks, closing the door, washing, and removing dishes
from the automatic dishwasher is just about the same as that involved in
washing the dishes by hand. Try it before you push your dishwasher out
to the curb. Actually time yourself. You will be convinced.

As you continue to reduce the number of appliances to which you have
become unwittingly enslaved, you will feel a rising sense of excitement
and exhilaration. You're simplifying your life without overburdening yourself. You will save money and feel good about taking charge of your own
destiny. No longer will you lie awake at night worrying about the funny
new sound the cooler or heater is making.

What you will find is that the chores which had become tedious and
meaningless when they were done with the aid of modern conveniences
may take on new significance and actually become pleasurable. Yes, folks,
opening a can of tuna can be fun if you do it by yourself. In a sense, the
situation parallels the ones we have been talking about where we increase
satisfaction by first increasing the need. Here, by eliminating an appliance
which has heretofore done the work for us, we increase the need to do the
work ourselves. And, because we need to do the work, the actual accomplishment is rewarding and pleasant. Somehow, running a carpet sweeper
around is really a kick after the noisy, troublesome vacuum cleaner has
been put out to pasture. Cracking ice out of a tray is fun after the ice maker
goes on the blink. Those appliances have been robbing us of satisfaction
because they have been doing too much for us. They have been eliminat-

ing the ordinary demands of life which are so essential to our sense of satisfaction.

As you make your way up through the ranks of the appliance-of-the-month club, tossing out unneeded appliances right and left, you will realize that there are even higher levels of freedom and satisfaction to be obtained. We have a friend, who lives in a cool but not frigid climate, whose furnace went out. After calling repair services and having them not return the call, and after making appointments to meet service representatives at his home only to have them fail to materialize, our friend said, "To hell with it. I'll just leave the thing (the furnace) broken." We asked what he did when it got cold. He said, "Put on a jacket." We asked how he felt. He replied, "Wonderful," and proceeded to describe the joys of furnace-free living. He said he thought he might eventually get around to having it fixed but he just wasn't going to worry about it. In fact, he enjoyed having to fight the climate a bit.

He felt a great satisfaction in proving to himself that he could be just as happy without a furnace. He enjoyed the new sense of resourcefulness which accompanied his successful efforts to keep warm in other ways. He used the fireplace and a small electric heater. He wore more clothes. He just stayed a bit cooler. He found he could live without the furnace. Two years later he still had not had his furnace fixed, and he still got a chuckle out of the whole episode.

When his oven went out he let that go, too. He felt that if he was clever enough he could eat pretty well just using the top burners which still functioned. He felt a challenge and responded with a renewed sense of independence. When his garbage disposal and then his dishwasher collapsed, he was positively gleeful. He laughed at how helpless and dependent all these conveniences had made him. He washed dishes by hand and threw his garbage in the trash. He felt particularly pleased to learn that he was, after all, self-sufficient and resourceful. If someone had told him that he would soon be without heater, stove, disposal, and dishwasher, he would have panicked and felt that sense of helplessness which a dependence upon technology fosters in all of us. But when the appliances did break, he felt a lifting sense of relief.

He finally began to replace the items, not because he needed them, but because, after his long period of deprivation without them, they became wonderful, magical toys again and not absolute necessities. It was a lot of *fun* to get the oven going again. (He never did bother with the disposal or the dishwasher.)

Oh, what would we ever do without electricity, running water, or plumbing? The answer is we would do very well. In fact, it can be a real source of pleasure to "make do" for ourselves without being dependent upon modern devices. Depending upon where you live, the loss of one or more of these services can be handled in many different ways. Try, for instance, turning off your electricity at the circuit box for two days. You'll do very well. You still have water and gas, and with them you can pretty well meet all your needs.

It's better if some external agent turns off your power, but doing it yourself is better than nothing. If you leave it off long enough, you will find things become quite "normal" in a short period of time. We are, after all, very adaptable critters, and we got along for thousands of years without any of these conveniences we now assume we are so dependent upon.

Another thing you can try is parking your car for a week. Pretend you don't have one. You'll find buses are perfectly acceptable and walking is downright pleasurable. Riding a bike is invigorating. Pride in your native survival instincts is a source of satisfaction. Then, after a week, driving your car will be pleasant again. You'll appreciate it more for not having had it for a while. Deprive and indulge, deprive and indulge.

Tearing your phone out of the wall can be a truly enlightening event. When you don't have a phone, three things become clear right away. First, at least half the calls you have been getting are more trouble than they are worth. It's usually someone who wants something from you. Second, if you really want to call someone you can walk down to the public phone booth. Third, most of the calls you have been making are not all that essential. They are not worth walking to the phone booth to make.

Again, after a period without a phone, reinstating the service can be a source of satisfaction. If you want to experiment with living without a phone, it is best to have the service cut off. If you just put the phone in a closet and promise yourself you won't use it, you may well break your promise when a "really important" something comes up.

Spending Money

There are, of course, many other areas of our lives where we can apply our principle of gaining satisfaction by first depriving and then subsequently indulging ourselves. Take money, for example. We are always hearing that money is the root of all evil. But we all have the sneaking suspicion, don't we, that money is also the root of a lot of pleasure, too? The problem is that we tend to get less from the money we have than we would like to. It doesn't go far enough. In this section we are going to see if we can increase our sense of satisfaction, not by actually getting more money, but by learning how to spend money in such a way that the sensations we have correspond to those which we would experience if we did have more money. We are going to feel rich, and act rich, even though we are not rich.

There are a few simple rules concerning the spending of money which can vastly increase our sense of getting what we want without actually having any more money. Without having any more funds, we can increase our satisfaction with what we do have. We can do it on our present income. It's all a matter of knowing how to spend what we do have.

Many of us, with poor spending habits, never seem to have enough money. We dribble it away. We say, "I just don't know where it all went." We don't especially enjoy it when we spend it. In fact, we often don't even notice or focus upon spending it. We just hand it over in a sort of preoccupied trance, never really marking its passage into other hands. As a result, we are often surprised to find it gone.

And then, as we have seen, we get into debt. If you are in debt, getting money is just not very exciting because you know there are always those spongelike debts waiting to soak up everything you have. As a result, we never seem to have any extra (How can there ever really be any extra if we are in debt?) for the things we really want. We are constantly plagued by a sense of having a lot less than we had hoped we would have. Here are some ways to avoid these problems and to increase your sense of getting what you want.

Rule 1: Attack your budget

A budget can be a wonderful thing if you treat it as the enemy. Your strategic stance is to try to make your budget as small as possible. Your war goal is to keep as much of your money as you can away from and outside your budget. Do it this way. Deprive yourself of the boring essentials of life. Figure out the *minimum* amount you need each month for the basic essentials of life. These include, among a few others, rent, food, and utilities. Determine how *little* you can get along on each day, after you have paid the monthly bills. Figure it out to the nearest dollar. How little can you get by on each day? Five, ten, twenty, thirty dollars? Whatever you can squeeze by on each day is exactly what you should spend each day on these ugly necessities and joyless maintenance tasks. Never any more. Put the month's allotment in small bills in a drawer. (Don't worry about it being stolen. That happens so seldom that it's not worth being concerned about.) Each morning put your daily allotment in your pocket. That's all you have for the day. If you run out, that's too bad. You'll just have to wait until tomorrow.

If you run out of some "essential" such as dish soap, don't buy it until tomorrow. If you need toothpaste but have spent your money for the day, use baking soda until tomorrow. If you want a magazine but have hit your limit, read an old one.

Be tough on yourself because everything you can save from that ugly, boring monster of a budget is pure gravy. It's your play money, your dream money. It's the money with which you are going to look, act, and feel like a rich person. If the budget gets it, it's gone down the tube of never ending, joyless maintenance demands.

If your budget whispers in your ear, "No, but it would be sensible to have some milk in the house for your cereal tomorrow morning," reply, "Forget it. You're not getting another cent out of me." Refuse to give in to even its most reasonable demands. The money you put into your budget is no longer yours to love and savor and spend with relish. It's gone. So be careful because budgets have a way of speaking ever so logically, ever so reasonably. Don't listen. Keep your money for yourself, and let tomorrow's budget allotment worry about the cat food, the margarine, the dish soap, the shaving cream, the pencils, the tea, and the Kleenex. You would rather have the money to blow, thank you very much. You're willing to do without "necessities" so you can have "extras."

Rule 2: Spend big

Assuming you are winning the war against your budget, committing fiscal atrocities in the hope of being able to squander a little, you should have some extra money or money that is not being eaten up by unneeded "necessities."

It is this money which will bring you the sensation of being richer than you really are. But only if you spend it properly. After all, it's probably not very much. Most of us can squeeze and press and torment our budgets all day long and not gain very much. But you do have something to show for your harsh cruelty toward your budget.

People often lose the pleasure to be gained from this extra money because they spend it here and there, in little amounts, on fairly unexciting things. Then they end up saying, "I know I had some extra money, but where did it go?" The problem is that their purchases were all so small and trivial that they became swallowed up in the flow of everyday living expenses. They were not significant enough to be remembered. When was the last time you heard someone say, "I'll never forget the day I bought a three-dollar box of candy."

Purchases have to be big and substantial if they are to be exciting enough to be marked or tagged in your memory. We have to indulge ourselves. So, simply enough, your task is to avoid buying little things and to concentrate upon buying big things which will get your adrenaline going, will cause some excitement, and will be remembered with satisfaction.

Clearly, you won't be able to buy as many things as you could if you concentrated on cheaper things. But what you do buy will mean a lot more to you. Which would mean more, fifty meals at the local hamburger joint or one meal at the best restaurant in town? Twelve ties from an inferior store or one tie from the most expensive shop in town? The point is clear. Given a certain amount of money, it's more exciting and memorable to spend it all on one grand, unusual, rare, or otherwise distinctive unit than it is to dribble the money away on innumerable, mundane, ordinary, boring things.

Save up your money (deprive) and blow it all at once (indulge). Think big. Go for the occasional expensive item rather than the more numerous, forgettable units. Gain satisfaction and a sense of being rich by walking confidently into an expensive shop frequented by well-to-do people and actually buying something. Notice with pleasure the way the shop clerk, upon seeing your roll of bills, begins to be obsequious. The condescension with which you and your ordinary appearance were greeted will always evaporate in the face of the big bucks. The proprietors will get all squeamy and cozy with you just as they do with the constantly rich. They don't have to know your fits of being rich are temporary and widely spaced. For the moment, as you select a ring to go with the brooch, you are as rich as anyone who goes into that store.

If you do it with flair and confidence, it can be quite exhilarating. Avoid being self-conscious and feeling inferior. Remember, for the moment, you've got the money and are ready to spend it. That's all that counts.

Then, when you leave the establishment, returned to the planet Earth by the precipitous drop in your ready cash, you can gain further satisfaction by ridiculing the rich. How silly and pompous they are. How so very much like everyone else they are.

At the same time, you begin to plot your next excursion into the world of the rich. Torture your budget, and then spend big.

Rule 3: Spend impulsively

A lot of pleasure can be lost in this business of spending money if too much time is spent tearing and comparing quality and price. Let's say you want to buy X. You go all over town looking at X's. You drive everyone crazy talking about X's, comparing prices and weighing features. By the time you get around to making a purchase even *you* won't be very excited by it, beyond perhaps some vague and not entirely convincing feeling that you got the best buy.

True pleasure and excitement, a true sense of having a lot of money, can come when you spend impulsively. On-the-spot, no-questions-asked purchases can be very exciting and memorable. "Remember the time I plunked down ten twenty dollar bills for the little Indian basket?" "Remember the time we dropped into the Bistro and spent eighty-five dollars for lunch?" "Remember when we bought new tennis rackets and gave our old ones to those kids on the street?"

Don't draw out the spending of the money you have saved from your budget. Not only is it a lot of work to compare prices all over town, but you will feel like a dullard doing it, too. "Well, we've narrowed it down to four possible restaurants. In another week or so, we'll probably have our final decision made!" Snore.

As long as you're trying to taste champagne on a beer budget, you might as well act the part once in a while. Get out there and splurge impulsively.

This is not to say that you have to spend *unwisely.* Impulsiveness and stupidity do not necessarily correlate. Your impulsive and spontaneous purchases of either objects or services can be good purchases. For example, if you are an expert on Chinese food or old records, you might be able to buy impulsively in these areas. But that doesn't mean you would necessarily also be willing to buy impulsively in the diamond market. Restrict your impulsive purchases to areas where you can quickly estimate value. If you know about opals, go ahead and buy them spontaneously. But don't do the same thing in uncharted areas. A lot of fun is to be gained when you make large purchases, impulsively, in an area where you have some expertise. Don't fritter your hard-won money away. Save it up and spend it all at once.

Rule 4: Buy investments

As long as you are making large, impulsive purchases in an area where you have some competence, you might as well take things one step further and not spend your money at all. More accurately, you might as well spend it in such a manner that you can get it back anytime you want.

Our culture is filled with lovely, useful, decorative, unique, and interesting objects that can always be resold in the future, often at a profit. Whenever possible, you might as well buy these kinds of things. As long as you are out there acting like a rich person, you might as well do what they do. Invest.

Of course, there are some purchases, such as a good dinner, which are difficult to turn into a profit. So there will be times when you don't invest your money. There will be times when, once you spend it, you'll never see it again. But balanced against these instances are literally hundreds of cases where you can buy exactly what you want, you can own it and love it, but you can also reconvert it to cash anytime you want.

Buying things that can be resold makes you feel rich in two ways. First, you know that's what rich people are doing (that's how many of them get and stay rich). Second, you will end up with more money and actually become richer.

So what are all these investments? Buy a house not a car. Buying cars is pouring money down a rat hole. Houses appreciate faster than the rate of inflation. Drive a 1967 car and live in a mansion. It's the way to feel, and get, rich.

Buy antiques. An antique bed costs no more than a new bed. It can be very attractive, and it can be resold at a higher price than your new bed. If you want to frame a picture, do it with an antique frame. Mix antiques into your home furnishings. Antiques have yet to go down in value. All home decor, from the bathroom, through the living room, to the kitchen, can be sprinkled with antiques.

The traditional definition of an antique is anything that is over a hundred years old. But now, in fact, anything that is no longer being manufactured is bordering on the collectible. Items from the '30s and '40s and even '50s can now be found which are being sold as "antiques." The kitchen utensils from your childhood are now "collectibles."

Buy gold, silver, diamonds, and other gems and precious metals. Nothing makes you feel richer. And while these purchases are becoming more valuable every day, extra color TVs and hedge trimmers are becoming worth less every day.

There is no need to run through endless lists of things which do and do not go up in value. What goes up and what goes down is common knowledge. The point is that, as long as you are going to spend large amounts of money, you might as well, at least part of the time, spend that money in such a way that you can spend it again in the future if you want to. It won't ruin your fun. In fact, once you begin buying investments, you may find buying is more fun than ever. It doesn't worry you at all because you know you'll be able to get your money back.

Stay away from modern appliances and technological gimmicks. They will fall apart before they are worth anything. Concentrate on things that you like but which also have lasting and growing value. Buy gold, silver, jewelry, furniture, antiques of all kinds, rugs, land, stocks, gems, old photographs, art, stamps, and so on. Many of the rich do, so why shouldn't you? Stay away from things that have no lasting value or that lose their value quickly, such as clothes, new cars, TV sets, electronic equipment (which is being made obsolete every year by new developments) and savings accounts.

The old argument is that in a period of inflation you should own objects and during a period of depression you should have cash. If the present siege of inflation continues, and it looks like it will, it makes sense to have your assets in objects. But not just any objects. They have to be things which will grow in value or at least not lose $3,000 in value as does your brand-new big car as you drive it out of the showroom door.

Rule 5: Upgrade, upgrade

There is another way you can increase your satisfaction and the sense that you are well off without actually having any more money. We are referring here to the process of upgrading your possessions. The idea is to constantly move toward ownership of fewer but finer and more valuable possessions. It doesn't make any difference what kind of possessions we are talking about. They can be stamps, horses, houses, land, antiques, paintings, or anything else you like to own. In each case, you should always strive to sell off your poorest items at a profit and combine that profit with money you have squeezed from your budget to buy a better example of whatever it is you collect. You should strive toward ownership of a few extremely valuable, choice items rather than own a lot of mediocre examples.

For instance, suppose you become interested in early American carpenter's tools. You begin by buying a few planes, saws, and braces. Nothing costs over twenty dollars. Then, as you begin to learn more about these objects, their relative values, and the fine points of collecting these tools, you can sell off some of your early acquisitions and combine the monies to buy one fine item, such as a cobbler's bench, for a couple of hundred dollars.

If you collect stamps, you can "trade up," or collect rarer and rarer items as you learn about stamp collecting.

If you buy land or houses, you can trade up, or use the profit from early acquisitions as leverage to purchase better, more expensive properties.

Upgrading your possessions can be satisfying in several ways.

1. You get to act like a big shot because, by selling smaller or less unique items, you have the ready cash to walk in and slap a bundle down on the counter and buy what you want.
2. You enjoy owning a finer and finer set of items. Pride of ownership and all that.
3. You experience variety and change. You don't have to stare at the same old goods all the time.
4. You will become an expert and feel proud about being one. When it comes to owning objects, you learn by doing. The only way to find out about what to buy and what to sell is through experience. By trying to upgrade your possessions, you will gain valuable experience and knowledge—knowledge that is not usually contained in books.
5. Your objects will be easier to care for. Instead of having boxes and boxes of who knows what, you will have a smaller number of choice items which can be stored or displayed with great ease. Get the clutter out of your life.
6. Fine pieces may appreciate in value faster than mediocre pieces. This is not always true, but it happens often enough to suggest that a few choice items will make you more money than will a group of less choice items whose total value might be the same as the one or two choice items to begin with. It pays to "buy good."

Rule 6: Use cash not cards

Throw away all your credit cards. In the long run they make you feel poorer. You use them without thinking, and you often don't enjoy the purchase. Then, when the first of the month rolls around, you have that depressing bill, saddled with 18 percent interest.

Forget about your checkbook, too. Your account is always slightly out of balance. You often forget to record at least one check. You often end up having less money than you thought you had. To cash a check they always want fourteen pieces of identification which makes you feel either indignant or criminal. When you use checks, you always hold up the line. All those people waiting and waiting while you write that check.

Use cash. No one argues with you. No one asks for identification. It's fast, simple, and you always know exactly how much you have left. Once it's gone, you're done for the day—but at least you won't go into debt.

Keep a bundle of cash in your purse or wallet. Don't worry about robbery. What makes you think you stand out? No one would expect you to be carrying several hundred dollars. They expect you to be carrying credit cards and a checkbook. And if they do rob you, they may be so overjoyed at the sight of all that cash that they will ignore you. They may take the money and run. If you only had seven dollars, they might get angry.

Carrying around a wad of bills makes you feel rich. Don't flash it around, of course, but think about it a lot, and when you whip it out to pay for a large purchase, watch the eyes of the seller; you'll experience what rich people experience all the time.

Rule 7: Don't earn too much

Money has a funny way of trapping us. When you look around, you'll see people who are so busy making money and then protecting it from each other and from taxes and from inflation, that they really don't have much time to enjoy it. Free time, the most precious gift of all, evaporates as you become a slave to your money. You end up frantically spending on things you don't really care about just to get *something* for all the time and effort you're putting in.

It may be better to earn less, have more free time, and act like you're rich even though you're not. As we have seen, you can have most of what the rich ones have with half the effort.

Deprive and Indulge: A General Concept and Some Examples

In this chapter we have pointed out some of the ways we can increase our pleasure and satisfaction first by depriving ourselves and then by indulging ourselves in whatever it is that we have been deprived of. We have also seen that if we have trouble depriving ourselves we can get around this problem by making it worth our while . . . we can reward ourselves for undergoing a period of deprivation.

The last point to be made in this chapter is that these principles may hold true in connection with just about any imaginable source of pleasure.

Our list of satisfactions (e.g., enjoying people, reading, watching TV, eating, going out on the town, drinking, using appliances, and spending money) is far from complete. But this does not mean that our principles are applicable only to the issues we have discussed. To the contrary, they can be adapted to any source of satisfaction. The satisfaction you wish to increase can be of a small and minor nature, such as shaving or getting a haircut, or it can be of a more lofty nature, such as gaining satisfaction from your career. In all cases, the trick is to discover what it is that you are getting too much of and to then deprive yourself of that element until your interest in it is rekindled. While we can't guarantee results and we acknowledge that these procedures have not been scientifically proved, we think that they work. We invite you to try them.

We will close this chapter with three diverse examples of the deprive and indulge principle. Specifically, we will consider how meditation, smoking, and insomnia are related to the general notion that satisfaction can best be achieved after a period of deprivation.

Meditation: Getting away from it all

At first, meditation may seem like a strange topic to discuss in connection with the deprive and indulge principle. But if you think about it for a moment, engaging in meditation actually is a form of depriving ourselves of the noisy, bothersome activity of life. It is a way of getting away from our busy, hectic life pace. After we have taken time out through meditation, we can return to our normal speedy activities and enjoy them more, feeling refreshed and ready for some action. When meditating we are depriving ourselves of intense, complex, varied external stimulation. By meditating we can bring about a renewed interest in these active phases of our lives.

Although an interest in meditation is relatively new in this country, various forms of it have been practiced for centuries in other cultures. It is difficult to define meditation because there are so many different varieties and because the basic nature of the experience is elusive. Basically, *meditation is an attempt to alter our state of consciousness through various forms of concentration.* Many meditation techniques have as their goal an inner sense of calm and quiet. The aim is to achieve a state of tranquillity. Other meditation techniques are designed to heighten or change the experience of conscious awareness. In these methods excitement, wonder, and distortion can be mingled with peacefulness.

Many forms of meditation can be thought of as efforts to shake off our concern for the past and the future and to live in the immediate present. The goal is to experience and to feel in an intense manner the "here and now;" to feel, in a calm, tranquil, and awed manner, what it is to be alive at this moment. Normally, our minds are filled with incessant thought. We wonder where we are going, what we have done, what we should do, what we should have done, and so on. The goal of meditation is to do away with this agitated mental activity, to gain a calmer perspective, and perhaps to understand that we are part of all that there is, and not some distinct, burning, overly self-important individual. A sense of inner quiet can be attained, at least temporarily, if we stop the wide-ranging, frantic activity of our minds and focus on the moment. We deprive ourselves of activity, only to enjoy it more later.

Meditation techniques vary widely. Some, such as Zen meditation, involve sitting perfectly quietly, while others, such as that practiced by the Sufi dervishes of Turkey, involve whirling dances and physical activity.

If you want to try meditation, the following are some simple forms. Remember, you are shooting for a sense of inner calmness and peace. Go ahead, don't be embarrassed, try it.

1. Sit quietly in a darkened, quiet room. Count your breaths as a means of eliminating extraneous, distracting thought. Clear your mind of everything except counting.
2. Repeat a simple phrase, or *mantra.* Do it over and over again, either aloud or under your breath. The mantra can be anything, even something nonsensical, such as "cellar door." Saying the mantra makes you focus on the present moment. It helps you concentrate without being distracted.
3. Sit quietly and "step back" from yourself. That is, watch or listen to your thoughts as though you were a second person in the room. Do not try to control your thoughts. Merely observe their flow. Seek a feeling of detached calmness. Become a quiet observer of your own mind's restless activity.
4. While sitting quietly, focus upon some part of your body. Some people "concentrate on the navel." This is really just a way to focus upon the rhythmic, calming rise and fall of the abdominal area as you breathe. Others concentrate upon the "mystical third eye," which is the spot halfway between your eyes.
5. Some feel meditation is nothing more than a way to relax. According to this view, there is nothing out of the ordinary about meditation. It just helps us ease the tensions and stresses of everyday life and attain a calm, relaxed state. It rids us of overstimulation. Here is a way to learn to relax. Sit in a chair. Take a deep breath and exhale as a signal to your body that you are now going to relax. Now continue to breathe evenly. Imagine a ball of tension in your stomach. Raise this ball up the front of your chest, cross it over to your back, and let it slide down your back, through your legs and away into the ground through your feet. Now do it again; circulate another knot of tension.

Now we will teach each part of your body to relax. Begin at the top of your head. Relax your scalp. If you can't tell whether or not it is relaxed, tighten it up for a moment. Clench it, and then relax it. Now move to your face. First relax the muscles around your eyes. Let them melt and be drawn down by gravity. Now your cheeks. Now your mouth and chin. Take your time. You will find little areas of tension that you weren't aware of. Dissolve these areas and let your face melt and sink toward the earth. If you can't tell if an area is tense, tense it up on purpose and then relax it so you can tell the difference.

Go back now and then and circulate another knot of tension up and out of your stomach. Go back occasionally and make sure your face has not tensed up again; it can without your knowing it.

Now move to your jaw and neck, especially the back of your neck. Relax all these muscles. Next relax your shoulders, arms, hands, and fingers, in that order. Take your time. Allow your spine to relax, then all the muscles in your chest and abdomen. Now, relax your lower back and the pelvic area. Then your thighs, your knees, your ankles, your feet, and your toes.

Now take another deep breath, exhale, and stand up refreshed and ready to face the world again. The whole exercise shouldn't take more than five minutes, but you will be surprised at how rested you feel.

Essentially, all meditation techniques take us away, at least temporarily, from normal forms of thought and behavior. In this sense, meditation is a deprivation technique. Of course, there is more to meditation than simple deprivation, but, by removing us temporarily from active participation in everyday life, it can lead to renewed interest in the more energetic paths we follow in our social lives and in our careers.

Smoking

Let's turn now to a less esoteric example of how the deprive and indulge principle can be applied in our lives: smoking. Although studies and experiments have yet to prove that there is one sure way to quit smoking, many people hold that the most effective method is to quit cold turkey or completely. How often have you heard people say, "I either have to quit completely or not at all. If I have even one cigarette, I'm a goner." There is some truth to the cold turkey theory. Some people do, in fact, find it easier to quit if they make a decision to stop entirely. On the other hand, many people can't bring themselves to quit completely. They may stop for a few hours or days or weeks, but, sooner or later, they pick up one cigarette, then another, and quickly fall back into their previous smoking pattern.

The cold turkey method is too hard, too stressful for these people because it requires them to go from a full-blown smoking pattern down to nothing, all at once. For some, that burden is just too great. In other cases, smokers who have resolved to quit cold turkey may become depressed and discouraged if they smoke even one cigarette. Suppose a smoker who has gone two weeks without a cigarette breaks down and smokes one. That single cigarette represents a major defeat because the smoker hasn't been able to abstain completely. Those who adopt the cold turkey approach either succeed (no cigarettes at all) or fail (any cigarettes at all). Once they have smoked one cigarette, many people may respond, "I failed. So, what the hell, I might as well smoke another."

For those people who just can't quit cold turkey, there is another method which illustrates the deprive and indulge principle we have been discussing. This method, based on gradual reduction rather than on the all-or-none principle, allows for occasional backsliding. Perhaps it will work for you.

Suppose you are one of those individuals who can't seem to quit entirely. It is just too difficult. Would you be satisfied with cutting down by half or even more? This method requires that you play a game with yourself. First, divide the number of hours you are usually awake each day by the number of cigarettes you usually smoke each day. Use rough approximations. Don't worry about exactly how many hours or cigarettes are involved. Just make a rough guess. For example, suppose you normally get about eight hours of sleep a day (you are awake for sixteen) and smoke about twenty-five cigarettes a day. Thus $16 \div 25 = .64$. This means that you tend to smoke one cigarette about every .65 hour, or approximately one every forty minutes. Now, suppose you want to cut that rate in half. That would mean you would want to, actually allow yourself to, smoke one cigarette every eighty minutes, or every hour and twenty minutes. That wouldn't be too bad, would it? Your lungs and heart would benefit from a 50 percent reduction in smoke while you still enjoyed, even relished, a fair number of cigarettes each day.

By having to wait just a little bit longer than your normal delay between cigarettes (eighty minutes instead of forty minutes), you will benefit in two ways. First, you will be smoking less. Second, *you will enjoy it more.* You will be capitalizing on the fact that, as we saw in Chapter 1, satisfaction is greater as time of deprivation increases. Because you will now be waiting an extra forty minutes for your cigarette, that cigarette will be even more pleasant once you do light it up. By depriving yourself for a little while, you will, in the long run, be *increasing* your pleasure rather than decreasing it. And you will be reducing your overall level of smoking while enjoying it more.

How often do you notice that you are smoking without really having wanted a cigarette, without having noticed when you lit it, and without actually enjoying it? With the technique outlined above, you can change all that. You can smoke less and enjoy it more. You can utilize the fact that satisfaction is greater following deprivation.

It's easy to implement the recommended procedure. Merely spend one day smoking cigarettes at half your usual rate. Keep an eye on the clock and discipline yourself a little. You will find that when you are allowed a cigarette it will be wonderful, better than when you have free access to them. It's worth a try, isn't it?

It's all a matter of avoiding that ugly situation where you have too much of something. By waiting a little longer between cigarettes, you are making yourself really desire what you can have and are then allowing yourself to go ahead and enjoy it.

Once you have seen the benefits of delaying your smoking behavior and, at the same time, guaranteed yourself that you will be able to smoke and will enjoy it more, you can move on a further step if you wish. Specifically, you can *increase* the time between cigarettes even further. You might, for example, decide that you could wait two hours or even three hours between cigarettes. Remember, the longer you can wait the better that inevitable, guaranteed cigarette will taste. There is no end to the length of time you can wait. Some people smoke only after 5 P.M. In this way, they build up a desire all day long and then, at five o'clock, it is heaven to light up.

So it was a flop?

This section is for those of you who tried the method described above and it just didn't work. The problem was you wanted a cigarette too badly to wait until the correct time, right? So you went ahead and had one, right? (But when you did smoke it probably tasted exceptionally good because you had deprived yourself a little.)

If you are one of us who finds it difficult to wait, there is a solution to the problem. Try spoiling yourself in the following manner. Think of some delicious bad habit you have. Make it something you love to do but don't do very often for one reason or another. It can be anything—going to a movie; buying an opal ring; calling up Barbara or Mitch or both; fantasizing about three penguins, two men, and a woman; eating toast; or buying a present for your aunt. Once you have an indulgence in mind, *reward yourself* with it if you can make it through the day sticking to your smoking schedule. If you manage to get through a day, go ahead and indulge yourself. It will be your payoff for depriving yourself. Reward your own virtuousness. You deserve it, and it will make depriving yourself a lot easier.

Suppose you do make it through one day, and you do reward yourself for being so self-disciplined. The next question that may come to mind is, "Is this going to cost me an opal ring a day forever?" The answer is again no. Fading, a technique that has been used in psychological labs for years, can be of value here. If the initial reward or indulgence you chose is relatively small, harmless, and inexpensive, such as watching TV, or sleeping a half hour later, you may continue to use that same reward from day to day. But if the reward you used initially is something you cannot afford or do not want to continue using, then fading can be of some help. Fading refers to the gradual lessening of reward as time passes. For example, suppose you began your experiment by allowing yourself to eat five cookies after your first successful day of cutting your smoking in half. On the second day begin to *reduce* the size of the reward. Allow yourself only four cookies. As the days pass keep reducing the size of the reward. Or shift to something else that is less of an indulgence. Settle for something you like but don't love quite as much as you do those cookies. If you use TV watching as a reward, cut down the time you allow yourself on successive days. If you reward your smoking reduction with a spending spree, slowly, over the days, allow yourself less and less money to spend. As you fade the reward or make the reinforcing indulgences smaller and smaller each day, you will find that you will still be able to hold to your smoking schedule.

Eventually, you will find that it will not be necessary to reward yourself for cutting down on smoking at all. As you continue to engage in this cycle of first depriving yourself of cigarettes and then smoking freely, you will find that the situation will be rewarding enough in itself. You will feel pride and a sense of accomplishment because you have reduced your dependency on a dangerous drug by half. At the same time, you still get to smoke, and those few cigarettes that you do allow yourself taste better than ever. You will *want* to continue the game because those cigarettes do taste so much better and because you are quitting. It's called having your cake and eating it too.

From insomnia to sweet dreams

As our third and final example of the power of the deprive and indulge principle, let's consider insomnia. Don't you love those wonderful nights when you lie in bed, wide awake, from 2 A.M. to 4 A.M. worrying about everything from the size of your bank account balance to the colonization of Mars? Your brain won't stop. It whizzes from one thing to another, exhausting you. You try to divert its pell-mell progress into slower, calmer channels. You try to think about kittens or tranquillity but, before you know it, you are off worrying about something else. You worry about not getting enough sleep, about what you will do if the roof springs a leak, about your miserable personality. You worry about worrying. Final, fitful sleep doesn't arrive until it's almost too late.

Methods for "curing" insomnia are common enough. Some people take sleeping pills, employing a chemical attack upon the problem. Sleeping pills will work, but wouldn't it be better if we didn't have to saturate our bodies with dubious chemical substances in our efforts to gain a good night's sleep? Then there are the psychotherapeutic methods or remedies. These approaches assume that you can't sleep because you have some kind of psychological problem. They attempt to resolve the problem, thereby eliminating the cause of the insomnia. This is all well and good except for the fact that psychotherapy is often expensive and time-consuming.

Before drugs or expensive psychotherapeutic methods are employed, there is something every insomniac might want to consider. This method is free, doesn't consume time, and does not involve drugs. It is based upon the principles outlined in the preceding section. First, if we deprive ourselves of something and then go ahead and indulge in it, the experience will be very satisfying. Second, if we have trouble depriving ourselves, we can always make the job easier by spoiling ourselves, indulging or rewarding ourselves in some other way.

These simple principles apply very nicely to the problem of insomnia, because being in a state of sleeplessness is often nothing more than not being able to enjoy because we are not deprived enough. For example, many insomniacs will spend extra time in bed trying to "catch up" on what they believe is needed sleep. This may be just the wrong thing to do. What insomniacs need is to be deprived of sleep so that when the opportunity to sleep does arrive, it will be welcomed with open hands. Insomniacs may need *less* not *more* sleep. They may need to stay *out* of bed not *in* it.

When we have insomnia, we often get up and knock around the house in a daze. This experience is seldom satisfying and sometimes seems to do little good. We need a carefully planned program of sleep deprivation to *prevent* the occurrence of insomnia before it happens, rather than try to resolve the problem once we are lying there, staring through glazed eyes at the ceiling.

We may distinguish two types of insomnia: chronic and occasional. The chronic insomniac is the one who has trouble sleeping, if not every night, then pretty close to it. The occasional insomniac is the one who will have a few sleepless nights here and there. The chronic insomniac might want to try a planned program of sleep deprivation and continue it until the method either works or seems to be doing no good. The occasional insomniac cannot always tell when a bad night is coming up. But there are some cues that many of us use in predicting an insomnia-filled night. For example, if we drink too much, eat too much, become overly excited, or overly stressed, we often sense that we may be in for an unpleasant night. When these cues are present, the occasional insomniac might consider staying up later in order to increase the need for sleep and the pleasure associated with that sleep.

Basically, what the insomniac needs to do is to stay awake longer. The longer one stays awake, the greater the need for sleep. Even an hour or two beyond the normal bedtime can work wonders.

There are two ways to increase your need for sleep. Some of you will find it easier to stay awake longer in the evening. Others will prefer to lengthen their days by getting up earlier in the morning. Either method will increase your need for sleep, will lessen your chances of insomnia, and will make those crisp clean sheets feel wonderful in the few minutes before you drop off into untroubled sleep.

Sleep may be less fitful and more restful following a longer rather than a shorter period of waking. Even if you are not an insomniac, slightly decreasing the amount you sleep can increase the pleasure gained from sleeping. Trying to sleep when you are not really tired can be an irritating experience.

Whether you prefer waking earlier or staying up later, the first step is determining the average amount of sleep you normally get. You can do this by keeping track of the hours you sleep over a week's time. Then increase the number of waking hours by one or two. You may find sleep will become even easier and even more refreshing when you sleep a little less.

If you decide to increase your waking hours by staying up later, you may run into difficulty because you just can't keep your eyes open. Lying there in bed, holding a book, you may drop off to sleep unintentionally, only to awake in a few hours feeling restless and unable to get back to sleep. The solution to this problem of premature sleeping lies in planning. You must plan your evening so you will not end up lying in bed bored to tears while you try to stay awake. You must *reward* yourself for staying awake. Make it worth your while. Depending upon what you enjoy, the reward for staying awake that extra hour or two can be just about anything. Some of us will be rewarded by making up a batch of popcorn, or working a puzzle, or playing cards with friends. The trick is staying out of that bed as long as possible. Try to think of something to do ahead of time. Don't wait until 9 P.M. to try to decide how to spend your evening. Make plans for pleasant diversion ahead of time. Use your imagination. Let your mind float freely over all your fantasies of pleasure, and then go ahead and do something you really like to do as your reward for staying up. Don't choose something that falls into the category of chores or maintenance or things you know you should do but don't want to do. That will just make you all the sleepier. Pick something that is fun for you.

The same holds true if you decide to increase your waking hours by getting up earlier rather than by going to bed later. When you wake up early, have something pleasant planned as an incentive to get out of bed. Go out for breakfast. Walk on the beach. Ride your motorcycle. It doesn't matter what it is, as long as it is something that you enjoy.

If you do this and increase your desire for sleep, you will find that not only is sleeping better but your waking hours will be better too. Ironically, even though you spend less time in bed, you will feel more rested and energetic.

Of course, you don't want to overdo this thing. You don't want to deprive yourself of so much sleep that you can't drive or do your job properly. Perhaps you might want to consult your physician concerning these suggestions.

5

Wanting Too Much

In the last chapter we considered the means by which we can overcome the first of two ways that American life robs us of pleasure. Specifically, we looked at the fact that we often don't enjoy what we can have because we are overindulged. Too much of a good thing is boring and unsatisfactory. We outlined simple means by which we can increase our desire for attainable goods and events, thereby increasing our satisfaction with those goods and events. While not guaranteed, these methods can help.

In the present chapter we turn to the second form of frustration which is so common in current American life: wanting more than we can possibly have, no matter how hard we try to get it. If you will recall, we discussed learned drives or motives in an earlier chapter. It is these learned or acquired needs, such as the need for material objects and the need for success and achievement, which are instilled in us by our culture and which lead to inevitable frustration. Because so many of us have been taught to want to succeed, to be the best, we are bound to experience a sense of failure and disappointment when we reach the limits of our ability and discover that there are always people more successful than we are. Similarly, our capitalistic society has taught us to value material goods by constantly associating objects or products with good feelings. You will recall from the section on capitalism and advertising that it is the constant, never ending association of purchases with "goodness" which can lead us to develop an acquired need for objects. If we are constantly told that we will be happy if we have objects, then we may develop a strong interest in material goods. But here again, just as with success, we are bound to fail. We simply can't have everything we have been taught to want. There is always a limit to how much we can afford, and, left unchecked, our acquired need for objects will inevitably be frustrated.

So this chapter will outline some of the ways we can gain satisfaction in spite of our culture's tendency to instill in us acquired needs for objects and success which are doomed to be frustrated.

Obviously, we can't use the techniques outlined in the last chapter. Depriving ourselves further of things we can't have makes no sense. Deprivation can lead to fulfillment only if we can eventually indulge in whatever it is we deprive ourselves of. And now we are talking about those things which are quite clearly beyond our means. We can't indulge in them. So we have to look for a new set of principles and techniques to handle these equally vexing problems.

The discussion in this chapter centers around the concept of *level of aspiration.* We will first define level of aspiration and relate it to the idea that we suffer from wanting more than we can have. Then we will look at some of the practical, applied ways that we can change our level of aspiration in a manner which will allow us to have a lot more fun in life.

It's All a Matter of Expectations

Consider the following situation. A young child, let's say two and a half years old, is placed in a warm, comfortable room with half of a telephone. That is, he is given the receiver portion into which we speak but not the dialing portion. He plays happily with the receiver, cooing into it and carrying on a minor fantasy conversation. Then another child is brought into the room, but she has an entire phone to play with. She can dial and talk into the receiver, which she does in front of our first child. What happens? The first child, upon seeing this, becomes grouchy, unhappy, and demanding. Unless prevented, he may go over and try to take the complete phone away from the young girl.

When he wasn't thinking about the complete phone, he was content. But once he saw what could be had but that he didn't have it, he immediately became dissatisfied.

Consider another situation. Two college students enter a foot race. They tie for second place. One is completely dejected and unhappy while the other one is excited, proud, and elated. Why? They both achieved the same thing, but one is very pleased while the other is unhappy. More than likely the marked difference in their reactions has to do with their *expectations.* The one who is unhappy probably expected to come in first, while the happy one probably never even expected to finish in the top ten. Thus, how happy or satisfied we are with any event depends upon our expectations. If we get more than we expect, we will be satisfied. If we get less than we expect, we will be unhappy.

Consider a presidential candidate. If he loses and must remain a senator, he will be unhappy. On the other hand, there are millions of people who would be more than satisfied if they could just get to the point where they could enter the race.

The same event or occurrence can make people either happy or unhappy, depending upon what they expect. Two people may each earn $30,000 a year. One may be desperately unhappy because she thought, was sure, she was going to earn $60,000. The other is overjoyed because he expected to earn only $20,000.

If we expect too much, we are letting ourselves in for trouble. If we expect less, then our chances of being surprised and receiving more than we expected are improved. In general, if we expect too much out of life, there is a greater danger of our being disappointed than if we expect less. If a child expects a fancy new bike for Christmas and receives only a tennis racket, she may be disappointed. If another child expects nothing more than socks and receives the same kind of tennis racket, she will be very pleased.

Level of Aspiration

This notion that satisfaction is relative to what we expect is very important when we consider the concept of level of aspiration. Your level of aspiration refers to what you expect to accomplish, achieve, or acquire in your life. In a sense, it corresponds to what people are talking about when they consider how ambitious a person is. If your level of aspiration is high, you will want to, and expect to, do big things in life. If your level of aspiration is high, you will be an ambitious person with big plans who believes in success and expects to achieve it.

In our culture a high level of aspiration quite often leads to the expectation that a great deal of money will be earned and that a position of power and status will be obtained. Money, education, status, power, and possessions are common goals in our culture. If you aspire to these goals and expect to achieve them, you will be considered ambitious.

Of course, these goals are not the only ones available in our culture. For example, an individual might want to live alone, or to be unnoticed by other people, or to be above the need for money, or to reject the ordinary goals of our society. But even these people have a level of aspiration. They, too, have goals and expectations concerning those goals. They, too, can suffer disappointment if they do not fulfill their aspirations. They, too, can have a level of aspiration which is unrealistic and therefore apt to lead to trouble. For example, an individual might desire and expect to become a holy person, completely devoid of selfish desire, completely free from the crass desires of ordinary mortals. If this state is not achieved, then unhappiness will result.

It makes no difference what the actual nature or content of an individual's ambition is; wanting too much of anything can lead to frustration and disappointment. It can be wanting too much money, or it can be wanting to be completely free from any desire for money at all. If you expect too much of yourself, you can run into trouble.

Expecting Too Much

It is our contention that people in America suffer from a chronic state of overexpectation. Our levels of aspiration are simply too high. Much of our unhappiness stems from the fact that we simply expect too much from life. We expect houses, cars, jobs, money, fame, and a whole host of other goodies which many of us will never realize.

Take the fact that we Americans typically expect our standard of living to keep increasing throughout our lives. The thought of our standard of living merely leveling off, much less declining, is slightly depressing. Think about it for a moment. Imagine that your income and assets are frozen at their present level. Imagine never having anything more than you have right now. Somewhere, deep inside, you will probably admit that this would be a disappointing state of affairs. We all want more and more and *expect* more and more, not necessarily in great leaps and bounds, but more and more nonetheless. If we don't experience a constant increase in income, we feel uneasy and restless. Staying in the same place is not enough.

Now think about what individuals from a poor developing country would feel if they were suddenly placed in your shoes. They would be ecstatic. Your condition, which you find mildly disappointing because you have been led to expect so much, would be beyond their wildest dreams. The last thing in the world they would do would be to worry about getting more. Their level of aspiration is very low compared to yours, so they are capable of obtaining pleasure where you are not.

If an unrealistically high level of aspiration is an American national characteristic, where does it come from? We have already seen, in Chapter 2, that our culture teaches us to (1) value and pursue success, and (2) value and covet material objects. These two acquired drives, the need to achieve and the need to own and control material wealth, lie at the heart of our overinflated levels of aspiration.

We have been taught not only to want goods and success but to expect them as well. It's the "American way." When we were children, most of us heard the statement, "Someday you may be president." Sure, sure. Not likely at all. But the belief persists that "in the land of the free the sky is the limit." You can achieve your wildest dreams if only you'll work hard. Wrong. Not everyone can do or be anything. First of all, limitations on our personal abilities severely curtail what we can become or achieve. There is just no way, in spite of the great American belief that we are all created equal and all have an equal shot at the pie in the sky, that a borderline mental defective can become a trial lawyer. There is just no way that a 118-pound person can play professional football. There are, when all is said and done, enormous constraints on what each of us can do and become. In spite of the American belief in equality, we are not all equal. Our abilities vary enormously, and some of us have a much better chance than others to achieve and to acquire material goods. Life is not fair and equal. The American belief that it is fair and equal leads to overinflated levels of aspiration, inevitable failure, and a great deal of unhappiness. We are led to believe anything is possible and then shown by experience that it is not. Life, and we, are limited.

The limitations on life are not restricted to the personal capabilities and abilities we have been discussing. Clearly, prejudice holds many groups of people back. Minorities of all sorts, blacks, women, children, and so on, receive less than their fair share in our culture. Women are still paid less than men for doing the same work. It is instructive to note that, at the time of this writing, the U.S. Senate contains no blacks. It contains one woman. Nearly 90 percent of the senators are Protestant. More than half of them are lawyers. Although the situation is complicated, it does suggest that if you want to be a senator, you'd better be white, Protestant, male, and a professional person.

There is another factor which has led to this American overestimation of what is possible and that is the unparalleled economic progress which this country has experienced since World War II. Since that war everything has been turning up roses. The standard of living has moved steadily upward. We *have*, in fact, gotten more and more and more. People born since the war have never experienced anything but progress, achievement, and growth. It's no wonder they expect it. They expect growth to go on forever because they have never known anything else.

But there will be a limit to growth. We are already beginning to realize that fact as natural resources are depleted and the rest of the world belatedly begins to demand its fair share and refuses to be further exploited by the developed countries.

We have noted in this section that Americans chronically overestimate the possibilities of life. Their levels of aspiration are often too high. Hence, they experience disappointment when they do not achieve or acquire what they have expected to obtain. This chronic overestimation is a complex issue, but it is probably influenced by the American economic system which teaches people to want and value success and material goods, by the belief that all people are equal, and by the unprecedented growth the country has experienced during the last three decades. The upshot of it all is that *Americans experience more dissatisfaction and disappointment than they would if their levels of aspiration were more realistic or if their expectations were lowered a bit.*

Getting It Down

Because overly inflated levels of aspiration are common in our culture, we will spend considerable time discussing means of adjusting them downward.

Insight

The first crucial step is to recognize the problem. Although an awareness of the fact that you are unhappy because you want too much success and too many things won't cure the problem, it will at least allow you to define the limits of the problem.

Ask yourself these kinds of questions. Am I disappointed with what I have accomplished in life? Do I want more success than I am experiencing? Do I feel frustrated because I don't have more material goods? Do I look with envy at other people who have more than I do? Does my stomach tie up in knots when I think about money and success? Am I jealous when I hear about other people making a bundle, getting promoted, or traveling to far-off, exotic vacationlands?

Do I feel life is passing me by? Am I missing out on love, respect, sex, fame, fortune, and excitement? Do I get a slightly panicky feeling when I read about the accomplishments of others? Does what I have seem ordinary and second-rate? Do I feel slightly dumb and uncreative? Does what I do with my time seem mundane and repetitive?

All of these questions, if answered in the affirmative, suggest that you are being eaten up by a high level of aspiration and that you would be happier, calmer, and more satisfied if you could bring your level down a bit. Expect less from life and less from yourself, and you may be happier.

Not all of the following bits of advice will work for everyone. Read through them and choose the ones that seem to help you. In essence, they all represent ways of thinking about yourself and the world around you. They can help you learn to cope with the world by thinking about yourself in a different light.

Look down, not up

We Americans often compare ourselves with people who are more successful and who own more material goods. We tend to compare ourselves with a very select, very tiny segment of humanity. Specifically, we measure ourselves against the "best" and most successful people. We wonder why we can't seem to write a great hit tune, land a great job, or develop a successful business like "all" of those people around us. We feel bad because we haven't got or haven't accomplished as much as the lucky few, the select few.

We tend to forget or ignore the enormous masses of humanity whose standing in the world of success is far below ours. Just *living* in America is something. Millions of people in the world envy the lowliest American. Millions of people have never owned or used, and never will own or use, the simplest things that we take for granted. We sit and complain to our friends about how little we have, never noticing that we are sitting in a warm room, well fed, talking over a telephone. These conditions, which we let pass unappreciated, would be a dreamland for most of humanity.

The problem is one of perspective. If we can step back and realize just how much we do have, relative to the rest of humankind, we may be more relaxed about it all. We really are, just by the fact that we live in America, far, far ahead of most of humanity. I mean, how would you like to live in a shelter made of branches, without heat, light, or water? It's happening all the time, right now. And yet we are grumpy because we have a Chevrolet instead of an Oldsmobile. We live in such a rarified atmosphere we lose track of our truly enviable, truly privileged position among the ranks of humanity.

Look down, not up. Realize you have an enormous amount relative to the rest of the people in the world. Don't pine over those last few remaining things in life, which you will never get. Rejoice in what you have. We in America, right down to the lowest levels, are filthy rich when compared to most of the people in the world.

The next time you feel disgruntled over not having something (e.g., Tom has a new stereo—why can't I afford one?) think about the millions of people who have never even heard a stereo and never will hear one, much less own one.

If you stopped right now and never did or received another thing, you would already have lived a life that is richer, fuller, and more varied than almost anyone else in the world.

Think about not only the 4 or 5 billion people alive on the planet today but the billions who have lived and will live. Most of them died or will die young and in poverty. You rank well up toward the positive end of all these individuals. We tend to narrow our focus so greatly. We tend to worry and fret about a mere handful of people and how much they have compared to how much we have. The rich, successful Americans we think about represent a tiny, a minuscule portion of humanity. Although we still want more, more, more, Americans really already have it made.

Relax, enjoy what you have, and realize that you are way ahead of the game. By looking at the world from this point of view, you will not need to compete with the last few ranks of ambitious people. Let them earn the heart disease, the inevitable failure, and the worn, stressed minds. Who needs it?

Readjust your sights

Take pride in a new outlook. Feel good about rejecting the money-success game. Choose your own goals. Laugh at the silly pursuit of money and success. Set as your goal the *absence* of these doomed desires. Be so snobby you won't even go into the stores, much less buy anything. Be above the heated rat race (knowing, at the same time, that you have already done very well relative to most of humanity). Understand that a Cadillac, after all, has only four wheels and a trunk, just like every other car. Become humorously ornery and rebellious. Reject the values of success and posses-siveness that have characterized your level of aspiration. Be contrary. Whatever they do, you do the opposite. Decide that if they want it, it can't be all good.

Choosing less

Get more out of life by preferring less. Don't be *forced* into settling for less, which will inevitably happen if you stay in the rat race. Make the choice yourself. If you continue to compete and to scrabble upward in the pyramid of success, somewhere along the line you will be blocked and feel frustrated. But if you decide to be satisfied with less ahead of time, then you will feel smug and content when you get exactly what you expected and wanted to get.

For example, think about what it is you want. Perhaps you want to be president of a manufacturing firm. You think you have a shot at it, but it is a long shot. Well, rather than hoping and wishing and perhaps failing in the end, choose as your goal the next lower level. Consider shooting for a *vice*-president's position. After all, the vice-president's position isn't all that bad—less responsibility, less stress, etc. Make a conscious decision to pursue a trimmed-back goal.

You can't lose

If you think about it for a moment, a trimmed level of aspiration almost guarantees success. If you expect less, you will probably be able to achieve that level. And, if by chance, you do go on and achieve beyond your level of aspiration why then you will be doubly happy.

Suppose, for example, a person sets as her goal the running of an eight-minute mile. If she attains this goal, she will be very satisfied. But if she should happen to exceed her expectations and run a six-minute mile, she will be extremely pleased.

If she expected in the beginning to run the six-minute mile and did, she would be less pleased than if she had initially thought eight minutes would be her best time. And if she failed to run it in six minutes, she would experience keen disappointment.

So by lowering our level of aspiration, we increase our chances for satisfaction enormously.

Death at any moment

Life is really very fleeting. Although the days may drag on, the years fly by. Elderly people often say that they can't believe all those years have gone by. They wonder where it all went.

Keeping this notion that life is very brief and tenuous firmly in mind can help us lower our level of aspiration. It underlines the fact that a level of aspiration is really future oriented. We want to do this or that, or get here or there, or acquire these or those. All of these goals are in the future. If we put too much effort into future accomplishment, time can pass us by. We can keel over any day. If we don't focus on today and its pleasures, if we constantly put off pleasure until we achieve whatever it is we are after in the distant future, we may miss the boat entirely. The fleeting quality of life tells us to spend a little time fooling around now. Enjoy the moment. Constantly driving toward some future goal can rob us of life.

Consider the case of Mr. X. He always wanted to own his own chain of hardware stores. He worked hard, incessantly in fact. He worked nights and weekends, first as a stock boy, then salesperson, manager, and so on. He put off all forms of relaxation and pleasure in his drive to the top. He finally bought one store. After several years he was on the point of buying two more. At this point he had a stroke and now sits paralyzed, looking out the window, wondering what happened. As is so often said, there are no guarantees in life.

That's an extreme case, to be sure. But it underlines the fact that being too future oriented can be dangerous. And as your level of aspiration goes up, your commitment to the future increases. So lower your sights a little and spend some time in the here and now.

Admit your limits

No one is perfect. We all have our limits. There are things we just can't possibly do. Some limits are physiological. If you're only four feet six inches tall, you'll have trouble playing for the Celtics no matter what your other attributes. Other limitations are social and psychological. Some people simply cannot feel comfortable dancing; others are nervous talking in front of a group.

Often we try to deny our shortcomings. We hide them and are embarrassed by them. We pretend we are more than we really are. We try to present ourselves in the best possible light.

If we fail to admit our limits to ourselves and to the world around us, we are letting ourselves in for trouble. A failure to admit limits is often closely tied to an inflated level of aspiration. We will take on more than we can handle. We will expect more of ourselves than is reasonable. We will get into a position where there is a discrepancy between what we want to achieve and what we are able to do.

But if we admit our limitations, if we are aware of our shortcomings, we will be much more likely to set our goals at an appropriate level. We will be much less likely to experience eventual failure if we are realistic about ourselves. Saying, "Oh sure, I can do *that*," without really thinking about whether or not we actually can do it can lead to eventual disappointment.

If we acknowledge our limitations, we will be much more likely to set our level of aspiration realistically (*below* our maximum capacity level) and will therefore be much more likely to experience success and to avoid failure.

Why don't we admit our limitations? For one thing, it's embarrassing. We've all had the experience of being embarrassed by our limitations, and we try to avoid admitting them. For example, a person who cannot read or write, or one who is tone-deaf, or one who knows nothing of current events, or one who can't cook, or one who is impotent, or one who gets carsick will feel uneasy if these truths come out in the open.

And yet, admitting our limitations may be the best course of action. By doing so we can avoid placing demands upon ourselves which we cannot possibly handle. Wouldn't it be better for the young man to admit he can't swim before he drives all the way out to the lake with the Esther Williams look-alike? Wouldn't it be better for the secretarial applicant to admit he types eight words a minute before the typing test? Wouldn't it be better for the business executive to admit he can't handle the stress of the next higher corporate level before he is thrust into it?

We have said that our level of aspiration will be more realistic if we can acknowledge our personal limitations. Given that it is downright embarrassing to admit our shortcomings, what can we do to get the job done?

1. *Take pride.* Take pride in your ability to admit your weaknesses. After all, it isn't everyone who is strong enough to do it. Suppose two people came to you seeking employment. Neither one had any experience. One of them admitted it right away, while the other one tried to hide the fact. Which one would impress you most favorably? The honest one, of course. It takes a special kind of person to say, "No, I'm not capable of that." So, if you can acknowledge your limitations, you have every right to feel proud about being able to do so. It takes a good, strong person to do it.
2. *Look for your limits.* It helps to think actively about what kind of a person you are and where your limitations fall. If you seek out your weaknesses and become aware of them, you will be much more able to tailor your goals to your abilities.
3. *Admit your strong and weak points.* One way to overcome the embar-

rassment associated with admitting your limitations is to remember that we all have our strong and weak areas of ability and training. So you can't do everything. So what? There are *some* things you can do very well, and they should, to a degree, balance or offset your limitations. If you can keep in mind that you possess a very fine array of good qualities, it is much easier to acknowledge your few weak spots.

Accept inconsistency and procrastination

Give yourself a break. Go easy on yourself. Allow yourself to be inconsistent and changeable. By thinking of yourself as changeable and often unpredictable, you will be less likely to demand too much of yourself. Realize that the human animal is, after all, frail and confused. And you are one of those animals, no better or worse. Your limitations and your inconsistency are the very essence of being human. Without them you wouldn't be recognizable. (If you were flawless and consistent, you would also drive everyone right up the wall.)

If you accept your own inconsistency, your level of aspiration will be less demanding. For example, you will not aspire to perfection or to unwavering commitment and labor. You may be sloppier and looser in your interests and endeavors. You may be happier, too.

We believe it is important to procrastinate regularly. Learn how when you are young. If you don't, your level of aspiration will be too high; you will suffer from the overdemanding goals you have set for yourself. Let things slide now and then. After all, as we have seen, we could drop over dead tomorrow.

Procrastination is a safety valve in our modern society. It allows us to say, "The hell with it!" at least occasionally. And everyone else does it, so why should you be so perfect and inhuman?

Success versus happiness

So far, in our search for ways to lower our level of aspiration, we have noted that we can alter our perspective by looking down not up; that we can consciously reject the pursuit of goods and success; that a lowered level of aspiration increases our chances of experiencing success; that life is too brief to be too future oriented; and that admitting our limits, accepting inconsistency, and procrastinating can all help us readjust our level of aspiration in a realistic manner.

What else can we do to lower our level of aspiration? Try this. The next time you find yourself eating your heart out because you have not achieved fame and fortune, think about the people for whom fame and fortune has been a disaster. Take the extreme cases. Think about the number of famous people who have committed suicide: Hannibal, Ernest Hemingway, Adolf Hitler, Marilyn Monroe, Freddie Prinze, George Sanders, Saul the first king of Israel, Socrates, and Vincent Van Gogh. The list of alcoholics is even more extensive. The number of plain old unhappy rich and famous people must be even greater. The point here is that riches do not *guarantee* satisfaction. In fact, they sometimes cause a great deal of trouble—perhaps more than they are worth.

Tell yourself you can keep striving for success—it's fun to have a goal and to work toward it. But also tell yourself that success and fame and possessions are not essential or necessary for happiness. There is no guarantee that you will be happier once you are successful.

Now think of all the plain, simple, ordinary people you know who seem quite content, who maintain a fine, satisfying sense of humor, and who do not torture themselves with thoughts of unfulfilled desires and lost chances.

Doesn't it seem there are as many happy ordinary people as there are happy rich and successful individuals? Although we have no good measures of the situation, it may be that, on the average, less successful people can be as happy as more successful people.

Success brings added stress and strain in many cases. Once you have power and money, you have to *keep it* or someone will take it away from you. What a drag, always having to plan and scheme to keep the money you had to plan and scheme to accumulate.

Pick out one particular rich and successful person who was, or is, extremely unhappy. Carry the thought of this person with you like a talisman. Whenever you find yourself sinking into remorse and self-incrimination over lost opportunities and broken hopes, think about this individual and realize that things could be a lot worse, even if you did achieve whatever it is you have failed to achieve.

Carry with you also the thought of an ordinary person who is very happy. Choose someone who knows peace of mind without having experienced success in the terms we have been discussing it.

Finding common denominators

As we seek ways to relieve the stranglehold that our overinflated levels of aspiration have upon us, we have considered a number of ideas which may further our cause. Basically all of these techniques have been what are usually called *cognitive behavior modification* methods. Essentially, they all try to alter our behavior and emotions by altering the way we *think*. If we can think about life a little differently and can view it from a different set of perspectives, then perhaps our emotional reactions to it will be more positive.

In this section we will describe a method of self-instruction, and "self-talk," which can be useful in reducing our levels of aspiration. It focuses upon common attributes of life's varied experiences. Let's begin with an example. Suppose young Maria wants more than anything else in the world to own a fancy sports car. She works hard, overborrows, and finally is able to swing the deal. At first she is immensely pleased with her purchase. But, as time goes on, she begins to focus upon things about the zippy new sports car which seem strangely, disquietingly *familiar*. It rattles here and there, just like her old car did. It doesn't really go that fast, and, anyway, the speed limit deters high-speed driving. Her old car was more comfortable. The control panel, although a little fancier in the new car, is really pretty much the same as the old one. Speedometer, gas gauge, lighter, lights, windshield wiper—and that's about it. Spare tire in the trunk. Doors, windows. In other words, she is beginning to realize that, in spite of the racing stripes and the sticker price, her new car has an awful lot in common with her old car. She begins to wonder if the new car was worth all that money. The new car is simply just not that different from the old one. Beyond a few frills they are essentially similar.

Life is, of course, filled with a wonderful array of differences, of shades and variations, of exciting diversity. At the same time, many of life's experiences and objects have a great deal in common. Resort hotels all have pools, dining rooms, bedrooms, waiters, clerks, driveways, tennis courts, and evening events. Bourbons all have a bite, a flavor, and an alcoholic content. Motel rooms all have a TV, a bed, carpeting, a bathroom, a chest of drawers, and a couple of lamps and chairs. Football games all have helmets, large people, scores, flying bodies, and crowds. Airliners all have steak, earphones, flight attendants, and noise. Most restaurants have food slightly poorer than we hope they will have. All diamonds sparkle and cost a lot.

We're not saying that life does not provide a rich and changing panorama of sights, smells, and sounds. But we are saying that *many* of life's experiences have an enormous amount in common. Socks that cost $15.00 feel quite a bit like socks that cost $1.98. Swimming in an Olympic-sized pool feels a lot like swimming in a smaller pool. There are more similarities between first- and second-class travel than there are differences. A $100 gold pen writes pretty much the same way a cheap pen does. Shopping with $1,000 in your pocket involves many of the same pleasures and displeasures that characterize shopping with $50 in your pocket. In each case you have to travel to a store, usually in a four-wheeled vehicle, park the vehicle, walk, talk to salespeople, buy similar goods, walk back to the vehicle, and return to your point of origin.

What has all this to do with our naggingly high levels of aspiration? Quite simply, *being able to see the common attributes of life's activities frees us from having to experience all of them.* There is a grain of truth in the old saying that if you've seen one you've seen them all. We don't need to be millionaires to experience approximately what a millionaire experiences. We go to the same baseball games, we see the same movies, and we read the same books. We get the same diseases and feel the same emotions. There are not special newspapers that rich people get to read while we don't. Shoelaces belong to all of us. Towels and toilet paper are similar among the successful and the unsuccessful. Rich people get caught in traffic. They breathe air pollution. They have to fight crowds. They itch.

If all this is true, and we can get, minus a few frills, pretty much the same things from life that rich and successful people do, then why should we kill ourselves trying to acquire and to succeed beyond our abilities? We shouldn't. To the contrary, we should giggle over the fact that we are getting away with murder. Without going to all the work and bother of getting successful and rich, we can see the same sunsets, go to the same concerts, and catch the same fish as those poor unfortunate people who think a little embroidery and a few fancy labels make things better. We can get 90 percent of the pleasures for 10 percent of the cost. The law of diminishing returns applies here. After a certain point, further success and further riches just won't buy you or get you that much more. Just how first class can first class be? No matter how much money you have you still sit on chairs, eat with a fork, walk to the bathroom, wash your hair, and put on a raincoat when it rains.

So here is the game you play with yourself. Instead of running after riches, wishing and hoping to have what the truly successful have, you lean back and laugh about how easy it is to have *most* of what the truly rich ones have. You look for attributes that are common to your experiences and to theirs. If they go skiing, you observe happily that you have already been skiing. If they buy a yacht, you recall that, in your experience, the bigger the boat the more boring the experience. If you watch TV, remember that they watch the same dumb programs.

If you do this, if you seek experiences of your own which approximate those of the truly rich and successful, you will find you probably wouldn't even want to do what they do.

Here's an example. A well-to-do young woman excitedly tells her less affluent friend that she and her husband are flying to San Francisco just for dinner! How romantic. But then the friend thinks for a moment. She's been to San Francisco, too. She can't afford to zip over for the evening, but she suddenly discovers she wouldn't want to. She knows what it's like driving to and from airports, riding in cabs, receiving less than excellent service, trying to sleep in strange places, and returning early in the morning. After a moment's thought, the young friend realizes she would actually pay good money *not* to go on this trip which only excessive money can afford.

Many of the activities of the rich and powerful can be experienced vicariously through reading. Read about an African safari. That way you don't have to undergo the incredibly uncomfortable traveling conditions which must accompany such a venture. Let your mind's eye roam the landscape while you are snug in bed. Reading allows you to do and see an enormous amount that would otherwise be denied to you.

In summary, you can cut back on your efforts to achieve and to acquire because you already have the ability to experience most of what riches will bring anyway. And the few things you can't have without money you can read about and feel good about not doing because half of them are uncomfortable anyway. And always remember that rich and successful people get bored, too. In fact, many of them, because life makes no demands upon them, may be bored more often than you are. It's a chore to think of twenty-four hours worth of activities each and every day. Better there should be some things you *have* to do. Leisure time can kill you.

Being "at one" with it all

By now most of us have bumped into the idea, imported from points east, about the "oneness," or the unity and wholeness, of the universe. We hear talk about being "at one" with the universe. It's a difficult and alien idea to the Western mind. But it can have some value in our efforts to rid ourselves of excess ambition.

Let's begin our investigation of this idea by considering the fact that the typical Western mind thinks of itself as being almost at odds with, rather than at one, with the universe. We emphasize our individuality, our distinctiveness, and our fight for survival. Don't you really think of yourself as the single most important thing in the universe? Aren't your mind and your body the most significant elements you can think of? Don't you think of yourself alone and there, set against you, "all the rest"? Most Westerners do. We tend to think of ourselves as distinct, incredibly important entities pitted against all the rest. We think about what we can get from the "not us," and we consider what the "not us" will be likely to take from us. We think of all the other animals and all the plants as distinct objects completely separate from ourselves. We think of rocks, oceans, and clouds as entities all separate from one another and from us.

There is nothing especially disastrous in thinking about the world in this way. But it does lead us to a position where we want to *get.* We want to have things and obtain success. We want to wrest these things away from the world out there and keep them for ourselves.

The alternative view, the one that proposes that there is a "oneness" about the universe, doesn't lead to this acquisitive position. To the contrary, it leads to the conclusion that there is no need to strive to take things from the world for ourselves because there really is no difference between us and the rest of the universe; we are all part of a single unity or whole.

If we Westerners could think that way, we probably would not feel quite so driven and ambitious. So let's pursue the oneness idea a little. What is meant by being at one with the universe? People interpret the idea differently, but here is our view. Being at one refers to the tranquil, pleasant emotional state which accompanies the thought that all things, although they may appear distinct, ultimately share the most mysterious and awesome quality with every other thing. Specifically, they "are," they exist, they are part of what there is, they are not absent. You are no different, or better or worse, or more significant or less significant than anything else because, in the last analysis, you both partake of the same inexplicable quality: you both exist. All that there is, is identical in possessing this fundamental quality of being. All the distinctions we make among things are overshadowed by this one fundamental attribute.

Being at one is as much a feeling, or an emotional state, as it is a logical position of thought. It has to do with a feeling of kinship to all that exists, with a feeling of being not different from all that there is. Another way to think about it is to consider the fact that you are composed of the forces which comprise everything else there is. You may appear to be clothes, nerves, meat, bone, shoes, muscle, and experience, but what you really are is some flux, some convolution, of the same unknowable forces which make up the stones, the birds, the trees, the stars, and the weeds.

Being at one is appreciating the common base that comprises all that there is. Being at one also plays hell with overblown ambition. Ambition of any degree tends to evaporate in the face of the sensation of being at one. Ambition involves wanting to take and get, but, if you're already a part of it all, what's the point?

"Cosmic" perspectives

It's amusing to think of humanity as a kind of mobile, carnivorous, carbon-based mold inhabiting the surface of the planet. Imagine you are an alien so large that our planet is the size of a bushel basket. Under a microscope you can detect humanity; a slightly damp form of life which tends to stink and stay undercover. Now imagine how surprised you would be to learn that each of these little bipedal symmetrical stalks thought of itself as the most important thing in the universe. Billions of tiny little egos screaming "me! me! me!" You would be taken aback, to be sure. But that is exactly how we tend to think of ourselves. It seems a little presumptuous, doesn't it? By understanding that there is so much more than ourselves, that we are really nothing more than tiny specks drifting in an endless universe, we can gain a sense of calmness and tranquillity. Our earthly concerns seem so trivial and, hence, so easy to neglect. Our worries become so infinitely small when thrown against the expanse of the universe that they hardly seem worth the bother. How important are a few more bucks, anyway?

Standing still isn't all bad

Inherent in the American level of aspiration is the concept of change. We desire, we aspire to, constant change and growth. If things stay the same too long, we become nervous and unsure about whether things are going along as they should. If nothing is happening, if we aren't moving, then we begin to feel depressed and dissatisfied. The higher our level of aspiration, the more change we want, demand, and need. Much of our frustration and anxiety results from not getting as much change as we want. We expect life to be a steady progression.

But of course life isn't all wonderful, exciting, never ending change. It's downright boring at times. There is no way we can get around that simple fact. Even the richest, most successful person in the world must have moments of boredom, of looking around and thinking, "There is nothing I want to do or can do right now." So, rather than thinking of our own periods of boredom and nonchange as terrible, unacceptable occurrences, and thereby driving ourselves crazy worrying about them, we should accept them as normal, as part of being human. In fact, the trick is *expecting* them. Actively anticipate these periods. Then, when they do arrive, you can at least have the satisfaction of knowing you were right. In addition, sometimes you won't be bored although you expect to be bored. Those periods are pure gravy. How wonderful to expect bland, listless boredom but to experience interest, excitement, and change instead.

This demand for constant change, growth, and progress, so inherent in the American level of aspiration, is not present in all other cultures. For instance, consider the native American. In many early Indian cultures, the level of aspiration was just as strong and controlling as it is in contemporary America. But it did not involve the same screaming necessity for constant change. Quite to the contrary, what the early native American wanted was a lack of change. What she or he wanted was a sense of continuity with the past. As things were, they should be now. As things are now, so should they be in the future. Satisfaction came in knowing that things were being done just as they had been done by one's ancestors. These early native Americans did not value change and progress the way we do. The absence of change was valued. To live exactly as their ancestors had lived, to cook the same way, to hunt and gather, to make love and war, to pass the same skills and beliefs on to the next generation were uppermost in their minds.

The point here is that there is nothing either biologically determined or God-given about this incessant demand for change and progress with which we seem to be saddled. There were people living here long before us who did very well, thank you, by valuing continuity and an absence of change. Their cultures were stable and prosperous. They lived all over the country, in many varied climates and geographical locations. But in each case there was a lack of desire to transform the environment, to mold and shape the forces of nature into ever newer forms, to tear down and reconstruct.

So, when you are being eaten by the need for change, remember the native American. Remember that a calm satisfaction and an inner sense of well-being can be achieved when "progress" is minimal. The idea seems peculiar and foreign to us because of our training and upbringing. But each of us is capable of attaining tranquillity through a lack of change. We should be able to laugh at our crazy neighbors as they ram their heads against the incessant demand for change, change, change.

Aversion Therapy

There is a behavior modification technique within the field of psychology which essentially eliminates unwanted behaviors by associating those behaviors with unpleasant events. This method is called aversion therapy. It has been successful in eliminating many undesirable behaviors and bad habits. For example, if a woman has a drinking problem she might be asked to drink six small cups of liquid. Two of the cups might contain whiskey or whatever she most prefers. The remainder of the cups would contain nonalcoholic beverages. Each time she drank the nonalcoholic beverages nothing would happen. But when she drank the whiskey, she would receive an uncomfortable shock. By experiencing this repeatedly, the woman came to associate drinking with nasty consequences. She would thus be less likely to drink because to do so would elicit the conditioned negative feelings. There are many reports of this technique being successful in at least reducing drinking behavior. It has also been successful with other bad habits, such as smoking, undesirable sexual activities, and overeating.

For example, if a man has been arrested for sexual assaults upon young children, he might be shown slides of young children or read descriptions of sexual acts with young children, while simultaneously being shocked. Chemicals which make the individual ill can also be used as the negative agent. In all cases an unwanted behavior is associated with a negative consequence. Aversion therapy can be used to help reduce stuttering by following stuttering very closely with a taped replay of that stuttering. It's very unpleasant to try to talk when a machine is giving you your voice back almost as soon as the words are out of your mouth. Stutterers will often reduce their amount of stuttering if smooth speech eliminates the noxious feedback.

There are at least two ways that the principles of aversion therapy can be applied to our concern about overly high levels of aspiration. In both instances the behavior we are trying to eliminate is obsessive thought about, and desire for, unattainable objects and successes. We do it by associating these frustrating, overly ambitious thoughts with negative consequences.

Stop thought

The stop thought technique is a very mild form of aversion therapy. It has been used most often with people who suffer from uncontrollable obsessive thoughts. One individual might have recurring hostile thoughts (I really do want to kill my child.) which are disturbing and frightening, but which seem unstoppable. Another individual might have recurring, disturbing, and apparently uncontrollable obsessive sexual thoughts (I am going to make a pass at my boss's husband, even if I lose my job!). In cases such as these the individual is instructed by the therapist to shout "Stop!!" either to themselves or out loud if circumstances permit such an outburst each time the unwanted thought occurs. The word "stop," spoken with such vehemence, is seen as a mild, self-inflicted punishment. In essence, the patient yells at him- or herself. Apparently the technique can sometimes be helpful in reducing these unwanted, repetitive, or obsessive thoughts. The thought becomes associated with the mildly unpleasant, self-condemning "stop!" and is thus avoided.

Well, the same method can be used in connection with obsessive thoughts about unrealizable ambitions. The next time you find yourself driving to work thinking, "I wish I had this, I wish I had that, I wish I had three of them, I wish I had a bigger one of those," simply yell at yourself, "Stop!" Do it out loud if you can. Keep it up. Every time you find you are driving yourself crazy with "woulda, shoulda, coulda" thoughts scream "Stop!" at the top of your lungs.

Sometimes the results can be quite satisfactory. If nothing else you will have a momentary sense of relief because the obsessive thought will have been blocked and the air will have been cleared. You will feel there is, after all, something you can actually do to stop your gnawing self-doubts and self-accusations. Some therapists believe there is a tendency to reduce the frequency of future obsessive thoughts, because they have been associated with a mild punisher (you screaming at yourself).

A level of aspiration which is too high can lead to all sorts of obsessive thoughts. These are primary candidates for the stop thought method. For instance, we can become obsessed about how younger or less experienced people have been promoted over our heads. Stop! We can worry about how our investments have been lagging behind other forms of investments. Stop! We can feel frustrated because we believe we have a best-seller inside of us but it won't come out. Stop! We can fret about the idea that there are ways of making money which require less effort than we are expending. Quit! We can spend a lot of time wishing we had a better house or place to live. Cease! We can worry about the fact that our friends have more possessions or money than we do. Hold it!

To use the stop thought method effectively you have to be aware of what you are thinking about. If you get too deep into an obsession and don't or can't think about anything else, then you'll never yell "Stop!" You have to cultivate a certain degree of self-consciousness. You have to monitor your thoughts, occasionally asking, "Am I obsessing now?"

Once you use the technique for a while it may become somewhat automatic. Each time you begin to fret, worry, and feel depressed and frustrated you will say "Wait a minute. Am I doing it now?" and will yell "Stop!" if it is needed.

Aversive thought conditioning

The second aversion therapy method is a little more complicated than the stop thought technique. It requires a little more preparation and thought, but it may be effective sometimes. Essentially, it involves associating more than a simple "stop" with the thought pattern you are trying to eliminate. It involves associating a series of negative consequences or attributes with a given obsessive desire.

For example, suppose your heart's desire is to become a dentist. Your parents, family, friends, and teachers have all encouraged you to do so. The concept of being a dentist is loaded with positive associations: status, money, freedom, professionalism, clean white clothes, exacting scientific methods, competence, superiority, good-looking assistants, adoring patients. All of these associations have been pounded into your head by our culture. In this culture the dentist is looked up to, and admired. But you fail every single test necessary for entrance into dental school. You start to brood about the situation, dreaming of the joys of working among glistening chromium instruments, soothing piped-in music blending with the hushed whisper of the expensive air-conditioning system in your expensive suite of offices located at the top of a high rise overlooking the bay. You feel frustrated and depressed because you can't have what you want.

Aversive thought conditioning to the rescue! What you have to do is break down this idealized conception of what it is to be a dentist. You have to replace some of these positive associations with downright negative ones. You don't have to delude yourself or rationalize. You can be quite realistic. First, make yourself a list of negative aspects associated with being a dentist. Start with bad breath. Can you imagine some of the startling olfactory experiences which await any dentist? Ferocious, to say the least. Can you imagine having to work inside mouth after mouth, breathing strangers' breath, all day long?

Then add to the list the thought of all the pain you must inflict. Some would enjoy this aspect of the job, but most of us would find it wearing and unpleasant.

Then think about malpractice suits. Add the problems of having to do constant public relations work. Consider the hassle of getting and keeping good office workers. Imagine standing in one room all day. Think about how medical doctors will be slightly, ever so slightly, condescending to you at cocktail parties.

Once you have a nice plump list of negative aspects of the job of being a dentist you must use them. Each time you think of being a dentist you must dwell upon one or more of these negative attributes. It takes a little self-discipline but it can be done. You must disconnect or extinguish all those lovely, positive, romantic ideas about what it means to be a dentist and replace them with some harsh, negative, but realistic aspects of the profession.

If you are driving along in your car or sitting quietly with a book, and you begin to get in a sweat thinking about what you are missing by not being a dentist, start thinking about your list of negative attributes. Carry a scrap of paper containing the negative aspects in your wallet or pocket if you have trouble remembering them all. Add new horrifying aspects of the job each time you think of them, and run them through your mind repeatedly.

Ask friends to think of things that are wrong with being a dentist. Add their ideas to your list. Think of your own most unpleasant dental experience (you remember—the time your tooth cracked under pressure of the drilling) and add that, too.

In other words, do everything you can to make your list true but gruesome. Then repeatedly dwell upon these unpleasant qualities each and every time dentistry pops into your mind.

This process, whereby you extinguish or disconnect pleasant associations and replace them with negative associations, is an example of what is called *counterconditioning* by psychologists. It may work for any goal or object that you desire but which is unattainable. The first step is to realize that the positive aspects of the desired goal or object have been forced upon you by our culture. You must next realize that there are many true but negative aspects of the goal or object. Then you must construct a list of negative attributes, drawing upon your own experience and the experience of acquaintances. Then you must think about and dwell upon these negative attributes each time the goal or object comes to mind.

After doing this for a while, you may realize that your feelings about the object or goal have begun to shift a little. The negative emotions stimulated by these thoughts about the shortcomings of the goal can become conditioned to the thought of the goal. Now, instead of having a sense of yearning for the goal or object when you think of it, you may discover that your reaction may well be somewhat less enthusiastic, if not downright negative.

If you want clothes but can't have them, think about expense, poor fitting suits, seams that tear, tiring and unsuccessful shopping trips, traffic, and, above all, the fact that by the time you get them home they will already be on the way to going out of style. Realize that as you buy them hundreds of people are scurrying about with only one idea on their minds—how to make your purchases obsolete as quickly as possible.

If you want a high-powered executive position but can't have it, think about boring meetings, phony greetings, rigid dress codes, unethical practices, lawsuits, competition, stress, heart attacks, and being fired. Above all think about the fact that everyone below you smiles but really wants your job.

If you want to be a doctor but can't, think about being called out at 2 A.M. to look into the orifices of a really diseased body. Think about living your life closer to germs than anyone else. Think about death and failure and unpleasant, disrupted bodily functions which fill most of your waking hours. Being an insurance salesperson can, by comparison, begin to look a little better.

If you want more money than you have, think about what having a lot of money means. It means, in these inflationary times, that you will be hard pressed just to keep what you have. If you simply try to save it, you will lose it because inflation will eat it up. There are no passive investments (e.g., savings accounts, T-bills) that can earn you anything. After taxes and inflation you will have lost money.

What you must do is *work* to keep the money you have already *worked* to get. It never ends, this labor. You have to be active and in a constant state of vigilance. Once you have money, there is no relaxing. Is it worth it? To keep your money you must invest it in such a manner that you incur risk. You can keep it only if you are willing to run the risk of losing it. And running all around you are people who are also trying to protect their money. To make things worse, the principal idea they have in connection with protecting their money is taking yours away from you. It has to come from somewhere, and you are it.

You can get into one of the popular "feeding frenzies." A feeding frenzy in the animal kingdom occurs when a large hunk of meat is thrown in among calmly circling sharks. Once the meat is detected, the sharks go crazy, ripping and tearing through the water, the meat, and occasionally each other, in their greed and blood lust. In the world of human economics, feeding frenzies occur during periods of inflation when people are trying to protect their money. They know that if they do nothing or put the money in a savings account, they will lose. So they circle one another looking for a "hedge," or something they can buy which will go up in value faster than the general rate of inflation. Gold has been subjected to several feeding frenzies in recent years. Once the price starts to rise, people want to buy quickly. They buy, which drives the price higher, which attracts more people, which drives the price higher, which attracts more people, and so on. Then, when the price gets ridiculously high, some people sell to make a profit. The price plummets, leaving the early investors way ahead of the game and the late investors way behind. In essence, the late investors have given their money to the early investors. Is that the kind of nightmare you want to think about every night?

Real estate, silver, and any number of other investments, including "pyramid" games, have experienced the same sort of feeding frenzy in recent years. Essentially, a frenzy redistributes money, taking it away from the people who got the timing wrong and giving it to people who, by luck or skill, had the timing down pat. It is our suspicion that many people who win, claiming afterward that they did it intentionally, actually just lucked out on the timing.

In your attempts to make unattainable money seem less desirable, think about the sorts of stomach-grinding concerns that come along with having money. Unless you don't care about keeping your money, there is no way you can avoid these cares, because to lean back and relax and to avoid competition will cause you to lose money, no matter how much of it you have. You end up so busy trying to keep your money that you don't have time to enjoy it. You add more concerns and doubts and requirements to your life. Perhaps it is better to have less money (just enough to live on) and more time and freedom from worry.

Try using this aversive thought conditioning method with anything you want but can't have. The essential point to remember is that you have to gather up negative attributes and then associate them in a regular and repeated manner with the unattainable goal. Remember, *nothing* is all positive in this world, so your search for legitimate negative aspects will be successful.

Summary

We have looked at a number of ways to lower our level of aspiration if we judge it to be too high. Some of these have involved nothing more than trying to think about the world and our place in it in a little different fashion, or from a different perspective. Others have involved actual mental exercises that we can use to encourage a reduction in our ambitions. These mental exercises roughly fall into the category of cognitive behavior modification techniques.

Because we have covered so many ideas it is useful to recall them here. In our efforts to lower an inflated level of aspiration we can:

1. look down, not up;
2. consciously reject the pursuit of goods and success;
3. prefer less and expect less, realizing that a lowered level of aspiration increases our chances of experiencing success;
4. understand that life is too brief to be overly future oriented;
5. admit our limits and be proud of doing so;
6. accept inconsistency and procrastination;
7. understand that success and money do not guarantee happiness;
8. find common denominators in life's varied experiences;
9. understand that we can already have most of what rich people have;
10. try to experience the sensation of being at one with what there is;

11. see ourselves and our concerns as mere specks in an unending universe;
12. realize that some cultures value continuity rather than continuous change;
13. use the aversion therapy technique of stop thought;
14. use aversive thought conditioning.

6

Expecting Too Little

Low Levels of Aspiration

Although overly inflated levels of aspiration may lead to the most trouble in America, there are some individuals who suffer from the opposite problem: their level of aspiration is too low. Levels of aspiration that are too high are probably more widespread than levels that are too low, but both can be a problem.

When your level of aspiration is too low, you feel as though you are hopeless and helpless. You are sure you are going to miss out on all of life's pleasures. You are convinced you won't be able to accomplish very much. You expect very, very little from life and, in general, feel disspirited, ineffective, and hopeless.

Thus an artist may denigrate her own work, claiming it is no good, worthless, and without value. She is convinced of her own inevitable failure. A student may be convinced that he will fail, no matter how hard he studies; so he doesn't study at all. He doesn't even try because he believes his efforts will be in vain anyway.

We will discuss possible methods of reversing this unfortunate state of affairs in upcoming sections. But for now we wish to point out a curious fact: an unrealistically low level of aspiration and self-esteem can be caused by an initially inflated level of aspiration. Take, for example, the young woman who is raised to succeed. From a very early age she is told by her parents that she will become a doctor. It is expected, as a natural course of events, that she will rise to the pinnacle of her profession. Hearing all of these constant, glowing, confident predictions, the young woman accepts them. She develops a high level of aspiration and, at first, never has a doubt about her eventual success. She has been told repeatedly that she is a winner and has accepted that evaluation as correct.

But now, as she emerges from the pleasant shadows of early childhood, and enters junior high school, she begins to experience a long, unbroken, and debilitating series of failures. She gets D's in her junior high school classes. Her parents laugh nervously, attributing these early failures to her high spirits and to the fact that she is so superior that ordinary educational activities bore her. But she secretly begins to wonder. She really *did* try on that math test but still received a C+.

By the time she is in high school, she has been severely bruised by a long series of frustrated expectations. It's not that she is a bad student. She passes all of her courses. But she can't achieve anywhere near the level of accomplishment that she has been led to expect. Hence, she feels a sense of failure. If she had expected and aspired to a C average, she would have felt fine. But she expected the moon and the sun and so crashed into depressed gloom when these goals were not obtained.

The final blow comes when she fails completely in her efforts to get into medical school. By this time she is sure she can't do anything. She is convinced by this unbroken string of educational failures that she is worthless. So she stops trying. What's the point of trying when all your past efforts have led to failure?

She ends up with an unrealistically low level of aspiration and a very poor self-image, all because she had been led to expect too much of herself. Her inflated level of aspiration has been punctured, leaving her completely and unrealistically deflated.

If she hadn't been led to expect so much in the first place, she would have been more pleased with what she could accomplish and would have avoided this unfortunate reaction.

In Chapter 3 we mentioned the concept of learned helplessness. Well, that is what we have been talking about here. Through a long series of inescapable punishments, the individual has learned to be helpless. If action in the past has led only to defeat and failure, why act now?

Reversing Learned Helplessness

In this section we will consider a method for raising low levels of aspiration. Specifically, we will discuss what is known about reversing learned helplessness.

According to current thinking in the field of psychology, the state of learned helplessness comes about because the individual has experienced an unbroken series of failures and defeats. The person begins to believe that things are hopeless and that further efforts will be futile. For example, suppose a young man goes to Hollywood full of hope and pleasant dreams. He wants to be a songwriter. Songs, both music and lyrics, just seem to pour out of him. He composes dozens of songs he feels are equal to or better than those currently on the charts. But no one buys any of them.

He presents his materials to every possible individual and company he can imagine. But they all reject his material, every time. For five years he tries. Nothing but unbroken rejection. You can see how, after this long string of failures, he would begin to believe that he is a failure and that to continue producing music would only lead to further pain and rejection. So he stops writing. His friends and acquaintances try to encourage him to continue. But he replies, "What's the use? They will just turn down anything I do."

So, even though that next song might be the big one, might be the one that justifies and rewards our talented friend's efforts, he never writes. He has learned to be hopeless and helpless. His level of aspiration is so low he feels he can't do anything and won't ever have anything.

How can this pattern be broken? How can the individual regain lost confidence and hope? Psychologists suggest that the individual must experience a series of small, very small, successes. To continue to dream of the top of the heap is futile. To go to the top in one step is, in fact, next to impossible. But there are small successes that the individual can experience which will help reestablish a sense of accomplishment and hope.

For example, suppose our frustrated songwriter has reached the point where he neither writes music nor works at anything. He stays home feeling trapped and labels himself a failure. He worries about where the next rent check will come from but doesn't seem to be able to do anything about it. What can he do? He can, with help and encouragement, experience a sequence of small successes. For example, if, on the first day, he can just get up, get out of the house, and buy a paper containing help wanted ads, he will experience a tiny sense of satisfaction. At least he will feel he has actually done something to help himself. It's a start. Then he should look through the ads, seeking not some high-level position which would be unrealistic for him to pursue, but rather some type of work for which he is qualified. It doesn't have to be a grand or important job. In fact, at this point the only essential aspect of the job is that it should be one in which success is virtually assured.

A job as simple as that of a night watchperson or a gardener's helper can, after years of failure, be a source of considerable satisfaction. The individual should be encouraged to take this kind of a job and to experience the sensation of doing the job correctly. It may not be much, but it's a start. Even if the work is temporary or part-time, it can be an encouraging source of success after failure-ridden years of songwriting. The individual will be able to say, "I can do *something!*" The regular paycheck can do wonders for a person who has been broke for years.

Further successes, and therefore further degrees of satisfaction, can be arranged if the steps are small enough. After working as a gardener's helper for a while, the individual should not say, "Well, now I'm ready to run General Motors." Doing so would guarantee failure and send the person back into the depths of learned helplessness. Shooting for the top of the heap all in one leap is what got the individual in trouble in the first place. The steps taken must be ones for which success is guaranteed. Hence they must be small ones, such as switching from part-time to full-time work, or switching to a different employer who offers more money and benefits, or switching to another form of work which holds out promise of more advancement.

As these small steps are taken and the individual experiences success, he or she will begin to feel better, more competent, and capable of wresting a living from life. Eventually the individual may work back to, say, songwriting. But that is not essential. If it happens, it happens, but it must occur only if it is done in a realistic way. Namely, it must not be attempted if unbroken failures will result. If nothing has changed since the initial period of failures, then perhaps it should not be attempted again. But if the individual has learned new skills, made more contacts, teamed up with someone else, or in some other way increased the chances of success, then it can be tried.

Many people who get into this learned helplessness state never get out of it because they say, "There are no jobs I can do." That seems unrealistic, doesn't it? After all, about 95 percent of the working force is usually employed. If they can all find work, so can the person who feels helpless. Saying, "There is nothing I can do," may really mean, "There is nothing I *want* to do." Saying there is nothing I can do may sometimes be an excuse for not wanting to work at all. But most of us engage in work that we're not entirely crazy about, so it is unrealistic to assume work must be all joy and happiness. After all, they don't usually pay people for engaging in fun and games.

The way to break the learned helplessness syndrome is to get the individual up and on her or his feet, engaged in some activity which will lead to a minor success. Once a minor success has been achieved, the next step can be approached. At all costs, shooting too high should be avoided.

Let's study another example which illustrates a second type of learned helplessness which is quite common. In this case the individual *is* fairly successful but seems to be stalled and without direction in her career. We are not talking now about someone who is a total stranger to success. This woman has been an instructor at a two-year college for fifteen years. She has job security and is competent in her work. But she feels as though she has reached her limit. She feels pretty hopeless about moving along any further. She can't see anything else she can do. She's afraid she will spend the next twenty years doing exactly what she is doing now. She sent her credentials to a couple of four-year colleges, hoping to move out of the two-year system, but they either didn't reply or politely indicated their disinterest in her. In a sense, she feels as helpless as our frustrated songwriter.

The solution for her is similar to that prescribed for the songwriter. She must choose steps which *can* be taken and which *will* lead to success. Applying to major universities may just not be realistic. It's like shooting for the top hit song of the decade. But there are other smaller steps which can lead to a sense of satisfaction. For example, she might find out about and apply for a grant in her area of interest. She might try doing some research. She might try writing a textbook. In other words, she should explore all facets of her current position. There are things she hasn't tried before but can accomplish. She has to set attainable goals for herself. "I will become vice chairperson of my department." "I'm going to go to New Zealand on my sabbatical." She must make sure her choice is something she can do, or she will slip back into feeling trapped by her own helplessness.

If she has already exhausted the opportunities offered by her present job, there are other things she can do. She can take on a second part-time job. She can try investing in something. She can take classes in real estate or auto mechanics. If she will just act, there are innumerable things she cannot only try but succeed at. Again the trick is to define goals which can be attained and then to pursue them vigorously. Overly ambitious projects should be avoided if the individual is prone to feeling helpless and hopeless.

Assertion Training

In the last section we described how a sense of learned helplessness might be overcome. Reversing learned helplessness can be thought of as raising a depressed level of aspiration. In this section we want to discuss one further technique for combating the negative aspects of a low level of aspiration. Specifically, we will consider *assertion training,* a method which has become very popular in psychology.

Assertion training is designed to do two things:

1. It teaches us to say no when unreasonable demands are made of us and when we would formerly knuckle under and say yes to these demands.
2. It teaches us to ask for what we really deserve when we would formerly not ask.

When our level of aspiration is low, we tend to give in to or be dominated by the world around us because we don't expect very much from it. It should be clear that learning how to demand a bit more from the world can help us here. If we learn to ask for more and actually get it, then our hopes will be raised and our expectations will be increased. Learning to be assertive can be very beneficial for the individual with a low level of aspiration. Assertion training can teach us how to ask for, and get, more out of life.

When we should say no

Suppose a friend asks you for money, say, fifty dollars. On your budget that's a pretty large sum. You don't want to lend the money, but it's your friend, and he says he will pay you back, "For sure, the end of the week." So, against your better judgment, you give him the money. Then you kick yourself for doing it. You become slightly irritated and angry. Off and on during the week your irritation with both yourself and your friend flares up again. You wonder if you will get the money back on time. Not only don't you get it back at the end of the week, you never see some of it again. These things have a way of ending up like that. One excuse leads to another, and before you know it the last payment on the loan is "forgotten," and it is too embarrassing to bring up the last owed fifteen dollars one more time. Wouldn't it have been better if you could have said no in the first place in such a way that no one was angry or hurt or disappointed? Well, assertion training can help you do just that.

What about all those people who knock on your door asking, in one way or another, for money? Don't you give in to some of them just to get rid of them? It's almost as if they know it will be worth a dollar or two to you to be done with them. After they leave, and you're standing there holding your latest box of peanut clusters from the Village of Heaven, don't you find you feel slightly disgusted with yourself? "What a namby-pamby," you think. "I should have politely said no to them." You peek out the window and see your neighbor refusing them and you feel all the more like a chump. Assertion training can help here.

What about the woman behind you in line at the grocery store who asks if little ol' her couldn't just pop right on ahead of you because her dog is waiting in the car? She has as much stuff to buy as you do. But you don't point that out. You act apologetic, as though you were guilty of something, and you let her go ahead of you, only to feel that you've been taken advantage of when she doesn't thank you.

What about the friend who calls and asks if you will watch her child because her baby-sitter is sick and she has a hair appointment? Sure, sure, you say. Good old easy going, helpful you. Then, when the kid arrives and completely destroys your sense of calm equilibrium, you wonder how you could have been so stupid.

What about the friends who want a ride to the airport because the bus is too expensive? What about the employer who gives you more work than your share, usually because you've shown willingness in the past and are much easier to approach than other workers? What about the spouse who insists upon going sky diving when you have a known genetic defect in that particular area? What about the children who manipulate you into the horrors of seeing *The Blob* for the fourteenth time? What about those wonderful people who have learned to sulk and make you feel guilty when you can't do something unreasonable for them, when you can't solve their problems. How do you like it when you find yourself feeling as though you have done something wrong when you can't lend your car to someone because it's in the garage. It's clear there are times when we could all benefit from an improved ability to say no in a diplomatic way. Assertion training can help.

When to ask for yourself

Just as there are times when we would do well to say no, there are as many times when we would be better off if we could just ask for what we deserve. If we have given a ride to a friend five times in a row, it is time to ask them to do the driving. Sometimes we don't ask because we are afraid of their reaction. You know, they act indignant and put upon in spite of the unfairness of the situation, and you end up feeling guilty about having asked.

Husbands, wives, and lovers should learn to ask for what they think they deserve, rather than hold grudges and bottle things up inside. These pent-up feelings may burst out in unpleasant ways anyway, so it pays to nip them in the bud. If you feel you've been doing too much of the housework, or making more than your share of the money, or getting stuck with the kids too much, it's time to ask for a little help.

If you feel you deserve a raise or a promotion, it would be better if you could step right up and ask for it in a clever, effective manner, wouldn't it? You might wait to be recognized forever.

In other words, being more assertive both by saying no and by asking for what we deserve can help us. There are some things in life which may seem unattainable but really are within our reach if only we will ask for them. Learning to be assertive without becoming pushy, obnoxious, and counterproductive can help us realize the goals we thought were beyond our ability to achieve. We don't always have to lower our expectations. Sometimes we can get more than we expected, simply by being assertive. Psychologists have developed steps to be taken in moving toward assertion behavior. The following list of steps is an example of the kinds of things psychologists have been talking about.

How to be assertive

1. The first thing to do is to look over your own behavior for excessive timidity. Do you let other people push you around? Do you bottle up your true feelings because you are afraid to express them? Are you hesitant to ask for what you really deserve?
2. Now look at your behavior in terms of excessive hostility. Do you blow up at people and rant and rave when you might better be calmer?

Being assertive means being neither timid nor aggressive. It refers to being calm and polite but firm in terms of our desires.

3. If you find you are either too timid or too aggressive, you can benefit from assertion training. If you are not sure whether or not you are less than assertive, keep a diary for a while. Write down how you handle interactions and how aggressive or timid you are.

4. If your diary shows that there are certain situations when you were either too timid or too aggressive, choose a couple of areas where it seems you need the most help. For example, you might find you tend to be huffy and indignant with co-workers or with your boss. Or you might be weak and submissive with these same individuals. Or you might be too hesitant or too aggressive with strangers or family members or school acquaintances. Try to define the situations where you seem to have the most trouble. Choose one or two of these areas to work on.

5. Now that you have selected, let's say, one particular area to concentrate upon, think about a recent example of your nonassertive behavior. Try to bring back the details of this particular incident. As you think about this incident consider how you appeared to the other parties involved.

6. Consider your bodily movements during the interaction. Were you smooth and relaxed? Or did you wave your arms about and tremble? Were you meek, nervous, and cowering? The assertive stance is one of relaxed repose. Cowering behavior suggests hesitancy while excessive movement and agitation suggests hostility.

7. How did you look at the other person? Eyes and eye contact are enormously important in communication. We probably say as much to one another with our eyes as we do with words. The assertive gaze is calm and direct. The aggressive gaze is direct but not calm; to the contrary, it is a flat, hostile stare. The timid person will avoid eye contact and keep her or his eyes averted.

8. The way you compose your face is important, too. The assertive person looks serious, because the situation is serious. But he or she does not look mad or angry or timid or hesitant. Firm, composed features suggest a serious quality which cannot be missed.

9. What was the tone of your voice during the interaction? You should try to speak at a normal level and in a normal tone of voice. Speaking too loudly suggests agitation. Speaking too softly suggests worry and hesitant anxiety. Speak directly to people in a modulated, normal tone of voice. Don't yell and scream and don't be wishy-washy.

10. Was your speech smooth, or did you stumble and mix up your words and sentences? If you are being effectively assertive, you will be coherent and grammatical. If you are angry or frightened, you will make errors, your voice will crack, and your speech will tremble.

11. Finally, ask yourself about what you said. Was it effective because it

was directed toward solving your problem, or was it either uselessly aggressive or hopelessly submissive? For example, suppose someone demanded that you do something you didn't deserve to do. Were you assertive as you clearly outlined the reasons why you shouldn't be expected to do it? Or did you rant and rave about how you damn well weren't going to do it? Or did you say, "Yes, yes. I'll get right on it"?

12. Pick out the areas where you have the most trouble. For example, you might be calm and collected except for the fact that you can never look anyone in the eye. Well, that would be what you would want to work on. Or you might tend to fly off into irrelevant, angry speech. Writing down what you have done in the past can help you focus upon what you need to do. You can't solve your problem until you know what it is.

13. Now make a list of things you could do which would be more assertive. For example, think about what kinds of things you might say instead of bellowing out angrily. Think of being calm and to the point. Now, using your imagination, construct situations where you might need your new assertive approach. Run through each situation, imagining exactly what you would do and say. For instance, imagine that some-one has denied you something you deserve. Think of specific sen-tences you could speak which would be fair, accurate, and assertive. Imagine the whole interaction, including what the other person says and does as well as what you say and do, without once slipping back into your former modes of aggressive or hesitant behavior. Invent and run through as many different situations as you can. This form of covert rehearsal can help you sharpen your assertive skills.

14. Once you have used your imagination, bring your new skills into a "role-playing" situation. Get a friend or acquaintance to play out a scene with you. Invent a situation where you need to be assertive and play it out with the other person. Keep track of your new skills and try to use them. Speak calmly, clearly, and to the point. Look directly at the other person. Keep your body relaxed and comfortable. Com-pose your face. Make your desires known in a manner that is forceful and direct, without being hostile.

15. Vary the other person's role. Sometimes the person can be hostile; other times, sneaky or condescending. In each case, work on develop-ing a set of assertive techniques which will work for you. Obviously, we are not all going to come up with exactly the same solution to the problem of being assertive.

16. Now it's time to move into the "real world." Try out your new ap-proach in a real situation. It's best to pick a spot where you know, ahead of time, that there is going to be trouble. Then you will be able to compose yourself, to get ready, and to select responses from within your new arsenal. You will probably be nervous and self-conscious. It

can't be avoided. Go through with the situation no matter what. Keep trying to remember what it is you want to do and what it is you want to avoid doing. "I will not look away from her. I will tell her what I want to do. I won't give in just because she starts to bristle. I won't let her make me feel guilty. I will be calm and reasonable."

17. After this first attempt, which can be pretty scary (and pretty much of a disaster), go back over what happened. Try to see exactly where you went wrong and exactly where you did well.

18. Don't be discouraged by your early efforts. After all, we're talking about some pretty substantial changes in your behavior, and we can't expect perfection overnight. Keep at it. Sooner or later you will experience the satisfaction of getting exactly what you want while, at the same time, keeping the other person fairly calm and satisfied, too. This does not mean you always have to worry about the other person's feelings, but it is an added bonus if you can keep them happy, too.

The Ideal Level of Aspiration

In the last two chapters we have seen that unhappiness can be the result of a level of aspiration which is either too high or too low. On the one hand, if our aspirations outstrip our abilities, we will feel frustrated and disappointed. If we want to be an English teacher but can't spell, we will be dissatisfied. If we want to be a car mechanic but can't remember which direction to turn a bolt, we will be disappointed. On the other hand, if we underestimate our capabilities and expect too little of ourselves and the world, we will also be unhappy. If we expect that we will be lucky to get on the welfare payroll when we could actually be earning a good living, we will be getting less from life than we should. If we have enormous energy and mental ability but feel that it would be useless to utilize these talents, then we will be bored, restless, and uneasy.

We have also outlined a whole series of techniques that may be helpful in both raising and lowering the level of aspiration. Now comes the important question. Given that we know how to manipulate the level of aspiration, where should it be? What level is ideal? How much *should* we aspire to? Quite simply, an ideal level of aspiration sets goals which, while requiring the individual to exert him- or herself, are attainable. Success must be possible. Our goals should not be so lofty that we will never reach them. They must be within our grasp. At the same time, they should require effort on our part. Very low level goals can easily be reached, but the satisfaction associated with their attainment is not very substantial. We can aspire to a position where we actually go to work almost every day. But so what? Most people do that anyway. It's difficult to get much pleasure from attaining low-level goals. I mean, how smug can you feel if you succeed every day in putting your shoes on the correct feet?

What we need is a level of aspiration that challenges but does not defeat us. We need a tussle, a struggle, and then success. A struggle followed by defeat is no fun. And neither will a total absence of struggle make us happy. We want to fight life, to respond to its demands, and to emerge victorious.

7

Pushed and Pulled

The Lure of the Environment

We have come to a turning point in this book. Now we are going to make a distinct change in our orientation toward the problems of human satisfaction. We will still be concerned with the American's sense of dissatisfaction and what to do about it, but we will address the issues from quite a different point of view.

This change in perspective can best be introduced with an example. Imagine a woman sitting in a chair on a terrace on a calm, lovely day. She is well fed, not thirsty, and sexually satisfied. She is a success and possesses just about everything she could want. In other words, in terms of all known drives, she is satisfied. According to the way we have been speaking throughout this text, all her drives are satisfied, and she is not pushed to get anything by some state of deprivation. She is not seeking food because she just ate. She is not looking for a drink because she has not been deprived of liquid. She is not searching for social companionship because she is not deprived of it. In a nutshell, all her drives are at zero.

But then, out of the corner of her eye, she spots a slight movement and a shiny something in the bushes at the edge of the terrace. What does she do? She immediately becomes interested, perks up, becomes more active, and actually walks over to see what the object is. She has been motivated, or energized, not by the push of some internal need or state of drive, such as hunger, but by the pull or the lure of the environment. Her curiosity has been stimulated, and it encourages her to act. It isn't a matter of being deprived and being pushed around by that drive but a matter of being stimulated by novel and unusual events in the environment.

So far in this book we have pretty much restricted our attention to the idea that satisfaction occurs when we indulge in something after having been deprived of it. That is what is called the drive, or *push,* conception of human satisfaction. We are driven or pushed from within to act in a manner that will reduce our state of need.

But there is another major conception of human satisfaction which does not rely on this push conception. It is the *pull* conception of satisfaction which argues that the environment, in all its wonderful novelty, complexity, and variety, can stimulate and satisfy us. We are drawn to variety and novelty and complexity like a bee to honey, like a moth to light. Complexity, novelty, and variety please us. They satisfy us. They are rewarding to us. We like change, we like movement, and we like unusual things and events. By our nature we are curious, which is to say we find pleasure and satisfaction in experiencing changing and unusual sensory experiences.

This capacity to feel pleasure by experiencing novel or complex events is very distinct from the kinds of push-drive motives we have talked about so far. It is not dependent upon internal needs which build up over periods of deprivation, such as hunger, thirst, or the need for sex. What stimulates this capacity for pleasure is not time of deprivation but the actual external stimuli themselves. Our woman sitting on the terrace was quite calm and unmotivated before she saw the movement in the bushes (you're still wondering what it was, aren't you?). But once she perceived it she became all interested and curious. It was the external stimulus (the bush movement) which not only aroused her but pulled her up out of her chair. She enjoyed being stimulated and being able to satisfy her curiosity.

It is our intention in this and the following chapters to show that the American way of life frustrates our capacity to find pleasure in changing, novel stimuli. Not only are we frustrated in the two ways described in the preceding chapters (by not wanting what we can have and by wanting what we can't have), but we are frustrated as well by the fact that the American way of life, in spite of its apparent diversity, robs us of novel, complex, and unusual experiences. We don't get enough variety and change in America. As a result we are dissatisfied.

In the upcoming chapters we will discuss how American life robs us of novelty and change, how we react in a maladaptive fashion to this lack of change, and, finally, how we may regain a sense of satisfaction through the pull mechanisms of motivation.

But for now, we need to consider some additional examples of the power of curiosity and the power of stimulus change, novelty, variety, and complexity. Let's return to our woman on the terrace. What would be most satisfying and interesting to her? She would be happiest if the thing in the bushes was unusual. Not dangerous, but unusual. She would be happiest if it was a peaceful, slightly bewildered Martian in need of her help, or an exotic bird using a tool, or an object no one had ever seen before. Such is the pull of the environment: we gain pleasure and satisfaction from unusual things and events without having to first undergo some kind of deprivation. More than likely, in spite of her wishes, the thing in the bushes will turn out to be something ordinary and slightly disappointing, like a piece of tinfoil in the breeze or a small child playing hide-and-go-seek. Life is never quite as interesting as our fantasy lives would like it to be.

The power of the novel and unusual environment to motivate and satisfy has been well documented in many laboratory experiments. For example, consider the lowly white mouse. Even this tiny creature appears to get a bang out of a changing environment. You can set up a situation in which each time the mouse presses a little lever the light in the cage goes off, plunging the animal into thirty seconds of darkness. Now, mice don't normally press little levers. But in this situation the animal will learn to press the lever and will do it repeatedly to have the light turned off. It's a kick for the animal, and it apparently enjoys it.

"Wait a minute," some say. "Maybe that little mouse is just afraid of being out in the light and likes the cover of darkness. Maybe it learns to press the lever so it can hide in the dark." Good idea, but not true. You can reverse the apparatus so that each time the mouse presses the lever the light goes *on* for thirty seconds. The animal will still learn to press the bar. It doesn't care if the lever press turns the light on or off, as long as *something* happens. Change is what the mouse likes.

Laboratory demonstrations are numerous. Monkeys will learn to open little doors when nothing more than the opportunity to look through the little door and out into the laboratory is provided as reward. Monkeys will learn to open and close latches just for the fun of it.

It should be clear that humans are capable of enormous curiosity and will experience great satisfaction through contact with varied external stimuli. Why else would we go exploring into those caves, why would we turn and look if we hear a piece of cellophane crinkling behind us, why would we gawk out the window of moving cars, and why would we want to learn about new things and go new places? We're possessed of a great deal of curiosity.

The drive conception of motivation discussed in previous chapters can't explain this form of satisfaction too well. The drive conception accounts for all those instances where we are pushed from within by a growing need. But these examples we've been talking about involve our being pulled and stimulated by the external world. One minute we're calm and unmotivated and the next, upon perceiving something unusual, we're all worked up and interested.

Try As We May

Boredom

Given that we know that the external world, in all its flux and change, is a source of great satisfaction to us, we can ask the opposite kind of question. Specifically, what would we feel if we were cut off entirely from the external environment? Imagine for the moment that you, for some reason, find yourself in the following situation. You are wearing opaque goggles, your arms are wrapped in mummylike bandages, and you are lying alone in a small, soundproof room. You've been lying there for twenty-four hours. How do you feel? Bored? Of course. Not only bored but more bored than you've ever been in your life. You are bored because you're not getting any change in your life.

Imagine you've been there for two days now. Then three days. Psychologists have actually set up this situation with volunteers so we know something about what happens when we are cut off from the environment. Most volunteers, in spite of good pay, will leave after one or two days. If they do manage to stick it out for a couple of days, they experience enormous frustration and anger. They actually have trouble thinking clearly. If you ask them to solve some simple problems after a few days in isolation, they don't do well at all. Some of them begin to hallucinate. That is, they begin to hear sounds that aren't there and to see things that aren't there. These kinds of studies suggest that we need external stimulation if we are to function properly. Without it we go a little cuckoo. Thus, external change and variety may not only be satisfying, they may be necessary as well.

Nothing lasts forever

When you walk into a kitchen filled with the delicious odor of fresh bread baking, you exclaim, "Mmm, what a wonderful smell." But what happens if you remain in the kitchen? Slowly the smell recedes until you barely notice it. The same thing will happen if you go into a fish market or a field of flowers. Your sensory systems initially react very strongly to a change in stimulation, but then they *adapt* to the stimulation; they, in a sense, stop telling you about it. In other words, our sensory apparatus detects and registers changes but does not continue to register unchanging stimulation. This effect is called *sensory adaptation,* and it refers to the fact that, in the face of continued, constant, unchanging stimulation, our sensory systems seem to stop responding. They really go wild when a change is introduced, but they will stop responding if things stay the same too long. We just can't continue to enjoy the smell of baking bread if we stay in the kitchen. Our sensory apparatus is just not set up to keep us feeling stimulated without change. We require change in external stimulation to have strong sensory experiences. About all we can do is go outside for a while and then return to the kitchen to again briefly experience the wonders of baking bread. Sensory adaptation adds to our problem of trying to seek satisfaction through change. It makes changes in stimulation interesting and exciting only for short periods of time.

There is an interesting experiment you can do to bring home the reality of sensory adaptation. First find three bowls large enough to put your hands in. Fill one bowl with ice water. Fill one with water as hot as you can stand it. Fill the third bowl with neutral or lukewarm water. Then begin by putting one hand in the hot water and one hand in the cold water. Hold them in the water for several minutes. Now take both hands out and simultaneously plunge them both into the third bowl containing the neutral water. What will you experience? The hand that had been in the cold water will tell you the neutral water feels very hot. But the hand that had been in the hot water will tell you the very same water is cold. You will have the unusual little sensation of experiencing a given bowl of water as both hot and cold at the same time. This is because the hand that had been in the hot water adapted to it. Specifically, it had begun to respond to hot water as though it were nothing special, as though it were neutral. Then, by contrast, the neutral water seemed cold to that hand. The hand originally in the cold water adapted to the cold, or made it neutral. Then the neutral water, by comparison, seemed hot.

Demonstrations aside, the point here is that sensory adaptation limits the amount of pleasure we can gain from any one change in our environment. Further changes are always required if we are to experience further interesting or exciting sensory experiences. Any one change, such as the change from no odor of baking to the odor of baking, will make us happy for only a short while. We soon adapt to the change and require further changes.

Satiation

Our problems in getting satisfaction from changes in stimulation are compounded further by the fact that certain changes, if they occur too often and repeatedly, become uninteresting. We get bored with the same old changes. We need a change in the changes we experience.

For example, suppose a couple buys a cabin overlooking the ocean. For months they are thrilled, watching the ever changing face of the ocean. The waves, the light, the sand, wind, and shorebirds, all provide a continually changing scene which constantly attracts their eyes and pleases their souls. But, within a year or two, this ever changing view has lost much of its appeal. The couple spends much less time looking out the window. They draw the shades against the glare more often. They occupy themselves with other things. They have become satiated with the view. They are tired of that particular form of change. The unending changes of the ocean no longer thrill them as they once did. They need to move on to other things.

Watching football is a prime example of how satiation with a certain form of change can set in. A person who once loved watching football may eventually tire of it. Even though each game presents changes and novelties which have never occurred before and will never occur again, the individual has tired of that *class* of changes.

Driving a car can become less than exciting even though it produces constant, new, unique changes. Sunsets, other people, careers, recreations, you name it, we can become satiated on any form of change if we experience too much of it. In short, we sometimes need change in the kind of change we are experiencing.

Preferred Level Theory

Let's recap what we have discussed so far in this chapter. We have seen that pleasure and satisfaction can be gained by the pull of the external environment as well as through the push of our internal needs. We have seen that without stimulus change, variety, and novelty we can become bored and depressed and may actually suffer mental disruption.

But we have also seen that to gain constant satisfaction from external change is not all that easy. First, any given stimulus change, although intriguing and intense at first, soon loses its impact; this is the sensory adaptation effect. Second, we can satiate on a given type or class of changes. That is, we may need changes in the kinds of changes we are experiencing to maintain a high level of satisfaction.

Now, in this section we want to present an overall view of the importance of stimulus change and variety in our lives. We will discuss what is sometimes known as the *preferred level of change* model. It's a simple model, really. It merely suggests that we have some level of change, neither too high nor too low, which we prefer and which we pursue. If we are getting too little change, we will seek greater amounts of change. If we are getting too much change, we will seek some lower level of change. There is some intermediate level of change where we feel most comfortable.

People differ in terms of how much change they prefer. Some like a lot and some not so much. The preferred level may change with age, too. But in all cases, the individual seeks to maintain some preferred level of change and novelty, neither too much nor too little.

For instance, there are times in your life when the thought of escaping into the privacy of your own house or apartment seems delicious. These feelings often occur when you have been experiencing too much change and variety. Perhaps you have been seeing too many people at too many parties. Or your work situation has been crammed with unneeded, un-wanted, and unappreciated extra bodies. You dream of unplugging the phone and relaxing in solitude. At other times the thought of doing these same things, of staying alone in your apartment, is enough to give you the willies. You can't stand the thought of being alone. Usually, if you think about it for a moment, these feelings occur during periods when your life is characterized by a lack of change. Your life may be filled with people, but it's always the same old people. You may be very active at work or school, but the activity is the same old activity. When you have these feelings, you are somewhere below your preferred level of stimulus change. You need a little more change than you are getting.

According to this view of humanity, we are all constantly tinkering with our level of stimulation, trying to get it just right. If we are faced with too much change, we feel overwhelmed and we try to reduce the amount of incoming change and complexity. When not enough is "happening," we try to stir something up. It's a very simple concept of motivation, but it probably accounts for a good deal of human activity.

In the next chapter we will examine how the American way of life makes it very difficult for us to stay within our preferred levels of stimulus change. There are forces in everyday American life which constantly thrust us to one end or the other of the dimension of stimulus change; it seems we are always experiencing either too much or not enough change, variety, and complexity.

Then, in Chapter 9 we will look at some of our maladaptive responses to these forces. Finally, in Chapter 10 we will suggest means of attaining and maintaining preferred levels of change in spite of the cultural pressures against such a state of affairs.

For now, in the final section of this brief chapter, we will look at how curiosity and sensory-seeking behaviors may be naturally selected.

The Natural Selection of Curiosity

We have outlined how the human gains great satisfaction by being stimulated by external stimuli, particularly those which are changing. We are "turned on" by novel, complex, unexpected, and unusual stimuli. We have also seen that too much change can be unpleasant and will be avoided by the human. Why?

It is easy to understand why animals are motivated to eat or drink; their bodies need certain substances without which the organism, and eventually the species, would disappear. But why are animals attracted to and intrigued by stimulus change? There is no need for change in the sense that the animal will die without it. A rat will live even when confined, without external stimulation, in a dark box. So there is no real physiological need which could account for our being so curious and so intrigued by external change. It's not like hunger or thirst which, if left unsatisfied, would lead to death.

We might be able to find an answer if we consider what advantages an animal with curiosity might have, in terms of survival, over an animal without curiosity. Specifically, the more curiosity the animal has, up to a point, the more likely it is to survive. Take two baby monkeys. Assume one has a great deal of curiosity while the other has none. The one that is curious and likes to experience new stimuli will be much more likely to *learn* how to be an effective monkey from its parents and peers. A new monkey has a lot to learn if it is going to be successful. It has to learn how to find food, how to eat it, which monkeys to stay away from, how to get along in the monkey troop, what wild animals to tease and which ones to run from, where not to go, where to get water, and what to do at night. Most likely these behaviors are not instinctive; they must be learned.

The more curiosity the individual monkey has, the more quickly and efficient the animal will learn these crucial behaviors. Consider the monkey without curiosity. It is fed by its mother at first. Because it has no curiosity and isn't interested in exploring, it just hangs around the tree. It doesn't go running and charging about with the other baby monkeys because it just doesn't care, it isn't interested. So it never learns where or how to get food on its own. Then suppose the mother dies. Where does that leave our lackadaisical little friend? In deep trouble. Because curiosity has not stimulated it to learn the skills and acquire the information that are absolutely essential for it to function as an independent, adult monkey, this little one may die. It may starve to death before it learns how to feed itself. It may be too late to learn what all the other monkeys learned long ago. The monkey with a great deal of curiosity, on the other hand, has a much better chance of surviving the death of its mother and reproducing because curiosity "got it going" at an early age.

In other words, animals with curiosity are probably naturally selected in many cases. Depending upon its ecological niche, an animal with curiosity has a great advantage in terms of survival. We would argue that the human being's high level of curiosity has been naturally selected. We are the kind of animal that gains satisfaction by being exposed to novel external stimuli because that trait is adaptive and because it has been naturally selected. It pays to be curious.

Now let's look at the other end of the dimension. Given that we like some stimulation and change because it is adaptive to do so, why is there a limit to how much change we prefer? How come we don't want *unlimited* change and variety? What accounts for our hesitancy with respect to ever increasing amounts of variability and change? Quite simply, this trait is probably also adaptive and hence also naturally selected. The individuals with it survive and those without it are likely to perish. Consider our monkeys again. We have one that is so uninterested it never learns anything and so dies. We have another that is substantially curious and learns all about its world by itself and from its companions. It does very well. Now imagine a third young monkey that has an unlimited capacity to enjoy change. There is no limit to this animal's curiosity or to its ability to be drawn to novelty and change. It's tremendously interested in anything which is new and unusual. How will this monkey get along? Probably not too well. It will be the one eaten by the snake because it couldn't resist coming close to see what the snake felt like. It will be the one to fall to its death because it was intrigued by the sensation of swinging on those tiny branches. It will be the one that dies lost in the forest because it wanted, couldn't resist, exploring around just one more corner.

In other words, curiosity in *moderation* is probably the most adaptive level. Hence, humans possess a preferred level of change because such a preference is inherited. It is the result of a long process of natural selection. Humans, as well as animals, with intermediate degrees of curiosity, or pull motivation, are probably the most adaptive. It probably pays to be curious, but not too curious.

8

Homogeneity in a World of Chaos

Too Much and Too Little

In the last chapter we developed the hypothesis that a moderate level of curiosity has been naturally selected in humans because to be moderately curious is adaptive. This naturally selected human trait forms the basis of the preferred level of change theory which proposes that there is some intermediate level of external change, novelty, and complexity which makes us most happy. We seek to maintain external variety at a level that is neither too high nor too low. We experience satisfaction and pleasure when we are within our limits of change and variety.

In this chapter we want to develop the suggestion that there are opposing, contradictory forces in American culture which tend to push us too far out on the ends of the dimension of change, either in the direction of too much change or toward not enough change. Some aspects of the culture, which are outlined below, tend to overwhelm us with change and complexity, thereby robbing us of the satisfaction to be gained through moderate levels of variety and change. But at the same time, there are opposing, somehow incongruent forces, which shove us toward the other end of the dimension, toward boredom through homogeneity, sameness, and lack of change.

We are pushed toward the extremes at the same time, never being allowed to rest, happy and satisfied, within the preferred intermediate level of change and novelty. In some ways, as we shall see, we are inundated with frightening, difficult complexity; in other ways, we are simultaneously deluged with a tedious sameness that leaves us irritable and dissatisfied. We want to be in the middle, but everything seems to drag us into too much or too little change.

In Chapter 9 we will look at some of our maladaptive reactions to this peculiar, almost paradoxical situation wherein we seem to have too much and too little variety and complexity at the same time. In Chapter 10 we will see what might be done to remedy this situation, to restore balance, and to locate and maintain ourselves within our preferred level of external change.

Homogenized Life

Let's simplify the problem by dealing with the two halves separately. We begin with a consideration of those aspects of American life which are rapidly becoming homogenized and boring, realizing that in a later section we will turn to the paradoxical fact that other aspects of our culture overwhelm us with too much change and complexity.

"Adjective-animal" restaurants

There are many aspects of American life where a sameness, a blandness, and a lack of variety seem to be appearing. Some of these forms of sameness or uniformity are trivial, and some are more important than others, but they all lead to a sense of dissatisfaction because they rob us of the change and variety which is so appealing to us. Take, for example, the curious phenomenon of the adjective-animal restaurant. A quick glance through the yellow pages of the phone book in any of our major cities will reveal the following kinds of restaurant names:

Red Pig	Leaping Frog
Intrepid Stallion	Hungry Horse
Cultured Steer	Crazy Lion
Black Bull	Golden Butterfly
Blinking Owl	Grey Whale
Velvet Cat.	

Cute, but how many of these restaurants could you bear to go to, unless you were after some perverse world record? It's boring to hear about one more animal-with-nifty-modifier restaurant. When you learn you are going to the Flying Goose or the Articulate Snake or the Presupposing Aardvark, you experience a mild deflation. You know it's going to be just like every other adjective-animal restaurant you've been in. You find yourself wishing they would vary the theme even just a little—maybe throw in a vegetable once in a while (Bitchy Rhododendron or Salubrious Artichoke), but they don't. They have to get that animal in there so they can cash in on the current fad.

Of course, there are variations on the theme. For example, there are the O' restaurants. Bit O' England. Tail O' the Rooster. Taste O' Honey. And the N' restaurants. Scotch N' Steak. Steak N' Soda. Soda N' Food. And there are many modified inanimate objects. Broken Lance. Silver Castle. Admiral's Table. Golden Gate. Hot Bagel. Blue Tree. Iron Chimney. Osprey's Roost. But it seems that the adjective-animal combination is the bedrock form upon which these derivative variations rest.

Love those banks

Don't you think the names of banks are grand? They all involve the same words including First, Federal, Security, Central, Savings, American, State, National, International, United, Western, of (state), Eastern, and so on. It's really a very limited set of words from which the names of all banks are constructed. Make up a few of your own. Go ahead, pick out three words from the above list. United National Security Bank, First Central Bank of California, American International Bank, United Federal Western Bank of Hong Kong. They're all the same, really.

How come you never hear of Tom Miller's Great Bank? Or Bit O' Treasure Bank? Or the Big People's Piggy Bank of Chicago? It's all symptomatic of this leveling tendency abroad in America today. We're being presented a more and more smooth and even pap or mush. Our environment is becoming homogenized.

Fast and identical

Who is responsible for this boring sameness creeping into American life? Some of the culprits can be clearly identified, and we will do so in a moment. But for now let's look at some more prime examples of American homogeneity.

When you go into older towns and look around, you find a pleasing array of unique business establishments. Old family business names abound. Cafes and restaurants are unique and one of a kind.

But what happens when you go into a new town or a recently developed area, such as a suburb? In each one you find the same predictable, recognizable fast-food outlets selling hamburgers, pizza, tacos, fried chicken, steak, hot dogs, and ice cream.

It's almost eerie the way you can predict the presence of these fast-food outlets. Drive down the street of any new American suburb and you will see them all, every time. If you don't see one, you can probably bet it will be just around the corner. It's spooky. Where are all the little interesting individual businesses? Not there. Gone. We are left with a group of predictable, prefabricated foods. In our opinion, about the only difference between the major hamburger places lies in the condiments used. Nifty-Wifty-Burger uses mustard while Bide-A-While-Burger does not. Our selection of eating places is reduced to a consideration of whether or not pepper is involved. To us the food itself is all pretty much the same and extremely tedious.

So, in America you have the choice of paying a lot to eat at the Graceful Abalone or paying less to eat at a fast-food outlet where the food is probably indistinguishable from the food served at all other fast-food outlets, except for, perhaps, the fact that if it has bones in it you would eliminate pizza as a probable label for that food.

Ever been in a fast-food outlet while traveling and suddenly had the feeling that you are in another city because this outlet and the one in that city are identical in construction, color, and activity? For a moment you are disoriented, not knowing whether you are in Kansas City or Sioux Falls, and you think dispiritedly what difference does it make anyway if they both look so much alike.

Department stores aren't much better. The country is being eaten up by large chains, particularly discount stores. After you've been in a few of them, the sameness of them begins to dim your enthusiasm. When you walk into a new example of one of them, you know exactly where the shirts made in Hong Kong will be and exactly where the rows of color TVs all tuned to Chuck Barris will be. It's enough to kill anyone's interest. Browsing isn't worth it because it's like going over the same pasture for the fiftieth time. The only thing those stores are good for is killing time with young children who are still too naive to realize they are being allowed to wallow in a homogeneous blend which will begin to bore even them within a short period of time.

Polyester as the bane of society

The preeminence of polyester fiber in the garments of America may foreshadow a dramatic change for the worse in terms of what we wear. Presently one is still able to find cotton clothes, woolens, blends, and the like. Different kinds of stores still specialize in various sorts of materials. But if things keep going the way they are we will soon have stores or departments displaying signs like "Blue Clothes," "Green Clothes," and "Red Clothes," all of which will be 100 percent polyester. Variety and, therefore, satisfaction and pleasure will disappear. Clothes requiring anything but the primary colors will have to be special ordered.

To blunt the boredom resulting from the loss of alternative materials, garment makers may put fins on clothing one year and replace them with simulated pages from the works of Dickens the next, all in 100 percent pure, virgin polyester. Can you wait?

Clearly, this sort of analysis is tongue-in-cheek, but the point is clear.

Culprit #1: The profit motive

What, or who, is the cause of this homogenizing, leveling process in America? The profit motive seems to be behind much of it.

Think about profits in abstract terms for a moment. Let's say you make and sell X's. To make the largest profit you raise the price of your X's while reducing the cost of making X's. One of the easiest ways to reduce the cost of making X's is to make them all identical. Mass produce them and they will be cheaper to produce, so your profit will be higher. If you have to make every X different from every other X, your cost per X would be enormous. These are simple facts of the capitalistic, profit-oriented system.

So what seems to be happening in America is that we are drifting further and further toward sameness because sameness is cheaper to produce and yields a bigger profit. Our buildings and homes are becoming plainer and less decorative because it's too expensive to introduce variety. Manufacturers and producers of the goods of America are, with or without being aware of it, moving toward "uniproducts," or identical, multiple instances of the same product. It's not a new process, it's been going on for a long time. But recently the process seems to be accelerating more and more. We're moving faster and faster toward uniformity in all that is available to us. Why? Because technology is moving forward at an accelerated pace. (By technology we are referring here to nothing more than the know-how to manipulate the forces of nature in accordance with our desires.) As our technological prowess accelerates, our ability to produce millions and billions of identical units of anything accelerates right along with it. The idea of lowering costs by producing multiple identical units is not a new one—but the technological knowledge required to put that old idea into action is new. And it's getting more extreme all the time.

Take the lowly bratwurst. Only a few years ago one particular brand of bratwurst was sold as unique sausages stuffed into unique casings. Each one was a little bit different from the next one. They all weighed different amounts and were often variable in shape. Then, all of a sudden, they all became uniform. All exactly the same size and shape. Every package now costs exactly what every other package costs. Someone, somewhere, finally figured out that the bratwursts could be made and marketed more cheaply if they were all identical. Somehow, they just don't taste as good to us as they used to.

You can pick just about any product in America and detect this profit-related trend. The way things are going it seems everyone in business is aiming toward uniproducts. It's easy to imagine a tongue-in-cheek science fiction conception of a business street in twenty-first century America. As you look down the street you see one sign which says "Food." Another sign says "Cars," and another "Clothes." When you walk into the food store, which is duplicated exactly in every other area of the country, you see coolers labeled "Bacon" and shelves containing "Peaches." Every can of pears is like every other can of pears, and they are all produced by The American Food Company.

There might be, in order to avoid our nation's abhorrence of monopolies, three food companies—the above AFC as well as The National Food Company (NFC) and the Federal Food Company (FFC). Obviously, this is an intentionally exaggerated characterization of the future. But it would not surprise us if the future did see fewer and fewer, but bigger and bigger, companies producing less and less variety and more and more homogeneity in product. For, you see, it is also the capitalistic way for companies to consume one another. Whoever gets there first with the cheapest, most uniform product will make the most money and be able to buy out poor companies that are still producing too much expensive variety.

Our antitrust laws probably will be fairly ineffective. Even now many major sectors of business are dominated by a few companies (e.g., broadcasting, oil, automobiles). It seems a natural growth pattern for a capitalistic society to produce a few massive organizations which dominate and which put out as little variety as possible in order to increase profits.

These monoliths need not stay within a given product area. Clearly, if a huge oil company wants to move into food or housing or any other area, it can simply buy whatever it wants, thereby further reducing competition in the business world.

The illusion of variety

The producers of uniproducts are not unaware of the fact that we, the general public, like variety and get bored and restless with sameness. At the same time, they don't want to go to the expense of producing varieties. So what's their answer to the problem? Window dressing. Tinsel. Make it *look* different without it really being different. American products are filled with, and covered by, differences which are, in the last analysis, superficial.

Take, for instance, the wonderful world of automobiles. It seems as though the array of available cars is enormous. On the surface it is quite impressive. But most of the differences are superficial and gimmicky. Once you've scraped off the racing stripes, removed the all-weather molding, and taken out the deep reclining bucket seats, what you have left is an internal combustion engine mounted on four wheels. An expensive car is an engine mounted on wheels. So is a cheap car. In our opinion the similarities between the two far outweigh the differences. Cheap cars have mufflers, shocks, spark plugs, and trunks, just like expensive cars.

But, through the magic of packaging, we are led to believe that there are much more substantial differences between the two than there really are. Window dressing, labels, and gimmicks are cheap compared to fundamental differences, so business people go in for packaging in a big way. It's so ingrained in our way of thinking that it almost seems sacrilegious to suggest that a luxury car is pretty much the same thing as an economy car. But when you strip away the veneer you find that they are not that different. As someone once said, cars are either big or little and either expensive or more expensive.

Car manufacturers have been known to use the same engine in different makes of car. Tell you anything?

It can be argued that as technology advances it becomes cheaper and cheaper to produce more variety. This may be true, but we would argue that the kind of variety which is produced is really superficial and not very fundamental at all. For example, years ago cigarette companies produced one or two brands of cigarettes. But now there are dozens of varieties. Long ones, short ones, very long ones, thick and thin ones, men's and women's, white and tinted, and so on. But, really, aren't they all just tobacco wrapped up in paper? When all is said and done, even though business may have the capacity to produce true diversity, the kind of variety we get is the window dressing kind because a little decoration and an assortment of packages are cheaper to produce than significant product differences.

Culprit #2: Follow the leader

This tendency toward homogenization in American life is probably multiply determined. As we have seen, the desire to cut costs by producing less variety can account for some of it. But probably not all of it. The impulse to copy a winner, stick with a winner, or follow the leader also appears to be strongly involved in the production of American homogeneity. Ever notice how so many cars have begun to look like the Mercedes Benz lately? The Mercedes became a popular status symbol so, consciously or unconsciously, other car designers apparently began to think along the same lines.

Textbooks in psychology often tend to be similar, covering pretty much the same topics in roughly the same order. Stick with a winning formula.

Think about TV programming. Aren't we constantly amazed at the "runs" of certain kinds of shows which will appear over a series of seasons? For a while it will be police shows, then doctor shows, then westerns. All of this seems to represent one way in which we get less variety because the people who develop the shows want to guarantee themselves some success. They probably think that if it was a winner once it can be a winner again. Our choices on TV are limited because most shows belong to one of a number of limited categories. They follow some proven formula.

Movies seem to run in variety-reducing cycles, too. We'll have a whole series of horror or occult movies. Or we'll have a series about two carefree, adorable guys knocking about. Or we'll have a series of science fiction movies.

The *first* of any of these series can be quite unusual and entertaining. But once one of them has been produced and has made a fortune, there is the inevitable sequence of imitations, all of which resemble slightly warmed-over fare. We have to live through the imitations of old successes waiting for that relatively rare unique movie.

You can't blame the producers, can you? After all, it's difficult and very risky to try something new. And an imitation of an old success can make money. Still, this tendency to follow the leader does reduce the variety and novelty in our lives.

Earlier, we mentioned how restaurants and banks tend to have similar names. Again this may be the result of following the leader. When you are about to open a new restaurant and want to choose a name that will assure success, you might well think that an adjective-animal name might be suitable because so many of them seem to be successful. Naming car models often seems to be an exercise in imitating what other manufacturers call their car. Fast, zippy, "up" animals such as colts, pintos, mavericks, and firebirds seem to be popular. So do slightly dangerous and powerful organisms such as cougars and chargers. No one names their cars after dumb or unexciting animals. "See the new Dog." "Don't miss the 1982 Hereford." "Be the first to own a Sheep." And then there is the tendency to develop a line of names around a company name such as Chevette, Chevelle, Camaro, and Corvette. All of these seem to be instances where proven winners from the past are emulated.

Culprit #3: The need for security

But the causes of homogeneity in American life are not all traceable directly to the capitalistic system. Some causes can be traced back to our own very basic desire for security, safety, and predictability. As we shall see, we get all tangled up and confused by our need for security. Obtaining security and predictability often involves losing variety and novelty which we also appreciate. Many times it seems we can have one or the other, security or novelty, but not both. Many times business merely produces the goods and services which our need for security demands. Business merely accommodates or fulfills our needs and, in the process, inadvertently further reduces variety in American life.

Take, for example, the matter of motels. When a young family of five pulls into town, tired and hungry, what do they look for? Some secure, clean, neat, predictable place. They don't want surprises. If they see a motel whose name they recognize and whose reputation they know emphasizes cleanliness, they will go there. They won't go to the slightly seedy looking, cheaper motel next door because they are afraid of germs, dirty blankets, and the unknown. At that point in the day, all they want is predictability, security, and cleanliness. Once they have checked into the motel, their choice of a place to eat will be dictated by this same need for certainty and security. They know that if they go to a national chain restaurant the kids will at least eat the hamburgers, the forks will be clean, and the prices will be known in advance.

It won't be very exciting or interesting, but at least it will be predictable and acceptable. The little cafe down the street might have truly good food, but who knows, and our young, tired family is not about to take any chances.

It is this very desire for certainty and predictability which leads to at least some of the boring homogeneity of American life. Business people, noting the public's desire for cleanliness and security, naturally respond. They build more and more chains of franchised business establishments. The name of the franchise can be very comforting to the public. At the same time, the unfortunate side effect of an increase in identical franchised establishments is a reduction in the number of unique, novel business establishments.

So, in a sense, we have ourselves to blame for some of the evolving American homogeneity. We want, and do like, predictability. So business naturally accommodates this desire. The result is a mixed blessing. We get the security we like, but we lose the excitement associated with uncertainty and change. We end up secure but slightly bored.

We certainly want our food homogeneous in this country. We feel slightly alarmed when we find a spot on our tomato or when our meat is even slightly discolored, even though these conditions are usually harmless. Because of our interest in clean, perfect food we end up with food which is overprocessed, oversprayed, and incredibly uniform. The food in one supermarket looks and tastes pretty much like the food in every other supermarket. There really aren't many differences among the major food stores.

Desire for safety and security leads to homogeneity and precludes real novelty. We give up a lot to have our processed, pasteurized, always-the-same cheese spreads.

Culprit #4: Snobbery

In a curious way, snobbery, or the attempt to demonstrate superiority by imitating and acting like those thought to be superior, may also lead to American homogeneity. Snobbery often revolves around a very limited set of possessions and behaviors. For example, in southern California the list of current status symbols seems to be about exhausted by:

big house	swimming pool
luxury car	tennis court.

It's just amazing how one can drive through the expensive parts of that section of the country and be overwhelmed by the preponderance of these few symbols or expressions of wealth and superiority.

It's almost as though people don't have any original ideas about what to do with their money, so they look around to see what everyone else is doing. Seeing that the house-car-pool-court constellation is very popular, they too go out and buy those same things. In spite of a lack of money, there is often more variety in lifestyle in the poorer sections of town than in the richer sections.

Homogeneity is fostered by the existence of groupings like the house-car-pool-court constellation. It's what many people dream of. If they do make money, they go right out and buy into that picture. They give up their 1959 Nash and buy another Mercedes. One more bit of character and uniqueness disappears from the American scene.

This is not to argue that people spend their money only on these few symbols. But at the same time, there does seem to be a tendency for people to try to keep up with their "superiors." And one way to do that is to buy what they buy and do what they do. The result is a leveling process. Rather than doing something unique and individual, people do what other people are doing. Instead of ending up with something novel and interesting, people end up with exactly the same things everyone else has. They are robbed of the satisfaction to be gained from truly unique experiences. The impulse to copy those whom we consider somehow superior to ourselves is an impulse which often comes into conflict with our desire for unique experiences.

Culprit #5: Sexism

Sexism takes many forms, but the most virulent type is that which holds that women are inherently inferior to men. Men are seen as strong, active, and dominant while women are seen as weak, passive, and unassuming.

Sexism robs *both* men and women of an enormous range of stimulation, because it demands that each of us only do one half of the things there are to do. Women do "women's things," and men do "men's things." Men make money, go to the office, fight, and play ball. Women sew, cry, take care of children, and stay home.

Sexism may have its roots in our ancestral times when it was adaptive to divide labor along sexual lines. But that is no longer the case. There is no longer a need to have strong, aggressive male figures engage in one set of activities while meek, submissive females do other things.

Men should be allowed to do what women do, and women should be allowed to do what men do. There is no need to limit anyone's activities, male or female. If a male wants to take care of children, or cry, or wear makeup, he should not be prevented from doing so by a social attitude which maintains that men don't do those sorts of things. If a woman wants to be a boxer, or smoke cigars, or wear a tie, she should be free to do so.

Sexism limits the lives of both men and women. It introduces homogeneity into the lives of both sexes by saying, "You are a man. Here is what you do," or, "You are a woman. All women do such and such."

Although things are getting better, progress is slow, and many of us are still frustrated because we are pressured into unnecessarily limiting our activities along sexual lines. Sexism, although perhaps here to stay and perhaps springing legitimately from a past born of necessity, has to be understood as one of the major limiting factors in American life. Not just for the female either. Do all men really want to be limited to the role of provider and protector? Wouldn't they enjoy, at least some of the time, staying home and taking care of the house instead of going out to work? Wouldn't they like to at least try the other role? Many women, of course, are being stifled by sexism. Although some enjoy and love the home life, which is complex and rewarding, many other women want to try something new but can't because of prevailing sexist attitudes.

To deny women equal rights, which is the case at the time of this writing, is medieval. It suggests that women are to be thought of as inferior or at least to be treated as inferiors. The failure to pass the Equal Rights Amendment is a bizarre tribute to the overblown American male ego. It is also sad, for it helps maintain sexist attitudes, and sexism shortchanges everyone, female and male alike.

Sexism is one more factor that limits novelty and change. It frustrates many people because it demands that they refrain from growing and exploring.

Canned towns

We have just reviewed some of the factors in American culture which contribute to the homogeneous quality of our lives. These have included the profit motive, the tendency to imitate a winner, the need for security, snobbery, and sexism. All of these, in one way or another, lead to a sameness in life which flies in the face of our inherited tendency to prefer change and variety.

The canned town is a recent phenomenon which seems to represent the culmination of all these forces. If you haven't run into a canned town yet, let me describe them for you. These towns (sometimes they are suburbs or additions to existing towns) are new developments. They seem to spring up quickly, sometimes between your vacation tours through the same area. One year there is nothing but farms and fields. Two years later there is the canned town. Canned towns are uniform, homogeneous expressions of every leveling tendency in America. Most of the business establishments are franchised. The motels and department stores belong to recognizable chains. All is new. There is no link to a variety-filled past. All buildings are plain and modern, with a tendency to emphasize earth colors, glass, and steel. The people are clean, well-dressed plastic figures placed along the streets, in the shiny cars, and in the condominiums. There is an unreal quality to the town, for it has no distant past and is composed of units (people, places, businesses) that you have seen before many times. There is nothing to distinguish this canned town from other canned towns springing up around the country. They are all the same—bland, clean, predictable, and above all, composed of newly developed units that you are already familiar with and on the verge of being bored by.

They are planned and placed with great order and forethought. They possess none of the random, chaotic development which characterized many of our older towns and eventually contributed to their uniqueness and charm. Canned towns have no charm beyond the charm of a waxed paper dispenser. They are without character. They are prefabricated and identical to one another, each possessing the expected units of business and housing. They possess no internal variety. You'll recognize one when you see it.

People like canned towns because they are safe, sure, and secure. At the same time, they frustrate our basic love of change, turmoil, confusion, and excitement.

Increasing Uncertainty

In the preceding sections we argued that a number of different elements in American life tend to homogenize the external stimulation that we experience. In many ways, American life is boring because it lacks variety.

In this section we wish to return to a point we made earlier. Specifically, at the same time that some elements of the culture lead to sameness and boredom, other forces simultaneously bombard us with increasingly complex and unsettling stimulation. Thus we are pushed in opposite directions at the same time. Some facets of the culture are increasingly boring, while other aspects of American life are increasingly complex and frightening.

In terms of the preferred level of change theory presented earlier, we are getting too much change in some ways and not enough change in others. We are not allowed to maintain our preferred level of moderate change.

Let's look at some of the things in American life which are overloading us with change.

When you pick up your newspaper in the morning, you have the problems of the whole world right there in your lap even before you've finished your coffee. Dangerous world developments occur rapidly and you know about them perhaps a little more quickly than you would like to. You are bombarded, not only with local, but also with state, federal, and international developments, by TV, radio, and printed matter. It's nice to know what's going on, of course, but at the same time you can find yourself driving to work worrying about a crisis in a country that is twelve thousand miles away. You're trying to comprehend, to get your mind around, too many complex changes that are beyond your control. You worry about the economy and your investments. You are bombarded with news of changes that may or may not affect you directly. This kind of modern communication is a little more than you really need or want. It may push you out of your preferred level of change.

It's difficult not to get involved in world events and to weigh and deliberate possible actions and counteractions. But events move so swiftly now. The rapid pace of change can lead to a sense that we lack control over our lives. Who knows when some crazy nut is going to drop a bomb on us? By knowing so quickly and so completely about world events, we are subjected to more stress and change than our preferred level dictates.

In times gone by the pace was more leisurely. News took time to travel, and events developed more slowly. People weren't faced with frantic, hectic events in faraway places that had the potential to directly affect their lives in a rapid manner.

It's not just the communication of great amounts of rapid change which is unsettling. It's the content of those changes as well. While science and the advancement of knowledge have reaped enormous benefits for humanity, they have also had their negative side effects. Very, very effective weapons, for example. The arsenals of the world change so quickly, and we know about the changes so soon, that we are bound to feel uneasy and wonder if anybody is keeping an eye on all of this. Too much change, too fast.

Science and technology have had some other nasty little side effects, too. Take, for example, pollution and the problems of harmful chemicals infiltrating every aspect of our lives. The list of potential dangers grows by leaps and bounds. Every day it seems a new cancer-causing substance has been detected. Even though the American life expectancy is increasing, which suggests that things are not all bad, we worry about all of these chemical substances which are so far beyond our understanding and our control. We can't keep up with all of them. When we talk about the dangers from cancer-causing substances, we are dealing in very small percentages. It's not like the plague where half the population dies in a year. But these newly discovered dangers are nonetheless frightening to people.

Because technology and knowledge are advancing at such a rapid rate, we often find ourselves feeling helpless and hopeless in the face of all the change. For example, just when we finally learn how to change the points and condenser in our car, the automakers switch to electronic ignitions which don't have those parts. If our watch breaks, we are at the mercy of a specialist. If our TV stops functioning, we have to take the repairperson's word for what is wrong. We can't keep up with all the new developments, and we feel uneasy about it. If you look under the hood of a new car, you will be shocked by the tangled mass of parts, none of which you can remember seeing in your 1959 Ford. The inner workings of computers are unknown to most people. The average individual has to accept that the machine does what it is supposed to do. What we eat is almost unknown, beyond the ever changing, ever expanding list of additives. What we drink is always changing, as pollutants seep into the nation's waters. What we breath in our cities is different every day, first this pollutant and then that. If you live in the city, you breath polluted air. If you live in the country, you live with thousands of changing chemicals sold as insecticides, herbicides, and fungicides.

We can't sort out what is important and what is trivial because there is too much change occurring and we're told about it all too quickly. We're inundated.

The expansion and change in our government contributes to our sense of being overwhelmed; too many fluctuating rules and regulations leave us slightly dazed and dazzled. We can't keep up with all the red tape and forms and governmental agencies. It seems the IRS forms change from complex to more complex. Hamburgers, and what they do and do not contain, are actually controlled by tens of thousands of separate regulations. Our minds are boggled by a whirl of new, unevaluated, sometimes scary information. We often want the rate of change to slow. We want to get back to the good old days. What we really want to do is to move into, and maintain ourselves in, our preferred level of change. The swift pace of modern American life often prevents us from experiencing the moderate level of change we desire.

9

The Cult of Extremes

Seeking Radical Change

We pointed out in the last chapter how American society overstimulates us in some ways and understimulates us in others. In this chapter we want to outline some of our common, and not particularly helpful, reactions to these dissatisfactions. Then in the next chapter we will present some more adaptive ways to handle these modern frustrations.

The discussion begins with a consideration of the effects of understimulation to be followed by a look at maladaptive effects of overstimulation.

Entertain me please!

American homogeneity leads to boredom. We've seen it all. We're jaded and dissipated. We're not excited by what there is because it's growing more and more homogeneous all the time. We crave new, exciting change. We demand extremes because extremes represent relief from the sameness that is creeping into our culture.

Take movies, for instance. Think about filmed car crashes. Just a few years ago one smashup would satisfy us. But not now. Now, before we can be excited, we have to see sixty-four cars join the junk brigade in flaming disarray. We like it even better when the cars are expensive cars. The more they cost, the more delicious the crash. We need, want, and seek greater and greater amounts of Hollywood destruction to offset our boredom because our lives are filled with so much routine and lack of change. It's almost addictive. Once we've seen fifteen cars bashed up, the next time we have to see thirty-five wrecked to gain the same sense of excitement.

Then cars being smashed up so often in so many movies begins to take on a homogeneous quality. It's all the same, in some sense. In our desperation to regain the excitement and fun we experienced the first few times we saw cars crash, we demand more and more extreme examples of car crashing. The movie industry responds, of course, and we get on the endless merry-go-round of trying to shake off the growing boredom with car crashes by increasing the number and flamboyance of these celluloid collisions.

Violence, blood, and gore in films also seem to be increasing dramatically. Whereas a stylized death, without blood, used to satisfy us, now we flock to movies which are quite explicit in their expressions of anatomical juiciness. It's as though we want more and more extreme examples of gruesome deaths and dismemberments in order to get a little excitement out of life, to stave off the boredom of ordinary, unchanging daily life.

Horror films and films of the occult are currently very popular. Each seems to try to outdo the last in terms of terror, fear, gore, spookiness, and general mayhem. These movies may represent an expression of the general population's need for extreme change, born of an ever increasing sense of tedium and sameness in American life. These darkened theaters are a place to experience intense emotion, to tingle a little, and to escape from the bland landscape of modern America. In a sense, these films represent the modern substitute for gladiators battling wild animals, or each other, in the stadiums of Rome. In a culture which has become rich, homogeneous, predictable, and slightly tedious, these excursions into the unreal and into the world of violence represent our attempts to increase the amount of change we are experiencing. We're trying to get back into our preferred level of change.

The problem, of course, is compounded by the phenomenon of satiation we discussed earlier. If you will recall, satiation refers to the fact that we grow tired of certain kinds of changes and need bigger or newer changes to regain our sense of pleasure. We can't watch the same level of car smashing, or body rending endlessly without becoming satiated. Hence we are constantly driven to seek more and more extreme examples of death, destruction, and violence to maintain the same level of excitement.

The moviemakers are doing their best, but it must get tougher all the time. Can you imagine sitting around trying to invent new forms or new expressions of violence which will excite a jaded audience?

Compulsive gambling

There are many examples of how our search for satisfaction takes us to extremes. The process is not limited to films. Take, for instance, compulsive gambling. Apparently the country is being swept by an epidemic of compulsive gambling. We're not talking about the occasional trip to the racetrack or the occasional visit to Las Vegas. We're talking about people who have to gamble every day. If they don't, they actually experience withdrawal symptoms. All they can think about is gambling. They will steal to gamble. They almost inevitably end up deeply in debt. Their lives are often in disarray because of their need to gamble. They prefer situations where it seems as though clever gamblers may beat the odds. Hence, they like to gamble on sporting events, football, baseball, and the like, because here they can study the players and past performances and "predict" the winner. They are less likely to enjoy playing a slot machine where the odds cannot be beaten; it's just a matter of pulling the lever.

We would argue that compulsive gambling can, at least sometimes, be an attempt to escape from an otherwise confining, unexciting, predictable life. Up at seven, drive to work, sit at a desk all day, drive home, watch TV, sleep. Nothing there that is nearly as exciting as laying down $200.00 on a Knicks game and then having to wait for the outcome.

In some sense, gambling can be the last remaining form of excitement for some people. Some compulsive gamblers say they like it better than sex. All they think about is that next bet. Gambling is so exciting because it is so unpredictable. In a sense, it is the epitome of change, variety, and complexity. You can't get much more excitement from change and variety than you can in a gambling situation. And the excitement seems to last. You're not satiated, because the outcome remains so unpredictable. If there is nothing else to do in life, if life is boring and tedious, you can always gamble.

The workaholic

The workaholic syndrome may sometimes represent another example of people seeking extremes in order to avoid boredom. Workaholics are often people who work so much that they may be harming themselves. They may put themselves under so much stress that their health may be in danger. But they keep it up anyway, because working at least provides some sort of change, variety, and challenge.

Suppose a workaholic is finally convinced to take a weekend vacation with his wife. They go to the shore for two days. They rent a cottage. What does the workaholic experience? To the outsider he seems tense and unable to relax. He keeps wanting to make business calls. He is restless and irritable. What is all this about? In some cases it may be that the individual is bored to tears by the cute little cottage, the predictable meals, his wife, and that damn silly ocean. There is not enough change here for the workaholic. It's too predictable and too homogeneous. He is, in this holiday setting, well below his preferred level of activity and change. He has no skills for inventing new forms of change in new situations, so he falls back on what he knows best—the change and tension involved in his work. Without assistance, he is apt to continue to find satisfaction in work, without ever becoming aware that satisfaction through other forms of change is possible.

Fill 'er up

Many of us turn to excessive consumption in our efforts to avoid sameness and to get a little something extra from life.

Exactly what is consumed can vary widely. Some people eat because there is nothing else to do, because they are bored, or because it makes them feel better. Some people drink. Excessive alcoholic consumption is obviously widespread. People probably drink for many different reasons, but some drink to fill a void. To not drink is to sit and be bored, edgy, restless, unsatisfied, and filled with a vague sense of the unending, unchanging uselessness of life. To drink is to gain relief, to become partially blotto, to escape the tedium of life, and to experience a partial lift or a sense of enjoying and partaking of the interesting quality of life. Drinking is a remedy for life's homogeneity. It blocks some of it out and, at the same time, provides a sense of well-being.

Drugs can fill the same sort of void. If life seems dull and uninteresting, there is always that grand array of chemical substances which can be sniffed, snorted, smoked, injected, and swallowed. Different drugs have different effects, but they all possess one crucial characteristic: they produce change. They can alter mood and/or thought. They can affect perception. They alter the individual's state of awareness. Some people prefer to elevate or depress their mood or emotional state, while others prefer to concentrate upon altering their thought processes. Some like to mix it up. But in all cases the crucial, common element is change from the nondrugged state to the drugged state.

In many cases the use of drugs is directly related to the individual's dissatisfaction with the nondrugged state. Many times the nondrugged state is seen as boring and "a drag." It's not interesting enough or variable enough. Drugs provide the experience of change and variety which is so precious to the human and which is lacking in many aspects of American life.

Obviously, the problem with drugs is that they can be dangerous. Drugs bought on the street can be impure and laced with alternative chemicals. Dosage can vary enormously. At this stage in American life it almost goes without saying that even clean, pure drugs can be dangerous. Our purpose here is not to lecture on the well-known problems of drug taking. Rather we wish to point out that drug usage is sometimes related to frustration with the homogeneity and sameness of American life. Because of the dangers involved in drug taking it would seem advantageous if we could outline some alternative means of avoiding boredom and attaining preferred levels of change.

"Kinky" sex

As we finally emerge from the restrictions of late Victorian morality, it is not surprising that many and varied sexual practices are becoming popular. This is not to say that the same kinds of actions did not occur during earlier periods of our history. They did, of course, but the difference is that we are now much more open about them. Sexual practices and topics seem much more explicit in our society now.

Whether this change is good or bad remains moot. It is our guess that it probably doesn't make much difference one way or the other. The proportion of sexually happy and unhappy people was probably about the same under the older, more rigid codes as it is under the newer, more relaxed mores.

But what does interest us here is that, in some cases, new and relatively unusual sexual practices occur as a means of fighting off the generally tedious, overly secure quality of American life which we have been discussing. If a person feels trapped by her job and her social life, seeing the rest of her life stretching before her as unchanging as the inside of a long lead pipe, then group sex might offer some relief from this depressing, boring outlook on life.

The current trend toward openness about sexual activities, which were previously limited to covert practices, suggests that the very act of going public makes the events themselves more delicious and tantalizing. Breaking a taboo in public is more exciting than breaking it privately. Swinger's clubs, pay-as-you-enter orgies, homosexual activities, and all-around promiscuity can be more exciting for the participants if others know about it. In a recent TV interview a swinging couple implied that sex with strangers was particularly exciting because it occurred in a social situation where others knew and watched what they were doing. To do the same things in total privacy does not represent the same degree of change and variety that public sex does. Hence, in some cases, group sex satisfies the underfed need for change and novelty which we have been discussing.

Clearly, people should not be hampered in their efforts to enjoy as much sex as they prefer and whatever varieties they choose (as long as no harm is done, such as might occur in a violent sexual crime). But when sex takes on a desperate quality, when the participants seem to be seeking, striving to find some meaning in life, without necessarily succeeding, then it seems there might be some better solutions to the lack of novelty so inherent in our culture. Sex is wonderful; do as much of it as often as you wish. But don't let others tell you what you should do (only you know what you really need), and don't use sex as the only means of trying to break boredom. It can help spice up your life, of course, but there are other things that can be done, too. It's not the only or the final answer to relieving the homogeneous quality of life.

The money game

Closely related to the workaholic syndrome discussed earlier is the tendency for people to try to use the earning or gaining of money as a means to maintain excitement and a sense of constant change. A workaholic can be interested in money, but not necessarily; she or he may be primarily concerned with the work itself and only secondarily with money. For example, a college professor may work long, compulsive, health-threatening hours on research or scholarly writing activities which will not bring any financial gain. People who are caught up in the money game as the only game in town may not necessarily be workaholics. They feel that earning money is the only thing which is interesting any more. Everything else is boring. Accumulating more and more money is the only thing which can satisfy their need for change. These individuals constantly seek new means of earning money. They seek new angles, new schemes, and new forms of investment. They don't necessarily enjoy working for money, but they will do it. In fact, they would prefer not to work, as long as the money keeps rolling in.

Counting funds and watching them grow, feeling depressed when they do not grow, represents, in many cases, a kind of less-than-perfect solution to the problem of needing excitement and change. The trouble with this solution is that it virtually ignores all the other wonderful possibilities of life. In a nutshell, it is too limiting. There must be more to life than little numbers written in bankbooks.

Shop, dress, and paint

Suppose Mrs. R's husband makes $100,000 a year. Mrs. R's basic needs are completely satisfied. She doesn't have to work. She has a big house, a live-in maid, and all the money she needs. It gets pretty boring sitting around that house all day waiting for her husband to come home at seven thirty. What can she do with herself? She can shop. Buy clothes. Keep up with the latest fashions. Spend money. She can seek change and variety in clothing and makeup. She can spend hours each day walking through stores. She can get her hair and nails done.

Sounds pretty luxurious, doesn't it? But for many women it can be a kind of prison. They, as bright, capable people, want to *do* something with a little more substance. But they are trapped by the sexist roles wherein the man provides and the woman spends. Mrs. R can't even take pride in keeping house because the maid does that. So she shops, sometimes in near desperation, sometimes without even knowing that her considerable talents are going to waste.

A degree of novelty is introduced into her life by the fact that styles are made to change rapidly. These style changes make the capitalistic garment industry happy, and they keep the women shoppers moving; money is made and variety is maintained.

While many women can find satisfaction in this realm, many cannot. They feel shopping is boring, tedious, silly, and above all, an expression of prevailing sexist attitudes. One woman we know points out that current women's fashions tend to reinforce the impression that women are helpless and dependent. The shoes which are in style are high heeled and unstable. When a woman wears them she automatically looks weak, helpless, and on the verge of falling over. How cute and fluffy her little dress. How adorable and helpless.

This same woman points out that makeup is bizarre. She asks us to imagine another animal within the animal kingdom doing the same sort of thing. Imagine a sea gull with eyeliner and lipstick. Imagine a fox with its nails painted and the fur on its head feathered back and streaked. Imagine a cow with earrings.

She feels, and we agree, that makeup reinforces the idea of the inferiority of women because it says, in effect, that women are not beautiful *unless* they wear makeup. The woman is drab and unattractive without it. But not so with the superior male. He may dash on a little scent, but essentially he is considered attractive, by both males and females, without decoration. The poor little inferior female, on the other hand, must paint and dress herself before she becomes alluring. The essential, naked, unpainted beauty of the female is denied by this social belief that makeup is necessary.

Women are, when all is said and done, most attractive when they are free of grease, powder, artificial color, and chemicals. But sexist attitudes demand that they paint, camouflage, and hide their natural beauty. In addition, it is becoming clear that many makeup substances are potentially dangerous.

Consider, for example, the fingernail. Many animals still use this structure for clawing, climbing, gripping, and tearing. But in the human, it is a vestigial growth, pretty much relegated to such functions as scratching your partner's back while lying in a water bed watching TV or lifting unused stamps from return envelopes mailed to you by nonprofit but internally well-paid charitable organizations.

You would think that relatively little attention would be paid to this digital outgrowth. But, no, the women of America are led to believe that they are somehow klutzy if their fingernails are not subjected to an enormous array of peculiar chemical treatments. Advertisements crow about the wonders of all the different chemical compounds which should be used to remedy an equally long list of fingernail problems. The bright, sexy, "hot" female is, we are told, the one who will recognize all of these horrible nail conditions and will rush to use the designated chemical remedy. Various compounds are designed to harden, soften, clean, mend, condition, smooth, and mysteriously improve the fingernail. The implication is that the female who does not use these chemical compounds is somehow inferior.

If there are this many chemicals to be used on the lowly fingernail, can you imagine the total number of chemicals recommended for use around and about the entire body? Must be thousands of them. The successful woman is one who walks around enveloped in a cloud of vapors, daubed, creamed, sprayed, and powdered. Sure.

In summary, shopping, dressing, and wearing makeup all represent examples of how women in our sexist society attempt to maintain change and variety in their lives. This is not to say that men never do the same thing. They do, but not to the extent that women do.

ESP and the occult

Extrasensory perception (ESP) refers to mental or physical events which are not controlled by known physical principles and which do not involve the activity of the known sensory systems. There are four types of ESP or psychic phenomena. First, there is telepathy which refers to thought transference or "mind reading." An example of telepathy would be a case in which an individual in one room can perceive and report what another person in another room is thinking. Clairvoyance refers to the perception of objects or events not influencing the normal senses. For example, if we place a card containing a number in a sealed opaque envelope and give it to an individual who is able to tell us what the number is, then we say clairvoyance has occurred. Precognition refers to the ability to foresee the future. One who professes to have precognition will claim to be able to predict future events such as election outcomes and natural disasters. Psychokinesis is the "mind over matter" phenomenon. It refers to the claims of some people that they are able to affect material bodies through their mental operations. They claim to be able to bend keys, move dishes, or make objects rise in the air.

For all their wild and wonderful qualities, ESP phenomena have *not* been scientifically established. If you believe in psychic phenomena, it is really nothing more than that—a belief based upon incomplete evidence. Psychology contains an entire literature which suggests that not one single instance of any type of ESP phenomenon has been conclusively demonstrated.

And yet a popular belief in ESP persists; in fact, it may even be growing. Why? We would argue that in a world such as ours, which is becoming bland and homogeneous in so many ways, the allure of weird, unusual ESP effects is especially appealing. Life would, after all, be a lot more interesting if ESP did occur. But, alas, unless you can believe or accept on faith that ESP exists, you must take the position that scientists have been unable to establish its validity. Of course, science hasn't disproved it either, so there is always hope.

A belief in ESP represents just one more instance of people yearning for change and novelty. The same thing can be said for belief in the occult. Belief in magic, alchemy, astrology, and the supernatural represents a further example of people's interest in finding and enjoying new and unique stimulation. In an otherwise drab world it's exciting to think that your next-door neighbor might be a witch who speaks to the devil through her Dalmatian. Let's face it, it's better than TV.

Summary

There are many other examples of the seeking of extremes in American culture which we cannot cover here. If you think about it for a moment, you will probably be able to come up with a few. The general point behind all of these examples is that Americans are constantly trying to increase their overall level of change in a homogenized world by turning to extreme forms of external stimulation. Countercultures, disaster news, disco dancing, and pornographic literature are some of the paths that people choose to increase the level of external change in their attempts to avoid being drowned in blandness and security. There is nothing at all wrong with many of these activities and events. Many happy, satisfied people enjoy them. But when they signal an underlying dissatisfaction with life because life has become boring, then some adjustments need to be made.

Reacting to Chaos

The hell with it all

We have seen that, in some ways, American life is too bland and predictable. In the last few sections we outlined some of our reactions to this pervasive blandness. But remember also that, at the same time, American life contains frightening, unsettled kinds of changes. In some respects it is too unpredictable and contains too much rapid, incomprehensible change. We are faced with too many changes of one kind while we lack enough change of another sort. In this section we outline some typical reactions to those aspects of our culture which contain or present too much change, such as overwhelming, frightening new scientific information and deluges of incomprehensible, instantaneous, uncontrollable world news.

One reaction to the confusion and doubt which are the result of too much change too fast is to deny responsibility. "It's beyond me. I can't do anything about it. Let someone else worry about it. It's not my job." Rather than fighting to control or at least understand the enormous changes going on around them, these individuals "tune out." They know change is occurring, but they do not attend to it. "Why should I read the papers? It's all bad news anyway, and I certainly can't do anything about it."

Thus we find people who "won't become involved" because the changes which must be dealt with are too different or too anxiety producing. People won't vote. They won't join organizations. They won't read the paper. They won't watch the news. They become withdrawn and refuse to participate. The reaction is one of cynicism and apathy. "I can't help it and it wouldn't even do any good to try."

Closely correlated with this denial of responsibility in the face of difficult change is the attitude that the individual might as well "go out and get mine before it's too late." It's the "fiddle while Rome burns" syndrome. It's the "eat, drink, and be merry" attitude. Rather than trying to control the direction of change, the individual chooses to have fun, to be oblivious to the need to control change, and to engage in excessive hedonistic activity. Difficult, seemingly chaotic change leads to a rejection of responsibility accompanied by an impulse to grab all the good things in life as quickly and firmly as possible.

This almost desperate desire to get all the pleasure as soon as possible ties in with the tendency to seek extremes which we described earlier in connection with the blandness of many aspects of American life. So it seems both too much and too little change can push us in the direction of overindulgence and excessive consumption. Calmness, tranquillity, and peace of mind are definitely not the typical outcomes of over- or understimulation. To the contrary, both tend to lead to a rather hectic, frantic, not altogether satisfying search for extremes.

True believing

Frightening change leads not only to a rejection of personal responsibility and a careless chase after pleasure. It can lead to true believing as well. By true believing we refer to the strict adherence to and belief in any illogical or arbitrary system which professes to contain or provide all the answers to our problems.

For example, a young man of our acquaintance believes that alien beings are here among us and, if we would only listen to them, we would learn the secrets of eternal peace and prosperity. The pyramids of Egypt, according to this individual, were built by aliens and stand as living proof of the ingenuity of these beings from other worlds. The pyramids are supposed to have special powers. This man has seen several flying saucers, and is currently trying to use the surface of a lake as an antenna to pick up communications from the UFO creatures.

Apparently his beliefs are shared by others. He is not alone in claiming that he knows, while the rest of us remain ignorant and skeptical, how to solve all of the problems of the world.

This is an extreme example. But it does represent the reaction of a mind overwhelmed and bewildered by unaccountable and frightening change. The true believer's system need not be so extreme in order to qualify as an example of how one attains a sense of safety, importance, and power through strict adherence to an unsubstantiated system of beliefs. The system can be economic, social, religious, or political. It can involve many people or just a few. It can be informal or formal. But in each case, anxiety produced by too much change encourages the individual to find certainty and power within the protective arms of some as yet unsubstantiated system of beliefs.

10

Restoring Balance

Getting Back into Your Preferred Level

In the preceding chapters we discussed how American culture gives us too much change in some ways and not enough change in other ways. We tend to find ourselves outside the satisfying limits of our preferred level of change. In this chapter, we will discuss, in random order, a number of different things we can do and think about in attempting to establish and maintain our preferred level of change. Most of these suggestions have to do with increasing, rather than decreasing, change, as we believe that a lack of change in American life is a more severe problem than is too much change. Some of these suggestions will appeal to you (we hope), while others will not. That's fine. Pick and choose the ones that seem to make sense to you, as they are, after all, nothing more than suggestions.

Escape from Security

Satiation: People, events, things

Mary and Joe are in their thirties. They have been married for twelve years. Two kids, two cars, two jobs. They feel restless and edgy because they have satiated on all the changes their current lifestyle has to offer. Sometimes at night they sit together, not talking, each secretly wishing something would *happen* to make their life more interesting. They don't want to talk for fear of hurting each other's feelings. So they bottle up their uneasiness, put on a brave smile, and pretend to be content. They don't have much to say to each other any longer. Through the years, they have about exhausted the list of common, shared interests. They find, without admitting it, that they are beginning to repeat themselves. Their conversations are old. They both have jobs and can talk to each other about them. But, when Mary talks about her job, many of the people and circumstances in the narrative are unfamiliar to Joe. Hence he is not directly involved and listens in a polite manner, without much excitement, waiting for his turn to talk about his daily experiences, which will, in turn, bore Mary. Sometimes they sit at home in the evening trying to think of something to do. They live in a fair sized town, but everything they can think of doing sounds slightly boring; they've done it too many times. Working on their home, which used to be so exciting, now seems slightly dreary and repetitious. There just doesn't seem to be anything they want to do together. They both have secret thoughts and fantasies about living alone, about having an affair, about old age and death.

And yet they don't *do* anything about the situation. They just go on from day to day wishing vaguely that "something" would come to their rescue. Nothing does, of course, because each of us is responsible for our own destiny. Waiting for the world to bring us good things never works; we have to go out and get them. Why doesn't the couple act? In many cases it is because to act would be to threaten their sense of security. After all, they do have quite a nice situation. Home, health, money, and so on. They don't want to threaten that. They don't want to do anything to upset the nice, comfortable, secure situation which they have worked so long to establish. And yet, at the same time, they sometimes scream silently to themselves in their need to break out and away from this predictable, safe pattern.

When you're done, you're done

The basic problem here is that the couple has satiated on the class of changes which occur within their lives. The very changes which once seemed so exciting are now boring. It's a fact of life that satiation occurs. No amount of denial or pretending will change the fact that events which were once wildly exciting become monotonous and dull.

When you were a child, little insects, water coming out of a tap, rubber bands, and candles all seemed incredibly interesting. But as we grow and develop, these things lose forever the charm and mystery they once had for us. We may still enjoy them, but never again do we recapture the immense excitement they brought to us when we were children.

Robins, hair in people's noses, dark stairways, frogs, evening rainstorms, climbing trees, pet turtles, and hot dogs just don't mean what they once did. As children we all satiated on an enormous range of things and events.

But the satiation process does not somehow miraculously stop when we leave childhood behind. It seems we continue to satiate throughout our lives. The process of satiation never ceases. As young adults, we may find fishing or bike riding or mountain climbing very exciting, but after a while even these glorious activities lose some of their edge. The avid skier one day notices that skiing is sliding down a hill on two pieces of wood or plastic. The dedicated trout fisherperson one day recognizes that all mountain lakes are strung in series down through successions of mountain valleys. The collector of antiques one day becomes depressed by the thought of musty old objects.

As we grow, we need new kinds of change. And yet many of us get into ruts where the amount of new change we experience is limited by our fear of the unknown and by our unwillingness to burn our bridges. Our natural need for security and predictability comes into conflict with our desire to experience new, novel changes. And yet satiation is inexorable. The longer we keep doing the same things, the greater will be our restlessness and uneasiness.

How can we escape this dilemma, this conflict between our need for security and our need for greater variety and change? There are two steps we can take to break out of our rut.

Step #1: Recognize and rate the problem

The first step, although it seems simple, is often difficult because it involves admitting that the problem exists. Our tendency is to say, "No, I'm satisfied. Everything is OK." Meanwhile we're getting more nervous and anxious by the moment.

The thing to do is sit down and make a list of your current life activities. Include major activities at work, at home, and in the area of recreation. List about fifteen or twenty major activities.

Once you have your list made up, go through it and *rate* each activity in terms of how boring or how exciting it is. Use a scale ranging from one to seven. One means the activity is completely and irrefutably tedious. Seven means the activity is truly exciting. Four means the activity is neutral. After you have rated all fifteen or twenty activities, add the ratings up and divide by the number of activities you rated. Thus, if you rated seventeen activities, divide the sum of all seventeen ratings by the number seventeen. If the resulting average rating is below four, you might want to consider the possibility that you are ready for something new in your life. A rating below four suggests that, on the average, your life activities are pretty unexciting. You've probably been at them too long and you are ready for a change.

Step #2: Act

Once you are convinced that much of your dissatisfaction stems from the fact that most of your life activities were once but are no longer very exciting, you have to *do* something about it. It's difficult to take charge of your life and actually make changes which are scary and threaten your sense of security. But that is what must be done.

Many of us sit and wait, hoping something will happen which will solve our problems for us. This is a pipe dream. Knights on white horses only come to the rescue in fiction. If you sit and hope that something outside yourself will help you out of your dilemma, you are mistaken; you will sit there forever. When it comes right down to it, you are the only one who can help. It's up to you, because nothing else, and no one else, is apt to do much for you.

It's easy to say, "Well, things aren't that bad. And maybe something will come up." But nothing ever does, and things get worse instead of better, as satiation progresses. Employees hope the boss will recognize their sterling qualities and take them in as partners. But all they get is a 3 percent raise instead. People needing contact with other people often wait for the phone to ring. But, when it does, it's someone selling something.

Waiting and hoping don't work. Action does. *If you don't like your life, change it.* It's such a simple message but so hard to learn. If you need more variety in your life, you have to take steps to get it.

Once the message sinks in, once people realize that it is up to them to change their life, they often say, "But I don't know what to do. I can't do anything. I don't know how to change."

It is often difficult to change, but it can be done. First, consider people who *do* know what they want to do. Sometimes they fail to act because they are frightened by the possibility of losing security. Well, few have ever made progress without taking some risk. And, in fact, the risk itself can contribute to the excitement of the change. For example, suppose a career woman is tired of her job. She wants to go back to school, but she is afraid to give up all that job security. What she should realize is that escaping from all that security can be exciting. She will feel stimulated, challenged, and exhilarated. She will feel the pull and tug of life's challenges, rather than the stultifying sameness of an old secure job. Fighting life can be fun. Humans enjoy a little tussle. They need some stress and strain to stay trimly alert and mentally active.

Step-by-step

If the fear of changing is too great, several things can be done. For example, the change can be made in a slow, step-by-step fashion. The career woman, discussed above, might take a few night classes first to see if she enjoyed the school atmosphere. Or she might take a leave of absence from her job to attend school full-time for awhile. After all, it is possible that she wouldn't like the change. Changing completely all at once, without first testing the waters, could be a mistake. On the other hand, there must be some change.

Step-by-step change is useful in many situations. A person who is interested in camping might try a one-night outing at a local campground before taking off for a two-week Alaskan adventure. For someone who wants to meet new people, perhaps a social contact of several hours with the new people might be a better first step than three weeks with them in Baja California. Ease into activities. Taste them and test them at first. But do something. Don't just dream about it—do it. Overcome fear and hesitancy by approaching change gradually.

Take a friend along

Another thing you can do to overcome the fear of losing security is to find someone to change with you. It's often easier to do something new if someone is doing it with you. Dieting is easier if a friend does it with you. Going out dancing is easier with friends than without. Selling out and moving to Idaho is easier if someone goes with you.

Trial and error

So far we have seen that the conflict between the need for security and the need for novelty can be broken if individuals will first recognize that they are bored and then act in a way that will bring about changes in a step-by-step fashion. Initiating these changes with a friend or acquaintance can make the transition easier and less fearful.

But what about the individual mentioned earlier, who doesn't seem to know what to do or how to change? In these cases, the use of trial and error can be useful. If you don't know which way to turn or what it is that would interest you, pick something randomly and try it. Don't worry if it seems ahead of time that it won't be interesting. Do it. Make flower arrangements, learn to play the harp, paint a house, buy and sell securities. Take up yoga, television repair, knife throwing, sheep raising, cookie box designing. Try a lot of things in a random order, with a friend, in a step-by-step fashion. You're apt to hit on one that will be of lasting interest.

Remember the five roads over the mountain discussed in Chapter 4. As we said then, if you don't know which road to take, just pick one and go. Don't brood about it. Just act. You can always backtrack and you will eventually find the correct one.

Romantic attachments

When your need for change involves someone else, such as in a romantic involvement, the situation can become complicated. With twice as many fears and twice as many needs, it's bound to be more complex. The final solution may involve dissolving the relationship, or it might just be a matter of finding some new common interests. It's curious, but people who are close together are often less experimental with one another than are less deeply involved people. In many ways, it's easier to be free with a stranger than it is with the one you love.

To break this hesitancy and to allow growth and change on both sides, the two people must act, even if emotional hurt is involved. The amount of emotional damage can be minimized if change is accomplished in an atmosphere of open communication and trust. No sneaky stuff. If your partner knows that you love him or her but that you hate the way things are going in your life, she or he will feel less threatened. If your partner knows you want change to protect your love, rather than to destroy it, then the threat will be eased.

On the other hand, if the change you finally decide upon requires leaving your partner, then you must be prepared for trouble. It's almost a law of human nature that the "leaver" is "up" while the "leavee" is "down." Even if the one that is left wanted the relationship to end, the act of being left can suddenly make the lost relationship seem a lot more desirable.

In cases where change involves the disruption of established, secure patterns, fear is a common emotion. And yet, as we have seen, change is necessary if a sense of awe and excitement is to be recaptured. So expect some anxiety as you move toward change, but don't let the fear deter you. After all, it's only fear. Escape from all that boring security. That's what your body and mind want.

The payoff

We've all heard people say things like, "You know I'll never know why I stayed with him as long as I did," and, "This is the best thing I ever did in my life. I don't know why I waited as long as I did."

What these comments indicate is that the fear and hesitancy we experience while making important changes in our lives often dissipate rapidly and can hardly be remembered later on. Our qualms over losing security become relatively unimportant and overshadowed by the consequences of the change itself.

If you find yourself hesitating because of anxiety or fear, try repeating to yourself, over and over again, that the fear is only temporary and really quite unimportant in your overall attempts to establish the kind of variety in your life which makes you happy. Think of the fear as a head cold. It will soon go away, and it is not serious enough to keep you from making changes in your life.

More Versus Better

In our efforts to maintain ourselves within our preferred levels of change, we often fall into the trap of trying to substitute quantity for quality. As we have already seen, Americans, in their drive for variety, tend to go to extremes in terms of the *amount* of stimulus change they experience. Thus we find Americans seeing movies with more sex, violence, and gore in them than ever before. To get the same "rise" more and more of a given form of stimulation is sought. Music is louder, sports are rougher, cars are faster, clothes are more expensive, lifestyles are more extreme, language is more explicit. Manners are circumvented. Lives are intruded upon. Frantic, frenzied activity, desperate competition, and a general orientation toward more volume, more noise, more "living" seem to characterize modern life. More money, more TV games, more clothes, more appliances, more of everything. But, somehow, no better. More of the same old thing just doesn't satisfy us as much as genuine qualitative change does. More of the same old thing just leads to saturation, which leads to further desperate, but equally unsuccessful, attempts to stir up flagging interest and to keep us at a peak of excitement.

To get out of this trap we must first catalog our current desires. We have to think very accurately about what it is that we have been wanting. If what we have been wanting really is just more of the same old things, then we must realize that the attainment of that goal will not be substantially satisfying. It will represent a quantitative rather than a qualitative change.

For example, suppose a young woman has her heart set on a new stereo. That's all she dreams about. Finally, she is able to buy her heart's desire. It's exciting at first, but the equipment soon blends into her life events and no longer becomes anything but "the stereo". Getting the new stereo was a change but not a very substantial change, because she has always had a stereo of one sort or another. Given that, like most of us, she does not have an incredibly sensitive ear, the added fidelity of the new equipment quickly becomes "normal" and not very exciting.

Consider a man working in an advertising agency. He wants to change jobs because his current position offers too little variety. It's the same thing day after day. So he moves to another bigger, more prestigious advertising agency. It isn't a month before he begins to wonder why he even bothered. If anything, he finds this job involves even more routine and even less variety than his earlier position. It is, after all is said and done, just one more advertising situation.

In both of the examples, the individuals thought that more of something would make it more exciting. But they both discovered that more isn't necessarily better. In fact, more of the same thing can seem like not very much change at all.

What is needed, rather than more extremes within a given dimension, is change which involves a more fundamental alteration in quality. For example, the advertising man might be better off moving into an entirely new field of work. Or he might even be better off staying within the same agency but taking on new, novel responsibilities he has never dealt with before. The woman wanting a bigger and better stereo might find more pleasure in seeking qualitative changes with the money she spent on the new stereo. She might spend it on riding lessons or books or a piano.

To stay within the confines of our current interests and to try to keep our excitement from slackening by increasing the intensity or amount of our involvement within those confines is to suffer a never ending series of defeats. The added stimulation will pale quickly. What we should do is seek more fundamental change.

If you will sit down for a moment and think about your latest set of dreams, you will be able to determine quickly whether you are dealing with quantitative or qualitative changes. Do you want more of whatever you are experiencing now? Or do you seek new forms of change? If your hopes are for qualitative changes, then you will probably experience more lasting satisfaction when you do realize them than you will if you merely want more of the same old things.

Consider the man who lived in the city and always dreamed of owning a farm. Finally he was able to purchase a small ranch where he derived great pleasure from learning how to raise animals and crops. The intricate knowledge he gained through reading, experience, and conversation with neighbors truly delighted his urban-raised mind. It was all so new and novel for him. It was exciting change and stimulating variety.

He liked it so much, he decided to buy a bigger ranch. After working hard to scrape together the funds, he did so. But, to his surprise, the new ranch wasn't all that much fun. He already knew most of what he was going to learn about ranching before he bought the second place. The larger ranch involved more headaches but not much more novelty. After the first understandable flush of proud ownership had subsided, our friend found himself wondering why he had gotten into this situation. He found himself thinking about what he might have done with the money he sank into this larger place. He thought he might have been able to keep the small ranch *and* travel, or buy a cabin in the mountains, or invest in something else. He was a victim of the fallacy that more of a good thing is better. He wanted more of something he already had, rather than something new.

The point here should be clear. In order to locate yourself in your preferred level of change, when you seek change, make certain that you do not only seek more of the same things you already have. Be certain that you attempt to bring about changes in kind rather than changes in amount.

Invent-a-Game

Many people find pleasure in life by inventing games to play with themselves. Some do it intentionally. Others do it without being aware of what they are doing. In either case, the idea is to increase novelty and change by engaging in an informal game. In either case, variety and novelty can be increased in the individual's life.

The kind of game we're thinking of involves competing against the world according to a rule or set of rules which you define either intentionally or unintentionally.

For example, you've seen those campers go by with stickers from the various states plastered on the back window. It may not be your idea of a good game, but it is a game nonetheless and probably one which is fun and amusing for the owners of the camper. The single rule is "see how many states you can accumulate." It's a fairly harmless game and it provides the players with a little pleasure. (Of course, it may also get a little out of hand if the owners start to feel bad if they see another camper with more, or choicer, stickers adorning its rear window.)

The point is that we all play games of this sort without thinking too much about them. Kids riding in a car sometimes count white horses or play guessing games. People jog against the clock or try to lose weight or collect stamps. These are all games of a sort, because they involve competition and rules.

To increase the pleasure we get out of life, we can intentionally make up games to play with ourselves. We can introduce a degree of novelty into our lives by establishing rules and trying to follow them. For example, we knew a woman who didn't like Eisenhower. So she set about collecting all the Eisenhower silver dollars she could find. She got quite a little sack of them and chuckled over the whole thing.

Another person we know started saving half-dollars minted between 1965 and 1970. At the time he started, coins minted before 1965, which were made of 90 percent silver, were being bought for more than their face value by coin dealers. The silver in the coins was worth more than their face value. Half-dollars minted between 1965 and 1970 were composed of 40 percent silver, but, at the time he started collecting them, no one was buying them yet. So he went merrily along collecting coins which he reasoned would soon be worth more than their face value.

The games you play can be of any type. You can collect just about anything, including interesting people, sexual experiences, travels, stamps, or, as did one youngster we know, dried wishbones. Saving money can be a game. Always having a joke ready when you meet a certain person can be a game. Surprising people in any number of ways can be a game. Giving money away can be a game. For example, you can pick out someone needy whom you don't know and put some money in their mailbox. Or you can put nickels on ledges in public buildings and see if they are there when you come back. Hobbies are really games, too. No wonder they are so popular. Use your imagination. Thinking of unusual games sometimes means nothing more than recognizing the potential for a game in many ordinary life situations. See if you can get to work without hitting a red light. Try smiling at every single person you pass. See if you can back the car into the garage without killing more than one rosebush. Train your dog to stand in a corner. Leave anonymous notes of praise on your colleagues' desks. Send packages to people who don't know you. Collect recyclable materials. The sky is the limit when it comes to inventing games to make your life amusing and interesting.

Be a Supersnob

We have already seen that snobbery is very limiting because everyone ends up doing and owning the same things. Everyone tries to out-snob the others by acquiring big homes, big cars, maids, pools, tennis courts, and so on. Snobbery has a way of reducing variety in life rather than increasing it.

So be a supersnob. What's a supersnob? A supersnob is someone who is so snobby that they wouldn't consider lowering themselves to the crass position of ownership and power so desired by ordinary snobs. The supersnob is above that. Whatever the snobs do, the supersnob does the opposite. If the snobs want big houses in exclusive neighborhoods, the supersnob intentionally looks for a small house in a racially mixed neighborhood. If the snobs want Mercedes, the supersnob wants a Datsun. The supersnob laughs at the snobs behind their backs. These supersnobs are so snobby the regular snobs don't even know they exist. The supersnobs' "in" place (the local junior college cafeteria) is so in, the regular snobs have no idea it even exists.

Be unique. Be contrary. Be something different. Be your own wonderful self without having to worry about how you measure up to all those regular snobs. If you do try to follow in their paths, it will cost you a bundle and reduce the variety in your life because you will have to do what they do. Lolling around a pool while Bert and Nancy bounce a tennis ball back and forth over a net can be grindingly boring.

Follow the Leader . . . Once

We have already noted that a lot of redundancy gets built into American culture because businessmen stick with a winner. If one venture (be it a movie or a book or a restaurant) makes money, there is sure to follow a long series of imitations capitalizing on the success of the first venture. For example, the world has never seen so much fancy pocket stitching as has appeared in recent years on the rear ends of style-conscious Americans.

The trick here is to try everything, once, but only once. After all, the first example of any of these trends might possibly represent some genuine change or variety. But after that, it's all carbon copying. So go to the first this and the first that, or one of your choice. But don't bother to waste your time with the seconds and the thirds. Better you should spend the time and effort seeking genuinely new changes.

Sometimes it pays to wait before you sample one of whatever the current fad is. Let the original and some imitations come out and be judged and compared by others. Then, when the dust has settled and a consensus has been reached by people you trust, drop in and sample the one instance of the fad which has been judged to be the best. This may be the best procedure, because, sometimes, the imitations are better than the originals.

For example, if a series of movies about life among the depraved comes along, wait until the choice instance of depravity has been identified for you. Then go and be depraved to your heart's content.

Be Not Misled by Tinsel

Directly related to our tendency to seek quantitative rather then qualitative changes is the problem of the overabundance of superficial variety in our culture. In our need for change, we look about us for variety. The capitalistic system, as we have seen, is very efficient at producing great superficial diversity superimposed upon underlying homogeneity. Sometimes, in our need, we are suckered in by this window dressing. For a moment we really do think one kind of dish soap is very different from another because the box is different and the advertising pitch is different. For a moment we think that there really may be a great difference between two kinds of spearmint gum or two kinds of menthol cigarette or two kinds of ball-point pen. But most of these highly touted differences are pretty trivial in the last analysis. Blindfolded, we would find it difficult to distinguish two kinds of standard white bread baked in America. Blindfolded, we could hardly tell the difference between two types of three-dollar red wine.

So we play a game with ourselves. We try to spot the underlying similarities among products that are described as being incredibly different. We avoid being disappointed by peeking under or peeling away the veneer of difference which covers underlying similarity. We are onto the profit game wherein cost is reduced by producing superficial diversity and underlying homogeneity.

Take the aspirin game, for example. Aspirin is a specific chemical compound. One brand of aspirin is pretty much the same as anybody else's. Yet we hear all sorts of claims about one brand of aspirin being better than another. To us it seems that aspirin is aspirin. But if you listen to these claims, you can end up spending a lot of money for a label.

And then there are the pain-relieving compounds sold over the counter. You hear claims like, "This product contains more of the pain-killing ingredient recommended most by doctors." Aspirin is often what they are referring to.

So don't be fooled by superficial differences. Look behind the labels, the hoopla, and the varying prices. You'll find a lot of similarity.

Reject Sexism

One of the easiest ways to introduce some new fundamental change into your life is to fight against the limitations imposed upon each of us by prevailing sexist attitudes. Basically, what this all amounts to is very simple. If you are a woman, try doing some of the things that are traditionally limited to men. If you are a man, break out of the limiting masculine role and try doing some of the things that are usually defined as women's activities.

Both men and women can benefit and prosper in this fashion. Change, novelty, and variety can be attained. For example, consider the things women can do that have traditionally been off limits to them. They can run for public office, drive taxicabs, join the army, hunt, drink beer with the boys, become electricians, fix the screen door, come home late, let someone else take care of kids, house, and laundry, swear, wear pants, be unintimidated by males, earn their own money, not raise a family, be dominant, refuse to hide their intelligence, work on construction jobs, forget about makeup and looking "feminine", throw away all artificial body scents, yell instead of cry, make obscene sexual references in mixed company, watch nude male dancers, drive fast, be a chief instead of an Indian, refuse to "save" their virginity, reject marriage, be assertive, be the household breadwinner, stop shaving legs and underarms, refuse to put up with sexist males, take charge of their own destiny, and, in general, raise hell with the traditional conception of what women are supposed to be and do. This doesn't mean there is anything wrong with the traditional role. It's just that some women might want to try something different.

Men, on the other hand, can break out of the limiting male role, and can enjoy new change and variety too. They can stay home and take care of the kids, sleep late, take naps, pay the delivery boy, let women support them, not earn very much money, cook, sew, nag, take the dog to the vet, be telephone operators, be delicate, be submissive, be helped, cry, be nurses, wear dresses, refuse to learn about plumbing, never look under the hood of the car, never play football, reject aggression, and, in general, do many of the wonderful "unmanly" things that there are to do in the world.

Sexism is really ingrained in our society. For example, in children's books the hero who does wonderful things is often a male, while the female characters, if there are any, usually sit around either sewing or watching the big, strong male. Advertising is filled with images of women as slightly ding-brained idiots who are talked into buying brand X by some slick, condescending, "understanding" male. Men are paid more than women for the same work. Women are excluded from many upper level jobs.

Our very language is filled with sexist references. Until recently, it was chair*man*, mail*man*, fire*man*, *man*kind, and even hu*man*ity. The pronoun "he" has been used almost exclusively in examples. Recently, many writers have begun to say "he or she," but that is still sexist because the masculine gender comes first; few say "she or he" yet.

Because the attitude that males are superior to females is so inherent in our culture, even the most well intentioned people still succumb to its influence. For instance, even couples who are firmly committed in their belief that behavior should not be defined along sex lines will still find little instances of sexist behavior within their own lives. For example, when they go out together, they may find the man "naturally" does the driving. Or they may find that the woman never opens a door for the man. They may find he orders dinner for her. He almost always pays the check and leaves the tip. Although these are not particularly serious examples of sexist behavior, they do suggest that even the most egalitarian of us probably still, without being aware of it, engage in sexist behavior.

This is nothing to be ashamed of. No one is perfect. In fact, it offers a fine opportunity for growth, change, and stimulation. Play the game called "ferreting out sexist behavior". Watch yourself when you are with a member of the opposite sex and see if you can spot examples of sexist behavior that you have been unaware of. When you do spot one, try reversing it. For example, have the woman pay the dinner bill and leave the tip. Waitresses and waiters, if you will think about it, automatically place the bill next to the male rather than the female. Having the female pay the bill is good for both male and female. The woman gets to be in charge, gets to whip out her wallet and treat for a change. The male, on the other hand, gets to sink back and doesn't have to figure, for once, what a fair tip is. Then have the woman drive home *and* unlock the front door *and* check to see if all the lights are out before going to bed.

You can see the point here, there can be lots of fun in reversing sex roles. Both females and males get to do something new. It provides relief and variety on both sides.

Have the woman tune the family car and change the oil. With the proper tools, it isn't hard at all. It seems mechanics like to make you *think* it is difficult, so they can charge you seventy-five dollars for about one hour's work and fifteen dollars worth of parts.

Keep a careful eye on who makes the decisions, on who has the final say. More than likely this sometimes odious task usually falls to the man.

What a drag, always having to make the decisions. Place some of this burden on the female.

All of this is not to say that men and women are identical. Clearly, they are different. But things have gotten a little out of hand. We don't have to limit our behavior so severely. Loosen up a little. Have the man put on an apron and get cute little flour smudges on his nose. Have the woman tell off the repair person when a job is poorly done. Get more out of life by doing things the opposite sex is "supposed" to do.

Making Up a Hierarchy

As a final example of the ways that we can maximize the time we spend at our preferred level of change, we will consider the construction of a personal hierarchy of activities.

We often find ourselves dissatisfied, disgruntled, and mildly uneasy. We don't know quite what's bothering us, and, more importantly, we can't think of what to do to make ourselves feel better. We run over several courses of action, but none of them seem particularly appealing. We are frustrated by our inability to come up with an activity which would please us at the moment. So we knock around, trying to make do with what we have thought of but without really enjoying it.

Wouldn't it be ideal if our memory could be aided by an extensive list of activities which we have enjoyed at one time or another in the past? We could look over this list and pick out something which might please us at the moment, something which we would never have been able to recall without the aid of the list. By constructing such a list, you do the work ahead of time. You don't have to wait until you are bored or over-stimulated to try to think of an appropriate behavior. The list of activities, ranging from quiet ones to active ones, is already there. All you have to do is run over the list and mentally savor several alternatives.

If you feel tired and overwhelmed, you may find a nice, easygoing, restful activity which appeals to you. In other words, if you have been receiving too much stimulation, you can move back into your preferred level of change by cutting back on the immediate impact of the environment. Your list provides you with a ready-made, extensive range of activities which you couldn't remember or retrieve without the help of the list.

On the other hand, if you are too far out on the other end of the dimension, receiving inadequate novelty and change, you can look over your list for stimulating activities which will help reinstate you within your preferred level of change.

Constructing such a list, or aid to your memory, is simple. Use three-by-five-inch index cards. Just begin writing down things you have enjoyed doing even if they don't seem especially interesting at the moment. Put one entry on each three-by-five card. Write down active and passive behaviors. Include things you have never done but might like to try some-time. Record activities that have to do with your career, the outdoors, indoor activities, recreational activities, loud activities, silent activities, things to be done alone, with friends, with loved ones, and with strangers. In fact, don't exclude any activity which has been, or seems like it might be, satisfying and fun.

Then, when you have about exhausted your memory for satisfying events and you have quite a stack of three-by-five cards, sort the cards into five piles on the basis of how much change and activity each recorded behavior involves. In the first stack, put all the activities which involve the least change. You know, things like sitting absolutely quietly in a chair with your eyes closed or reading alone in bed. In the fifth stack, put all the behaviors involving the most change. For example, this might include catching chickens in a small barn or attending a rock concert or street fighting. In the intermediate piles (two, three, and four), put activities of correspondingly intermediate levels of change. Now combine all five stacks into one deck.

By arranging the cards according to degree of change, you will have constructed a hierarchy of activities ranging from those involving very little change to those involving lots of change and action. Which of these many activities you will like to engage in, at any given moment, will depend upon how bored or how overstimulated you have been lately. If you have been bored, you will gravitate toward the active behaviors. If you've been doing too much, the more passive activities will be most appealing.

Here's the way you use your hierarchy. The next time you feel dis-satisfied, because you are either too bored or because you are over-stimulated, pick up your deck of activities and flip through it, considering how each activity would make you feel. If you recognize that you are bored, start looking through the deck somewhere toward the active end. If you perceive that you have just about had it with all of the change going on in your life, start toward the passive end. If you don't know how you feel, start in the middle and flip toward either end of the deck. If that doesn't get you anywhere, if you can't find anything appealing, reverse your search and seek satisfaction in the other direction.

The success of your hierarchy will depend upon its completeness. If you only have five cards and five activities, it won't work. The list has to be extensive. It has to include all sorts of activities in all kinds of arenas. It has to have so many items that, when you flip through it, you will be able to say, "Hey, that's a good idea! I didn't think of that, and I probably wouldn't have thought of it without my list."

So it should be clear that you can't complete your list all at once. It will take time to build it up. Each time you think of a new activity, write it down on a card and put it into your deck of cards in the appropriate level of change. If you think of something at a time when you do not have your deck with you, scribble it down on a scrap of paper and transfer it to a card when you can. If you don't write it down, you will forget it and say, "Now what *was* that activity I thought of?"

Don't worry about the exact location of cards in the deck. As long as they are *roughly* in the appropriate order, it will work.

Keep adding to your list. It should be an ongoing, growing thing. Whenever you hear of something or read about something that you have never done but which sounds like something you might like to try, add it to your list. Use your friends and acquaintances, what you read and what you hear, as well as your own imagination and memory to add to the deck.

Then, the next time you are colossally bored or overexcited, you will have a ready-made, handy list of activities which far exceeds your ability to recall, on the spot, potentially satisfying activities. Because this simple memory aid offers such an array of choices, you will be much more likely to find an appealing activity appropriate to your current need for change and variety. Try it.

11

Time for Professional Assistance?

You Can't Do It All

This book is crammed with new, potentially useful ways of looking at and dealing with our problems. Many of these new outlooks may be of assistance, and we hope you have gained something from reading about them. However, as we all know, there can come a time when all the helpful hints in the world won't do us a bit of good. We can get so tied up in knots, so distraught and frightened, that we really need help from a professional. There is, after all, a limit to how much we can do for ourselves.

So, in this chapter, we want to describe briefly some of the more severe forms of mental disturbance. Specifically, we will talk about *neurotic* behavior and *psychotic* behavior. It is these two forms of behavior which might best be dealt with in conjunction with professional assistance. If your problems are of the everyday garden variety, then much of what we have discussed in this book might be helpful. But if your problems are more severe perhaps it would be a good idea to talk to someone with appropriate training and experience. In the final section of this chapter we will consider some of the types of therapy which are available to us.

Neurotic Behavior: Close But Still on Our Own

Neurotic behavior is moderately disturbed behavior. There are a number of quite distinct behaviors, which we will discuss shortly, that are classified as neurotic. Each of these neuroses has three things in common:

1. All of the neuroses involve high levels of *anxiety.*
2. All of the neuroses are *disruptive.* That is, they lead to a condition where the individual gets less from life than would be obtainable if the neurosis were not present.
3. While all the neuroses are troublesome, and, in a sense, cheat you out of the pleasures of life, they are *not completely incapacitating.* The neurotic individual can usually function on her or his own. Most neurotics do not require hospitalization.

In a sense, we're all a little neurotic, aren't we? We all have fears and anxieties that keep us from enjoying parts of life. If you are afraid to swim, you will miss out on some forms of pleasure. However, this does not mean that you are seriously disturbed. It merely means that fears and anxieties can vary in strength as well as form. The more severe the disturbance, the more likely it is to be called neurotic. So don't worry if you recognize some of the neurotic symptoms in yourself. It's all a matter of degree. Mild neurotic tendencies are nothing to worry about. It is only when the individual is severely hindered in the pursuit of happiness that the label neurotic should be considered. Now let's look at some of the specific neuroses.

Anxiety neurosis

One of the most common neurotic reactions is called the *anxiety neurosis.* In this condition, waves of uncontrollable anxiety sweep over the individual, for no apparent reason. The attack may only last for a few moments, or it may go on for hours. Sometimes the person feels panicky. Heart rate can increase. Sweating and insomnia, as well as loss of appetite, can occur. It is an unpleasant, frightening experience.

While most anxiety neurotics are able to muddle through life without requiring hospitalization, it seems clear that the condition shortchanges them. They can't concentrate. They are often afraid to go certain places and do certain things because they are afraid they will have an attack. In other words, not only the attack itself, but the fear of the attack and the person's attempts to avoid an attack can be quite a waste of time. Can you imagine sitting around not going anywhere for fear of not being able to cope? Not good. If severe enough, the anxiety neurosis is best dealt with by a trained professional in the mental health field.

Phobic neurosis

Phobias are strong, uncontrollable, *unreasonable* fears. People can have phobic reactions to just about anything. One of the more common phobias, claustrophobia, is an unreasonable fear of closed places. We're not talking about the uneasiness any one of us would feel if we were packed and sealed into a four-foot lead box. That kind of fear is to be expected. But if we are made very anxious by being in a room, or even indoors at all, then we may be suffering from claustrophobia. The fear has to be intense to be classified as a phobia.

Acrophobia is a fear of heights. Now, we'll all feel a little nervous if we stand at the very edge of a four thousand-foot cliff. But that's not a phobia. A phobic neurotic might be one who is terrified of nothing more than the *thought* of standing on the roof of a house.

There are fancy names for all sorts of phobias:

Name of phobia	Feared element
ailurophobia	cats
anthropophobia	people
ophidiophobia	snakes
mysophobia	dirt
astraphobia	lightning
anthophobia	flowers
equinophobia	horses
nyctophobia	darkness

Phobias are not well understood. Some psychologists feel that they have a lot to do with inner impulses that we are afraid to express. Others are convinced that they are merely learned responses which we acquired long ago and which have stuck with us. At present there is no real agreement about the causes of phobias. About all psychologists have been able to agree upon is that if the fear reaction is intense and if it interferes with the individual's life, then it should be called a phobic reaction.

Obsessive-compulsive neurosis

Have you ever left the house and then worried for the rest of the morning about whether or not you turned off the stove? You are convinced that when you return home in the evening you will find nothing but smoldering ruins and looters scattering in every direction. There is nothing particularly unusual about such a repetitive thought pattern. We all go through that sort of thing occasionally. But when uncontrollable, repetitive thoughts begin to take over and disrupt your life, then they are called obsessively neurotic thoughts. For example, if you repeat "I'm going to kill someone" two hundred times a day, or if you can't rid your mind of the thought that everything you touch is covered with, crawling with, germs, then you are suffering from an obsessive neurosis.

Compulsive neuroses refer to repeated acts rather than repeated thoughts. For example, if you wash your hands seventy-five times a day, you are in the grip of a compulsion. Mildly compulsive behaviors, such as avoiding cracks in sidewalks, are not particularly unusual or serious. But if the compulsion begins to dominate your life, then it is labeled neurotic. Compulsions come in many forms. The compulsive neurotic may feel impelled to touch every corner of his or her apartment upon rising in the morning, or to check under the bed twenty times before retiring, or to adjust the window shades repeatedly.

Obsessive and compulsive neuroses are usually discussed together because they often occur together. For example, if you are a compulsive hand washer then you may very well be experiencing obsessive thoughts about filth and microbes.

Again, psychologists are not in agreement about the causes of this form of neurotic behavior. Some have argued that these ritualistic forms of thought and behavior can be anxiety reducing. If you wash your hands because you believe they are filthy, then you will feel less anxious after you have washed them. If you feel generally anxious and frightened, then checking under the bed can be reassuring. At least you will know that nothing is under there right at the moment.

Being obsessive and compulsive can be anxiety reducing in a more general way, too. Let's say that you are frightened and upset about what seems to you to be a chaotic and confusing world. You just don't think you can face it. It's too scary, unpredictable, and difficult. Well, if you can get involved in a rigid program of housecleaning, as some people do, then you will experience some predictability, order, and certainty in an otherwise frightening world. If you *know* you are going to vacuum this afternoon, just as you did yesterday, and nothing can keep you from this comforting, familiar task, then the booming confusion of life will be momentarily lessened. Going through familiar, repetitive acts can be reassuring if you are anxious. They are called neurotic acts if they get out of hand. If you fail to graduate from college because you are too busy cleaning your house to attend any classes, you might want to talk to someone about it all.

That's not all

We have not exhausted the list of neurotic behaviors. For example, hypochondriacal neurotics are unreasonably preoccupied with their physical symptoms. They exaggerate their physical problems, complain about all sorts of imagined diseases, and stuff themselves with pills, vitamins, and thermometers. While there are many different interpretations of exactly why hypochondriacs do all of this, everyone seems to agree that the behavior can be very disruptive and that it is appropriately called neurotic.

Then there is the conversion hysteria neurotic. This is the person who displays some apparent physical impairment, such as blindness, loss of the sense of touch, paralysis, or deafness, when there is no physical basis whatsoever for the disorder. (People who are simply faking these symptoms are not classified as neurotic. The true neurotic with a loss of, say, skin sensation can be pricked with pins and feel no pain.)

Some have argued that the conversion hysteria neurotic unconsciously develops these symptoms to avoid some unpleasant task. You know, if they are going to be shooting real bullets at you in a war it couldn't hurt to develop a quick paralysis, especially if you aren't even aware of what you are doing.

Other neurotic patterns include depression, loss of memory, and fleeing from one's life into a new life. All of these patterns involve anxiety and self-deception. While the neurotic can often function without hospitalization, persons suffering from the more severe psychotic reactions we will now discuss do often require care and treatment.

Psychoses: Losing Touch

In extreme cases, the kinds of frustrations, fears, and anxieties we have been discussing may contribute to the appearance of *psychotic* behavior. Psychotic behavior is what most people refer to when they speak of insanity, craziness, and mental illness. It is more extreme than neurotic behavior. The psychoses are extremely serious psychological disorders often requiring hospitalization or some other kind of special care. Generally speaking, psychotic behavior is broken down into two types: schizophrenic reactions and manic-depressive reactions. We will deal with each of these two major forms separately.

Schizophrenia

Schizophrenia is a name applied to a large group of disorders. These disorders all have something in common, and yet they can vary quite a bit, too. Let's look at some of the symptoms.

Withdrawal. Many schizophrenics are extremely withdrawn and "out of contact" with the rest of the world. They seem to be off in their own world. If you speak to them, they either fail to respond or they respond in some peculiar way. It's as though they have moved behind some invisible barrier which breaks all the communication links between them and the rest of us. Sometimes their withdrawal takes the form of silence. They won't talk to you, look at you, or *focus* on you. At other times they are extremely talkative, sometimes yelling and shouting. In either case, silent or noisy, they are withdrawn. They tend to avoid other people, as though the world were too difficult and painful to deal with.

Flattened affect. Schizophrenics often, although not always, display flattened affect. Their emotions seem to be blunted. Their faces may be blank and their speech may be monotonic. Again, it's as though emotions are too painful, and the schizophrenic prefers to avoid them too.

Hallucinations. Hallucinations refer to false sensory experiences, and schizophrenics experience them quite often. If an individual sees something that is not there, then that person is experiencing a visual hallucination. A person may wake up screaming that her room is filled with hairy brown spiders. Another individual may report that his dead relatives visited him. Schizophrenics may see God, aliens, and other assorted impossibilities. Auditory hallucinations, where the individual hears sounds that are not there, are much more common than visual hallucinations. Many schizophrenics report hearing voices. Occasionally, if you are sensitive to this sort of thing, you can spot a schizophrenic in everyday life. The next time you see an individual talking to himself, laughing, waving his arms, shouting, and generally acting in an extremely unusual manner, you may be observing a schizophrenic. Although some schizophrenics are dangerous, most are not and many manage to survive outside the hospital. If they do not commit themselves, if they have no family to commit them, or if they do nothing to alert the authorities, they may continue to live on their own in their wildly isolated worlds.

Hallucinations almost seem to take the place of contact with the outside world. Schizophrenics spin their own reality, all within the mind. Since they do not interact with the external world, the imaginings of their own minds seem to take on added significance. Not all schizophrenics appear to hallucinate, but it is a very common reaction.

Delusions. Delusions are false beliefs. Not all schizophrenics are delusional, but many of them are. Delusions can be quite elaborate. Again this symptom seems to be consistent with the fact that schizophrenics don't check their ideas against reality because of severe withdrawal.

Delusions of *grandiosity* are common. Here the individual believes he or she is Napoleon, or Christ, or some other important, powerful figure. The person may preach aloud, give advice, and generally act in a grand manner. Although the true causes of delusions are unknown, it does seem that this grandiose form could help an otherwise helpless, hopeless, frustrated individual feel more important. If you have failed in your life and been beaten down by the rat race, a little delusion elevating you to a position of power and influence couldn't be all bad.

Delusions of *persecution* are also common. Here the person believes the world is out to get her. She thinks people are trying to kill her, to poison her food, to poison her water, to tap her phone, to steal her money.

We all feel paranoid on occasion, but the true delusion of persecution is much stronger and more persistent than our occasional bouts of uneasiness.

A New York State mental hospital was built in the flightpath of a nearby Air Force base. Consequently, jets flew with some regularity over the hospital. A surprising number of patients worked this fact into their delusional systems. One believed that his mind was being controlled by radio waves from the aircraft. Another believed that she was controlling the planes. Thus delusions can be quite unusual and very complex.

Not all schizophrenics are paranoid, but when they are they usually have a delusional system. Paranoid schizophrenics may seem perfectly normal—until you hit upon their delusion. Then you may find they believe they are being followed and that the followers are government agents trying to thwart an important cosmic mission.

Bizarre behavior.   Schizophrenics often do things which appear very bizarre. They may make peculiar gestures, movements, and repetitive acts. They may sing, dance, and shout. They may sit motionless.

Catatonic schizophrenics sometimes show muscular rigidity. That is, they assume one position and hold that position for long periods of time. If their arm or leg is moved by another person, the limb will stay in that position. They appear to be in a stupor and it is difficult to tell if they are aware of what is going on around them.

Other schizophrenics may display wild, erratic, eccentric, and sometimes violent behavior. They may laugh for no apparent reason. They may giggle and act childishly. They may take showers while fully clothed, occasionally masturbate in public, put foreign objects in their bodily orifices, wave objects in the air, tear their clothing, and, in general, display an incredible variety of unusual behavior.

Disturbed thought.   The thinking and speech of schizophrenics seems to range from normal to extremely bizarre. It often involves strange connections and associations that are difficult to follow. One schizophrenic, moving through a cafeteria line, pointed at a jello salad and said, "Parakeet salad!" and laughed. Then he pointed at another salad and said, "Radio salad!" To us this speech and thought seems unusual. But within the schizophrenic's delusional system it may all make perfect sense. It's just that we are cut off from his thinking and so can't follow the connections he is making. Sometimes schizophrenics' speech appears to be completely nonsensical such as, "Here we can't use after feet color teeth." Schizophrenics often seem to jump from one topic to another, changing the subject constantly.

Manic-depressive reaction

The second form of psychotic behavior is usually referred to as the manic-depressive reaction. Persons with this disorder experience extreme mood swings. In the manic phase, which can vary in intensity, the individuals may feel enormously elated and be hyperactive. They may show unbounded confidence, rush about pursuing grandiose, impractical plans, avoid sleep, sing, shout, pace, and, in general, display great excitement. In some cases they may be confused and disoriented and experience some hallucinations and delusions. In some cases they may give up moral restraint and display sexual and aggressive behavior. In extreme cases, what we have here is the "raving maniac." People in the manic phase may buy things they can't afford, claim they can solve the problems of the world, decide to run for the presidency, give or spend money that they don't have, and get into overextended, doomed-to-fail business deals. They move restlessly, whistle, and drive people to distraction by being irritatingly "playful."

The depressed phase is just the opposite of the manic phase. Individuals in this phase may feel worthless, hopeless, guilty, and often suicidal. Sometimes they won't eat, talk, or engage in sexual activity. If they have hallucinations and delusions, they usually have to do with something bad the individual has done. For example, a person may believe that he caused all the diseases in the world or that she assassinated Martin Luther King. People in the depressed phase are indecisive, indifferent, tired, and, in general, very sad and mournful.

A single individual may experience both manic and depressed phases, but there is no predicting when one or the other of the phases will occur. For example, a person might experience three depressed phases before going through a manic phase, or vice versa. Each phase may last days, weeks, or months. Days, weeks, months, or years may pass between phases. During these interludes the individual appears perfectly normal. Sometimes a person experiences only one or two phases in their entire life. Others experience multiple phases. The occurrence and length of the phases is irregular and impossible to predict. Some people experience only the depressed phases, while others experience both. Interestingly enough, people who experience only manic phases are rare.

The causes of psychoses

The causes of psychotic behavior are not well understood. One popular interpretation argues that the psychoses are the result of an interaction between our genetic makeup and our experiences. Specifically, it is argued that a predisposition to become psychotic is inherited, while whether or not we actually become psychotic during our lifetime is determinal by how stressful a life we lead. If we lead an easy, comfortable, relaxed, successful life, where everything breaks just right and we feel good about ourselves, then we will not become psychotic. On the other hand, if we lead a stressful, unpleasant life where we feel we are inadequate and the world seems to concur, then we may well become psychotic *if* we have the inherited predisposition. When those of us who have not inherited the tendency to succumb to psychosis are faced with stress, we will not become psychotic, regardless of the unpleasant pressures we face.

Evidence for the genetic component in the determination of psychotic behavior comes from studies of families and twins. Schizophrenia tends to run in families. So does the manic-depressive reaction. If one identical twin is schizophrenic then the other twin is something like fifty times more likely to become schizophrenic than average. If one identical twin is a manic-depressive, the other twin is roughly seventy-five times as likely to have a similar mood disorder. In other words, the evidence for genetic determination of psychotic behavior is quite strong.

But not *all* twins become psychotic if their identical twin is psychotic. Thus there must be something more than genes that determines psychoses. The most widely accepted candidate for this additional cause of psychosis is a stressful environment. If the external environment is too demanding, does not provide you with satisfaction, denies you reinforcement and reward, denies you pleasant experiences, requires you to try to surpass your abilities, makes you feel inadequate, forces you to dislike yourself, and makes you feel helpless, then you may be in for a psychotic episode, given the appropriate genetic makeup.

These are just the sorts of conditions which we have been discussing throughout this book. Our culture leaves us having things that we don't want and wanting things we can't have. We are expected to succeed when we are bound to fail, and we are taught to want things that are unattainable. We experience a sense of futility, failure, and frustration. In other words, the very conditions and factors we have considered throughout this book may well contribute to psychotic breakdowns.

Therapy: Paying for a Captive Audience

Thousands of people are spending millions of dollars in their efforts to gain satisfaction through, or with the help of, some form of therapy. If you are not having fun, not feeling satisfied, and you can't seem to get what you want, it's only natural to look for help. And if someone with a fancy degree advertises, "I help people," well, then, it is only natural to consider that person's services. On the other hand, most forms of psychotherapy are very time-consuming and very expensive. A typical hour with a typical therapist runs around fifty dollars. Depending upon how many times a week you see the therapist, this can deplete your budget rather quickly.

Although there are three major approaches to psychotherapy in the

United States, and we will discuss them shortly, the number of available variations on the theme is quite astounding. You can find just about anything you want if you are willing to pay for it. Some of these forms are traditional and well established, while others are faddish and experimental. Just a partial list of therapies includes psychoanalysis, client-centered, behavior modification, existential-humanistic, Gestalt, rational emotive, T-group, encounter group, and marathons. The list goes on and on as everybody gets into the act.

Before we review the three major forms of therapy, two points should be made. First, the essence of most forms of psychotherapy is talk. You pay someone to listen to you. You hire a captive audience. You may converse in different ways, you may talk in a group, and you may mix action with words, such as in most behavior therapy situations, but the bottom line on psychotherapy is conversation. You try to feel better by talking to others. Paying them makes them all yours. You can really be the center of attention because this therapist has got to listen to you. You don't have to feel guilty about monopolizing the conversation, about focusing strictly upon yourself without a care for what the therapist is feeling, because you are paying. You've hired someone to listen to and think about nothing else but you. That has to be a luxurious feeling. We can't get it with friends because we have to give them a turn. We can't monopolize the conversation with them. But therapists can't, aren't supposed to, talk about themselves. Just you. For a whole hour—there has to be some value in this. It's exciting to talk about yourself and have someone pay attention. Just getting things off your chest and having someone react to your concerns can help.

The second point to consider is that there isn't a whole lot of evidence for the success of most forms of psychotherapy. Strange as it may seem, we don't even know if many kinds of therapy work. Many people swear by it, say they couldn't have felt as good as they do now without it. But who knows? Maybe they would have felt better anyway, without pouring nine thousand dollars a year into the therapist's bank account. Perhaps a close friend could have been just as helpful. Even though psychotherapy has been around for years, and it seems to be growing, there is little evidence concerning its overall usefulness.

Psychoanalysis

The first of the three major approaches to psychotherapy is based upon Freud's work and is called psychoanalysis. Psychoanalysis can take years and involve several meetings a week. You'd better have a fat bankroll if you want this form of therapy, even though it is deductible. During the sessions the patient typically lies on a couch and says anything that comes to her mind. She sometimes free associates to words given to her by the analyst. She describes her dreams. The therapist actively interprets what she says, particularly in relation to her early childhood experiences. Psychoanalytically oriented therapists believe our current problems stem from our very early experiences, especially our relationships with our mother and father. As therapy continues the patient begins to see the therapist as a kind of father figure. The therapist feels this is a good step that will help the patient feel better later because it helps the patient understand her relationship and conflicts with her real father. The therapist wants the patient to gain insight into unconscious and repressed desires, thoughts, and especially conflicts. Usually these buried, early conflicts, which must be brought to light, are thought of as sexual and aggressive.

Client-centered therapy

In client-centered therapy, the second of the three major approaches, the therapist does not interpret what the patient says. Rather, the therapist is an accepting, passive person who tries to help the patient discover for himself what is bothering him. Early childhood sexual and aggressive conflicts are not emphasized. The therapist doesn't ask questions or "analyze" statements. She merely restates what the patient says because she believes the patient can help himself. The therapist must show "unconditional positive regard." You know, "you're great no matter what you do." She must show sympathetic understanding, and she must be honest and sincere. In essence, the patient "cures himself" in this warm, understanding, supportive situation.

Behavior modification

The third approach is called behavior modification. Here emphasis is placed on changing behaviors instead of on changing thoughts and personalities. There are many types of behavior modification techniques available. For example, in assertion training patients are taught to be able to ask for what they want and deserve and to say no to unreasonable demands. Much of this training occurs through role playing where the patients actually practice being more assertive. In another technique, an alcoholic receives a mild shock as he drinks a cup of whiskey. He quickly associates booze with pain and, consequently, reduces his drinking. In another procedure, mental patients are rewarded with tokens each time they engage in some desired behavior, such as being nice to another patient. These tokens can later be redeemed for food, candy, cigarettes, or other privileges.

Behavior modification is the least dependent of all the major approaches upon talk. In fact, many behavior modifiers are interested in avoiding the traditional dependence upon talk. They want to deal directly with behavior rather than conversation. The methods for gaining statisfaction outlined in this text have a good deal in common with behavior modification in that they outline actions, not conversation, that can be taken to increase pleasure and lead to a sense of well-being.

Drug therapy

Finally, treatment of mental illness through the use of drugs has grown tremendously in recent years. New developments are appearing so rapidly that it is difficult to summarize the pharmacological approach in a few words. Years ago, when one visited a mental hospital, "raving maniacs" and people exhibiting bizarre behavior were often seen. Now the visitor will see much less of this extreme behavior. This is because most hospitalized patients are under some form of medication, whether it be for depression, overexcitement, or just good old tranquillity. There is some question whether these new drugs merely treat symptoms (e.g., calm people down) or actually get at the underlying problems. But, whatever the final answer to this question, it appears that drugs are here to stay.

Summary

In this chapter we have taken an excursion into the realm of truly disturbed behavior. We have done this to avoid giving the impression that the techniques introduced in this book can solve all our problems. When psychological disorder becomes severe, then the simple techniques we have outlined will not be sufficient. Further help should be sought. If you feel you need additional help, you should know that *psychiatrists* are medical doctors with special training in the area of psychological disorders. They can provide medical as well as psychological assistance. *Psychologists* are usually Ph.D.'s with extensive training in psychology. While they have no medical training, they often have more psychological training than psychiatrists. Counselors can be just about anything; it is not difficult to call yourself a counselor, so you might check the credentials of a counselor before being treated by one. Whatever form of help you seek, don't just pick a name out of the phone book. Seek a referral from someone who knows what is going on (e.g., school or college counseling personnel, your family doctor, experienced friends, university instructors).

12

Help Is on the Way

Up or Down?

There we sit, all wrapped up in this B movie on TV. Jane loves Bob but we're not sure Bob loves Jane. It's getting late, but we want to know how the movie comes out. Will Bob's true love for Jane finally be revealed? Or will Jane murder Bob and die a broken woman behind bars? We can't bear to flick off the set and never learn the ending, in spite of our knowing it is a dumb movie and in spite of our knowing the ending is really quite arbitrary. By that we mean the story could end either way (and it has, many times). Still, we are drawn to the conclusion of the story. It may be an "up" ending or a "down" ending, and we want to know which it will be.

The same holds true for books such as the one you are reading now. The ending could be harsh, severe, pessimistic, and full of warnings. Or it could be an "up" ending, full of hope and optimism.

If you are looking for a negative ending, crammed with dreary predictions about what a miserable life you will lead unless you shape up, then you will be disappointed. We're going for a positive ending.

It's All in Your Mind

As we have seen, two people faced with the very same life circumstances can react very differently. One will be gloomy and depressed, while the other will be cheerful and happy. This leads us to conclude that a great deal of happiness and unhappiness is determined, not by "life out there," but by how we think about ourselves and our experiences. And if it is "all in your mind" you might as well fill your mind with pleasant thoughts. Lighten up, as they say. Remember not to take yourself too seriously. Life is full of good and evil, positive and negative. It's a real mixture. The happy person is the one who accentuates the positive and accepts, but does not dwell upon, the negative. Look for, and directly at, the good side of everything. Refuse to be dragged down into looking at the negative aspects of life. They are there, of course, but who needs them? It's a bore to be depressed, especially when that depression is of your own making.

For Example

For example, consider how people might react to this book. Some will read it and become depressed. "Oh my God, there is so much for me to do and remember. I can't possibly keep all these suggestions straight, much less apply them in my life. I'm worse off now than before I read this stupid book. I hate this book. So much responsibility is placed on *me*. I have to do it all myself. I don't want a lecture, I want help!" Etc., etc., etc.

Then there is the person who will look at the bright side of things. "It's true that the burden of responsibility lies on me, but I can do it. It's not all that complex, and I can pick and choose what I want and need from this book."

So you see, much of our own sense of happiness depends upon what we choose to make of the mysteries of life. A flower can be beautiful, or it can be a source of allergic reaction. Storms can be beautiful, or terrifying. People can be wonderful little gardens of surprise and delight, or they can be swamps. All things can be read either way, positive or negative, so you might as well look at the bright side.

A Pleasant Irony

Let's end this book with a perfect example of how outlook or attitude can affect degree of happiness. Let's turn two negatives into a positive:

1. The first negative is the fact that many of the techniques and suggestions outlined in this text do, in fact, require the individual to be responsible for her or his own happiness. According to this book, we have to act to help ourselves. So far we have talked as though no one is going to do it for us.
2. The second negative is the fact that this country, and the world in general, appears to be moving into a period where less of everything will be available to us. We hear and read constantly about how resources are being used up, about how life's pleasures are being de-

pleted, about how we will all have to do with less, and about how we must learn to live with lowered expectations.

Now, if you think about it for a moment, it becomes clear that these two negatives dovetail and form a positive. They work with one another to reduce the negative quality of each other. In a sense, worldwide shortages of goods, materials, and opportunities are going to do some of the work for us.

For example, consider the principle that to experience pleasure we must first be deprived. We have noted that if we deprive ourselves then pleasure can be regained. We have outlined some of the ways we can deprive ourselves. But depriving ourselves is difficult. At this point we can look at the positive side of the situation and say, "Hey, I'm going to be deprived without even trying. World shortages and conservation measures will do some of the work for me." What could be better? We just get through discovering that to increase pleasure we must experience some deprivation only to discover that deprivation is on the way. To a degree, the depriving will be done for us. If gasoline goes to four dollars a gallon (and I hope it does, with some of the profits being circulated back to the poor), then driving may again take on some of the fun and excitement it once had. It will be a treat rather than a smog-bound inevitability. If hamburger becomes very expensive, then a tiny bit of hamburger will be a succulent morsel instead of just one more piece of cardboard. Inflation can, ironically, lead to increased rather than decreased pleasure. Food probably never tastes better than when it is rationed. As someone said, less can be more. We are going to have less, but perhaps enjoy it more. And some of this will happen without our having to struggle to deprive ourselves.

We will no longer be overindulged with the things that bore us to tears now. When we get something, it will mean more to us. Our levels of aspiration will be lowered by the events occurring around us. We won't expect, demand, and want so many of the things we can't have.

Let's hope big changes are on the way. If we experience major shifts in our lifestyles, brought about by changing economic conditions, we can expect to experience novelty and variety. And it is, after all, novelty and variety that we crave, not one more appliance made in Taiwan. Gone will be the boring, endless, deadening homogeneity of American life. New, exciting, varied lifestyles will emerge. We will be freed from the prison of success and materialism.

At the same time, many of our present fears which are related to runaway technology will be reduced. For example, if the economy slows, fewer new poisons will be developed to be spread, invisibly, into our environment. If technology slows and we learn to live with what we have, the new unseen dangers inherent in technological advance will be reduced.

Look forward to less. It will be (1) more interesting and (2) less frightening. Relax, because help is on the way. You won't be completely responsible for everything. The boring, depressing, frightening excesses of American life are already on the way out. Try to arrange your own life in such a way that your happiness is maximized, but be optimistic about the future. Positive change is on the way, no matter what you do.

Good luck and best wishes.